John C. Clyde

Guide to non-liturgical Prayer for Clergymen and Laymen

John C. Clyde

Guide to non-liturgical Prayer for Clergymen and Laymen

ISBN/EAN: 9783337209704

Printed in Europe, USA, Canada, Australia, Japan

Cover: Foto ©Lupo / pixelio.de

More available books at **www.hansebooks.com**

GUIDE

TO

NON-LITURGICAL PRAYER,

FOR

CLERGYMEN AND LAYMEN;

Consisting of one hundred and eighty outlines, formed by selecting suggestive passages of scripture and so arranging them that Clergymen may use a separate outline for each Sabbath-day and Week-day service throughout the year.

The whole is equally adapted to the use of Laymen as a general Guide to edifying non-liturgical prayer.

BY

REV. JOHN C. CLYDE, A. M.,
*Pastor of the First Presbyterian Church of
Bloomsbury, New Jersey.*

EASTON, PA.:
PUBLISHED BY THE AUTHOR.
1885.

Entered according to act of Congress, in the year 1885, by
JOHN C. CLYDE,
In the Office of the Librarian of Congress, at Washington.

PREFACE.

The experience of clergymen, in non-liturgical churches, has been different from that of the author if they have not at times felt the need of some guide or manual by which the field of contemplation in spiritual things could be enlarged, and whereby there would be suggested to the mind themes suited to the necessities of the worshipers as they were led by them in the service of prayer in the sanctuary. Also the need of something to keep the mind from always falling into the same line of thought, and thus causing the use continually of stereotyped phrases or forms of expression. Laymen also have felt the need of some manual whereby they might be directed in their efforts to become proficient in the service of public prayer. To meet such felt needs as these has been the aim of the author in the preparation of the following pages. Whilst laying out and elaborating his own plan, he has consulted several liturgies, with a view of divesting this work, as far as possible, of liturgical characteristics. The Sabbath-days are divested of all special terms of designation. As there are five Sabbaths, possible, in each month, there are two outlines for each Sabbath, making one hundred and twenty for the year; and in addition, sixty outlines for as many week-day services. As the work is viewed in its completed form, the author sees a number of particulars in which it might be improved; as for instance in reducing to one head those subjects which are substantially identical although inserted under slightly different forms of expression. Also the eliminating of such passages of scripture as do not suggest lines of thought other than those found in the passages with which they are connected. However, recognizing the many imperfections of the work, it is sent out with the hope that it may be of some service in aiding clergymen and laymen in the important matter of non-liturgical prayer.

BLOOMSBURY, N. J., MARCH, 1885. J. C. C.

INTRODUCTION.

That some aid or direction in prayer is needed, is manifest from the experience of professing christians. In the prayer-books of the liturgical churches we see an effort put forth to supply the felt need. In the non-liturgical churches, the ministry and laity, whilst eschewing set forms of prayer, feel that they would be benefited by such helps as would enable them to pray more intelligently and earnestly with the spirit and with the understanding. It seems strange that the means of preparation for this part of divine service, in non-liturgical churches, should be so meager, whilst the helps in the preparation for the other parts are so ample; this too when it is recognized that such help is not only appropriate, but has the direct sanction of the inspired word. In the standards of a large and influential branch of the non-liturgical churches we find this truth formulated in the words: "Prayer is an offering up of our desires unto God, for things agreeable to his will, in the name of Christ, with confession of our sins, and thankful acknowledgement of his mercies." Also: "The whole word of God is of use to direct us in prayer; but the special rule of direction is that form of prayer which Christ taught his disciples, commonly called, The Lord's Prayer." For the truth thus formulated there is ample warrant in the scriptures.

Feeling that both scripture and standards were on our side, we have made an attempt to supply, if only to a limited degree and in an imperfect manner, an apparent need in the non-liturgical churches, viz.: a Guide to Prayer. In doing this we have kept close to standards. It is declared that the whole word of God is of use to direct us in prayer. When we had wrought out our plan, we discovered that we had unconsciously laid under tribute every book in the Bible except the short prophecy of Nahum.

We have warrant for a form of prayer, and also for varying characteristics of the form. In our form or outline of prayer we have adhered to the warrant. We have divided the outline into 1. Address to God; 2. Confession of sin; 3. Asking for blessings; 4. Thanking for mercies; 5. Interceding for others, beyond the immediate assembly in which the prayer is offered. This form is preserved in each prayer, but the characteristics of the prayers themselves vary continually. To the left of the page we have placed the constant part of the outline, and to the right the varying part, and underneath both, selected passages of scripture suggestive of a line of thought appropriate. Thus whilst the form remains the same, in each successive prayer the subjects and passages of scripture change. Thus is furnished a new and independent line of thought for each service.

The design is to use these outlines only for what is known as the long, or comprehensive, prayer of the service. The clergyman may either prepare his prayer from the outline before going into the pulpit, or take the outline with him into the sacred desk and follow it as he leads the congregation. In preparing for the service, the design is to take the outline designated for that particular day and service. Let the general division found at the left of the page engage the mind; and then the particular phase of the division as indicated by the subject at the right of the page; then let the spirit and understanding express themselves in a line of thought suggested by the scripture passages inserted under the particular head dwelt upon. In using the outlines, they may be taken as found arranged for the various services of the year; but if any circumstances should exist which would make a change advantageous or desirable, the outline need not be adhered to. Nor is it essential that all that is suggested in each outline should be used. So much only may be taken as is appropriate to the time and circumstances, and agreeable to the one officiating. Thus the prayer may be made long or short at pleasure.

If a particular passage of scripture is under consideration, by turning to the index to scripture passages it very likely will be found among the more than fifteen hundred citations made, or if not found, passages of similar import, and so by turning to the body of the work an outline will be found containing the subject in hand. If a particular subject is under consideration, it, or a kindred one, will doubtless be found in the copious index to subjects, and so one or more outlines will be found containing it.

In the plan adopted in this work, it is thought practical advantages are gained. Those who might object to anything like a liturgical form in the service, cannot consistently take exception to the word of God as collated and made available in these outlines. Also the danger of rendering a lip service, without the mind and heart, so common in the use of liturgical forms, is here obviated; for no use can be made of the outlines without the mind, at least, if not the heart, is engaged in the service. Thus the individuality of the one offering the prayer is retained. Further, the people will be led in a new line of thought at each service, and by the use of the more than three hundred and eighty subjects, with their subdivisions, in the progress of the year, each one will be more likely to receive his portion of spiritual meat in due season. Finally, the work may be adapted, in an almost endless variety of ways, to existing circumstances. The index to subjects will enable the one officiating to pick out and associate together suggestive passages of scripture suited to any and all ordinary occasions.

It is thought that by the use of such outlines as these throughout the year, and from year to year, with such modifications and variations as circumstances require and the mind of the one officiating suggests, not only may the servie of prayer be made more edifying, but the "vain repetitions" and meaningless platitudes, so often complained of, may be avoided in the service of prayer.

BLOOMSBURY, N. J. MARCH, 1885.   J. C. C.

GUIDE TO PRAYER.

PART I.
SABBATH DAY SERVICES.

FIRST SAB. MORN..   **JANUARY.**   LESSON, PROV. 8.
Address to God.   *Present bodies.*

Rom. 12 : 1. I beseech you therefore, brethren, by the mercies of God, that ye present your bodies a living sacrifice, holy, acceptable unto God, which is your reasonable service.

Ps. 118 : 27. God is the Lord, which hath shewed us light: bind the sacrifice with cords, even unto the horns of the altar.

Confess sin.   *Sin self-accusing.*

Josh. 7 : 19. And Joshua said unto Achan, My son, give, I pray thee, glory to the Lord God of Israel, and make confession unto him; and tell me now what thou hast done; hide it not from me.

Ask for blessings.   *Spirit of prayer.*

Ezek. 36 : 37. Thus saith the Lord God: I will yet for this be inquired of by the house of Israel, to do it for them: I will increase them with men like a flock.

John 6 : 6. And this he said to prove him: for he himself knew what he would do.

Mark 11 : 24. Therefore I say unto you, What things soever ye desire, when ye pray, believe that ye receive them, and ye shall have them.

Thank for mercies.   *Spirit of praise.*

Ps. 147 : 1. Praise ye the Lord: for it is good to sing praises unto our God; for it is pleasant; and praise is comely.

Ps. 92 : 1, 2. It is a good thing to give thanks unto the Lord, and to sing praises unto thy name, O Most High: to shew forth thy loving-kindness in the morning, and thy faithfulness every night.

Intercede for others. *Propagation of the gospel.*

Is. 13 : 5. They come from a far country, from the end of heaven, even the Lord, and the weapons of his indignation, to destroy the whole land.

Is. 60 : 7, 8. All the flocks of Kedar shall be gathered together unto thee, the rams of Nebaioth shall minister unto thee: they shall come up with acceptance on my altar, and I will glorify the house of my glory. Who are these that fly as a cloud, and as doves to their windows?

FIRST SAB. EVE.. JANUARY. LESSON. ACTS 26 : 1—29.
Address to God. *Holiness.*

Rev. 4 : 8. And the four beasts had each of them six wings about him; and they were full of eyes within: and they rest not day and night, saying, Holy, holy, holy, Lord God Almighty, which was, and is, and is to come.

Confess sin. *Humiliation of sin.*

Dan. 9 : 8. O Lord, to us belongeth confusion of face, to our kings, to our princes, and to our fathers, because we have sinned against thee.

Ask for blessings. *Pardon and forgiveness.*

Ezek. 18 : 30. Therefore I will judge you, O house of Israel, every one according to his ways, saith the Lord God. Repent, and turn yourselves from all your transgressions; so iniquity shall not be your ruin.

1 Sam. 12 : 19. And all the people said unto Samuel, Pray for thy servants unto the Lord thy God, that we die not: for we have added unto all our sins this evil, to ask us a king.

Rev. 2 : 11. He that hath an ear, let him hear what the Spirit saith unto the churches: He that overcometh shall not be hurt of the second death.

Thank for mercies. *God's goodness.*

Ex. 33 : 19. And he said, I will make all my goodness pass before thee, and I will proclaim the name of the Lord before thee; and will be gracious to whom I will be gracious, and will shew mercy on whom I will shew mercy.

Ps. 145 : 10. All thy works shall praise thee, O Lord; and thy saints shall bless thee.

Intercede for others. *Church in distant parts.*

Deut. 33 : 19. They shall call the people unto the mountain; there they shall offer sacrifices of righteousness: for they shall suck of the abundance of the seas, and of treasures hid in the sand.

SECOND SAB. MORN.,   JANUARY.   LESSON, JOB 37.
Address to God.   *Glory.*
Ps. 104 : 1, 2. Bless the Lord, O my soul. O Lord my God, thou art very great; thou art clothed with honor and majesty: who coverest thyself with light as with a garment: who stretchest out the heavens like a curtain:

Ps. 18 : 11. He made darkness his secret place; his pavilion round about him were dark waters and thick clouds of the skies.

Job 37 : 19. Teach us what we shall say unto him; for we cannot order our speech by reason of darkness.

Confess sin.   *Plead promises.*
Ps. 130 : 3, 4, 7, 8. If thou, Lord, shouldest mark iniquity, O Lord, who shall stand? But there is forgiveness with thee, that thou mayest be feared. * Let Israel hope in the Lord: for with the Lord there is mercy, and with him is plenteous redemption. And he shall redeem Israel from all his iniquities.

Ask for blessings.   *God's forbearance.*
Neh. 9 : 17. And refused to obey, neither were mindful of thy wonders that thou didst among them: but hardened their necks, and in their rebellion appointed a captain to return to their bondage: but thou art a God ready to pardon, gracious and merciful, slow to anger, and of great kindness, and forsookest them not.

Ps. 103 : 9. He will not always chide: neither will he keep his anger forever.

Thank for mercies.   *God's goodness.*
Ps.104 : 5, 9. Who laid the foundations of the earth, that it should not be removed for ever. * Thou hast set a bound that they may not pass over: that they turn not again to cover the earth.

Is. 54 : 9. For this is as the waters of Noah unto me: for as I have sworn that the waters of Noah should no more go over the earth; so have I sworn that I would not be wroth with thee, nor rebuke thee.

Job 38 : 8, 11. Or who shut up the sea with doors, when it break forth, as if it had issued out of the womb? * And said, Hitherto shalt thou come, but no further: and here shall thy proud waves be stayed?

Intercede for others.   *Church universal.*
Ps. 28 : 9. Save thy people, and bless thine inheritance: feed them also, and lift them up for ever.

Ps. 29 : 11. The Lord will give strength unto his people; the Lord will bless his people with peace.

Ps. 5 : 12. For thou, Lord, wilt bless the righteous; with favor wilt thou compass him as with a shield.

GUIDE TO PRAYER.

SECOND SAB. EVE., JANUARY. LESSON, II COR. 11 : 12—33.
Address to God. *Revealed in works.*
Ps. 19 : 1. The heavens declare the glory of God; and the firmament sheweth his handywork.
Rom. 1 : 20. For the invisible things of him from the creation of the world are clearly seen, being understood by the things that are made, even his eternal power and Godhead; so that they are without excuse:
Ps. 14 : 1. The fool hath said in his heart, There is no God. They are corrupt, they have done abominable works, there is none that doeth good.
Ps. 58.: 11. So that a man shall say, Verily there is a reward for the righteous: verily he is a God that judgeth in the earth.
Confess sin. *Original sin.*
Ecc. 7 : 29. Lo, this only have I found, that God hath made man upright; but they have sought out many inventions.
Ps. 49 : 12, 20. Nevertheless man being in honor abideth not: he is like the beasts that perish. * Man that is in honor, and understandeth not is like the beasts that perish.
Ask for blessings. *Reliance on Christ's righteousness.*
Ps. 11 : 7. For the righteous Lord loveth righteousness; his countenance doth behold the upright.
Ex. 34 : 7. Keeping mercy for thousands, forgiving iniquity and transgression and sin, and that will by no means clear the guilty; visiting the iniquity of the fathers upon the children, and upon the children's children, unto the third and to the fourth generation.
Matt. 18 : 26. The servant therefore fell down, and worshipped him, saying, Lord, have patience with me, and I will pay thee all.
Is. 64 : 6. But we are all as an unclean thing, and all our righteousnesses are as filthy rags; and we all do fade as a leaf; and our iniquities, like the wind, have taken us away.
I Cor. 1 : 30. But of him are ye in Christ Jesus, who of God is made unto us wisdom, and righteousness, and sanctification, and redemption.
II Cor. 5 : 21. For he hath made him to be sin for us, who knew no sin; that we might be made the righteousness of God in him.
Thank for mercies. *God's goodness.*
Acts 17 : 25. Neither is worshipped with men's hands, as though he needed anything, seeing he giveth to all life, and breath, and all things.
Ps. 119 : 64. The earth, O Lord, is full of thy mercy: teach me thy statutes.

Intercede for others. *Conversion of unbelievers.*
I Pet. 3 : 1. Likewise, ye wives, be in subjection to your own husbands; that, if any obey not the word, they also may without the word be won by the conversation of the wives:

I Cor. 14 : 24, 25. But if all prophesy, and there come in one that believeth not, or one unlearned, he is convinced of all, he is judged of all: and thus are the secrets of his heart made manifest; and so falling down on his face he will worship God, and report that God is in you of a truth.

THIRD SAB. MORN., JANUARY. LESSON, Is. 8.
Address to God. *Incomprehensible.*
Job 11 : 7. Canst thou by searching find out God? canst thou find out the Almighty unto perfection?

Confess sin. *Depravity.*
I Cor. 2 : 14. But the natural man receiveth not the things of the Spirit of God: for they are foolishness unto him: neither can he know them, because they are spiritually discerned.

Ask for blessings. *Pardon.*
Rom. 11 : 27. For this is my covenant unto them, when I shall take away their sins.

Jer. 50 : 20. In those days, and in that time, saith the Lord, the iniquity of Israel shall be sought for, and there shall be none; and the sins of Judah, and they shall not be found: for I will pardon them whom I reserve.

Thank for mercies. *Man's wonderful creation.*
Ps. 139. : 14. I will praise thee; for I am fearfully and wonderfully made: and that my soul knoweth right well.

I Cor. 2 : 11. For what man knoweth the things of a man, save the spirit of man which is in him? even so the things of God knoweth no man, but the spirit of God.

Intercede for others, *Revival of the church.*
Jas. 1 : 27. Pure religion and undefiled before God and the Father is this, To visit the fatherless and widows in their affliction, and to keep himself unspotted from the world.

Rom. 14 : 17. For the kingdom of God is not meat and drink: but righteousness, and peace, and joy in the Holy Ghost.

Hab. 3 : 2. O Lord, I have heard thy speech, and was afraid: O Lord, revive thy work in the midst of the years, in the midst of the years make known; in wrath remember mercy.

Heb. 9 : 10. Which stood only in meats and drinks, and divers washings, and carnal ordinances imposed on them until the time of reformation.

THIRD SAB. EVE.,　　　JANUARY.　　　LESSON. REV. 4.
Address to God.　　　　　　　　　Matchless perfections.
 Ex. 15 : 11. Who is like unto thee, O Lord, among the gods? who is like thee, glorious in holiness, fearful in praises, doing wonders?
Confess sin.　　　　　　　　　　　　　　Sinful heart.
 Jer. 4 : 14. O Jerusalem, wash thine heart from wickedness, that thou mayest be saved. How long shall thy vain thoughts lodge within thee?
 Prov. 24 : 9. The thought of foolishness is sin; and the scorner is an abomination to men.
 Matt. : 15 19. For out of the heart proceed evil thoughts, murders, adulteries, fornications, thefts, false witness, blasphemies:
 Micah 2 : 1. Woe to them that devise iniquity, and work evil upon their beds? when the morning is light they practise it, because it is in the power of their hand.
 Prov. 17 : 24. Wisdom is before him that hath understanding; but the eyes of a fool are in the ends of the earth.
Ask for blessings.　　　　　　　　　　　Divine aid.
 Ps. 25 : 21. Let integrity and uprightness preserve me; for I wait on thee.
 Ps. 40 : 12, 13. For innumerable evils have compassed me about: mine iniquities have taken hold upon me, so that I am not able to look up; they are more than the hairs of mine head: therefore my heart faileth me. Be pleased, O Lord, to deliver me: O Lord, make haste to help me.
Thank for mercies.　　　　　　　　God's preserving care.
 Ps. 35 : 10. All my bones shall say, Lord who is like unto thee, which deliverest the poor from him that is too strong for him, yea, the poor and the needy from him that spoileth him?
 Ps. 34 : 20. He keepeth all his bones; not one of them is broken.
Intercede for others.　　　　　　　　Defeat church's enemies.
 Zech. 12 : 3. And in that day will I make Jerusalem a burdensome stone for all people: all that burden themselves with it shall be cut in pieces, though all the people of the earth be gathered together against it.
 Judg. 5 : 31. So let all thine enemies perish, O Lord; but let them that love him be as the sun when he goeth forth in his might.

FOURTH SAB. MORN.,　　　JANUARY.　　　LESSON, Is. 53.
Address to God.　　　　　　　　　　　　Omniscience.
 Heb. 4 : 13. Neither is there any creature that is not manifest in his sight; but all things are naked and opened unto the eyes of him with whom we have to do.

Confess sin. *Affections misplaced.*

Col. 3 : 1. If ye then be risen with Christ, seek those things which are above, where Christ sitteth on the right hand of God.

Matt. 6 : 21. For where your treasure is, there will your heart be also.

Ask for blessings. *Pardon.*

Eph. 1 : 7, 8. In whom we have redemption through his blood, the forgivness of sins, according to the riches of his grace; wherein he hath abounded toward us in all wisdom and prudence:

Rom. 8 : 1. There is therefore now no condemnation to them that are in Christ Jesus, who walk not after the flesh, but after the Spirit.

Thank for mercies. *God's bounties.*

Lk. 22 : 35. And he said unto them, When I sent you without purse, and scrip, and shoes, lacked ye anything? And they said, Nothing.

Intercede for others. *Deliver from persecution.*

Is. 63 : 4. For the day of vengeance is in mine heart, and the year of my redeemed is come.

Is. 34 : 8. For it is the day of the Lord's vengeance, and the year of recompenses for the controversy of Zion.

FOURTH SAB., EVE. JANUARY. LESSON, I TIM. 1.
Address to God. *Eternal, Immortal, Invisible.*

1 Tim. 1 : 17. Now unto the King eternal, immortal, invisible, the only wise God, be honor and glory for ever and ever. Amen.

Confess sin. *Corrupt nature.*

John 3 : 6. That which is born of the flesh is flesh; and that which is born of the Spirit is spirit.

Gen. 3 : 19. In the sweat of thy face shalt thou eat bread, till thou return unto the ground; for out of it wast thou taken: for dust thou art and unto dust shalt thou return.

1 Cor. 15 : 49. And as we have borne the image of the earthy, we shall also bear the image of the heavenly.

Rom. 7 : 18, 19. For I know that in me (that is, in my flesh,) dwelleth no good thing: for to will is present with me; but how to perform that which is good I find not. For the good that I would, I do not: but the evil which I would not, that I do.

Ask for blessings. *Reconciliation.*

Is. 27 : 4, 5. Fury is not in me: who would set the briers and thorns against me in battle? I would go through them, I would burn them together. Or let him take hold of my strength, that he may make peace with me.

Job 22 : 21. Acquaint now thyself with him, and be at peace: thereby good shall come unto thee.

Thank for mercies. *Temporal blessings.*
Job 21 : 9. Their houses are safe from fear, neither is the rod of God upon them.
Ps. 118 : 15. The voice of rejoicing and salvation is in the tabernacles of the righteous: the right hand of the Lord doeth valiantly.

Intercede for others. *For nations.*
Dan. 2 : 44. And in the days of these kings shall the God of heaven set up a kingdom, which shall never be destroyed: and the kingdom shall not be left to other people, but it shall break in pieces and consume these kingdoms, and it shall stand for ever.
Prov. 19 : 21. There are many devices in a man's heart; nevertheless the counsel of the Lord, that shall stand.
Ps. 33 : 11. The counsel of the Lord standeth for ever, the thoughts of his heart to all generations.

FIFTH SAB. MORN., JANUARY. LESSON, JOB 2.
Address to God. *Omnipresent.*
Jer. 23 : 23, 24. Am I a God at hand, saith the Lord, and not a God afar off? Can any hide himself in secret places that I shall not see him? saith the Lord. Do not I fill heaven and earth? saith the Lord.

Confess sin. *Unfaithfulness.*
Lk. 13 : 6, 7. He spake also this parable; A certain man had a fig tree planted in his vineyard; and he came and sought fruit thereon, and found none. Then said he unto the dresser of his vineyard, Behold, these three years I come seeking fruit on this fig tree, and find none: cut it down; why cumbereth it the ground?
Matt. 3 : 10. And now also the axe is laid unto the root of the trees: therefore every tree which bringeth not forth good fruit is hewn down, and cast into the fire.
Is. 5 : 4. What could have been done more to my vineyard, that I have not done in it? wherefore, when I looked that it should bring forth grapes, brought it forth wild grapes?

Ask for blessings. *Converting grace.*
Heb. 8 : 10. For this is the covenant that I will make with the house of Israel after those days, saith the Lord; I will put my laws into their mind, and write them in their hearts: and I will be to them a God, and they shall be to me a people;
Ps. 110 : 3. Thy people shall be willing in the day of thy power, in the beauties of holiness from the womb of the morning: thou hast the dew of thy youth.

Thank for mercies. *Land blest.*
Deut. 8 : 10. When thou hast eaten and art full, then thou shalt

bless the Lord thy God for the good land which he hath given thee.

Deut. 11 : 12. A land which the Lord thy God careth for: the eyes of the Lord thy God are always upon it, from the beginning of the year even unto the end of the year.

Intercede for others. *Our land.*

Jer. 3 : 19. But I said, How shall I put thee among the children, and give thee a pleasant land, a goodly heritage of the hosts of nations? and I said, Thou shalt call me, My father; and shalt not turn away from me.

Is. 8 : 8. And he shall pass through Judah; he shall overflow and go over, he shall reach even to the neck; and the stretching out of his wings shall fill the breadth of thy land, O Immanuel.

Is. 22 : 1. The burden of the valley of vision. What aileth thee now, that thou art wholly gone up to the housetops?

Ezek. 37 : 26, 27. Moreover I will make a covenant of peace with them; it shall be an everlasting covenant with them; and I will place them, and multiply them, and will set my sanctuary in the midst of them for evermore.

FIFTH SAB. EVE., JANUARY. LESSON, 1 JOHN 3.

Address to God. *Omniscience.*

Heb. 4 : 12. For the word of God is quick, and powerful, and sharper than any twoedged sword, piercing even to the dividing asunder of soul and spirit, and of the joints and marrow, and is a discerner of the thoughts and intents of the heart.

Confess sin. *Unworthiness.*

Lk. 15 : 18. I will arise and go to my father, and I will say unto him, Father, I have sinned against heaven, and before thee.

Rom. 3 : 23. For all have sinned, and come short of the glory of God:

Dan. 5 : 23. And the God in whose hand thy breath is, and whose are all thy ways, hast thou not glorified:

Ask for blessings. *Divine favor.*

Ps. 119 : 58. I entreated thy favor with my whole heart: be merciful unto me according to thy word.

Ps. 30 : 5. For his anger endureth but a moment: in his favor is life: weeping may endure for a night, but joy cometh in the morning.

Ps. 63 : 3. Because thy lovingkindness is better than life, my lips shall praise thee.

Thank for mercies. *Spiritual mercies.*

Tit. 3 : 4, 5. But after that the kindness and love of God our Saviour toward man appeared, not by works of righteousness which we have done, but according to his mercy he saved us, by the washing of regeneration, and renewing of the Holy Ghost;

Hos. 13 : 9. O Israel, thou hast destroyed thyself; but in me is thy help.

Intercede for others. *Humble for national sins.*

Jer. 51 : 5. For Israel hath not been forsaken, nor Judah of his God, of the Lord of hosts; though their land was filled with sin against the Holy One of Israel.

FIRST SAB. MORN.. FEBRUARY. LESSON, JER. 9 : 1–16.
Address to God. *Wisdom.*

Ps. 147 : 4, 5. He telleth the number of the stars; he calleth them all by their names. Great is our Lord, and of great power; his understanding is infinite.

Confess sin. *Pride.*

II Chron. 32 : 26. Notwithstanding, Hezekiah humbled himself for the pride of his heart, both he and the inhabitants of Jerusalem, so that the wrath of the Lord came not upon them in the days of Hezekiah.

Rom. 12 : 3. For I say, through the grace given unto me, to every man that is among you, not to think of himself more highly than he ought to think; but to think soberly, according as God hath dealt to every man the measure of faith.

Mic. 6 : 8. He hath shewed thee, O man, what is good; and what doth the Lord require of thee, but to do justly, and to love mercy, and to walk humbly with thy God?

Ask for blessings. *Divine blessing.*

I Chron. 4 : 10. And Jabez called on the God of Israel, saying, O that thou wouldest bless me indeed, and enlarge my coast, and that thine hand might be with me, and that thou wouldest keep me from evil, that it may not grieve me! And God granted him that which he requested.

Ps. 133 : 3. As the dew of Hermon, and as the dew that descended upon the mountains of Zion: for there the Lord commanded the blessing, even life for evermore.

I Chron. 17 : 27. Now therefore let it please thee to bless the house of thy servant, that it may be before thee for ever: for thou blessest, O Lord, and it shall be blessed for ever.

Thank for mercies. *Redemption.*

Heb. 10 : 5, 6, 7. Wherefore, when he cometh into the world, he saith, Sacrifice and offering thou wouldest not, but a body hast thou prepared me; in burnt offerings and sacrifices for sin thou hast had no pleasure. Then said I, Lo, I come (in the volume of the book it is written of me) to do thy will, O God.

Ps. 40 : 7, 8. Then said I, Lo, I come: in the volume of the book it is written of me, I delight to do thy will, O my God: yea, thy law is within my heart.

Intercede for others. *National mercies.*
Ps. 85 : 7—13. Shew us thy mercy, O Lord, and grant us thy salvation. I will hear what God the Lord will speak: for he will speak peace unto his people, and to his saints: but let them not turn again to folly. Surely his salvation is nigh them that fear him; that glory may dwell in our land. Mercy and truth are met together; righteousness and peace have kissed each other. Truth shall spring out of the earth; and righteousness shall look down from heaven. Yea, the Lord shall give that which is good; and our land shall yield her increase. Righteousness shall go before him; and shall set us in the way of his steps.

FIRST SAB. EVE.. FEBRUARY. LESSON, 1 COR. 13.

Address to God. *Sovereignty.*
Ps. 115 : 16. The heaven, even the heavens, are the Lord's: but the earth hath he given to the children of men.
Ps. 24 : 1. The earth is the Lord's, and the fulness thereof; the world, and they that dwell therein.
Ps. 95 : 3, 4, 5. For the Lord is a great God, and a great King above all gods. In his hand are the deep places of the earth: the strength of the hills is his also. The sea is his, and he made it: and his hands formed the dry land.
Ps. 50 : 10. For every beast of the forest is mine, and the cattle upon a thousand hills.

Confess sin. *Anger.*
Prov. 14 : 17. He that is soon angry dealeth foolishly: and a man of wicked devices is hated.
Ecc. 7 : 9. Be not hasty in thy spirit to be angry: for anger resteth in the bosom of fools.
Ps. 106 : 33. Because they provoked his spirit, so that he spake unadvisedly with his lips.
Eph. 4 : 31. Let all bitterness, and wrath, and anger, and clamor, and evil speaking, be put away from you, with all malice.

Ask for blessings. *Divine presence.*
Ex. 33 : 15. And he said unto him, If thy presence go not with me, carry us not up hence.
Heb. 13 : 5. Let your conversation be without covetousness; and be content with such things as ye have: for he hath said, I will never leave thee, nor forsake thee.

Thank for mercies. *Early indications of grace.*
Gen. 3 : 15. And I will put enmity between thee and the woman, and

between thy seed and her seed; it shall bruise thy head, and thou shalt bruise his heel.

Rev. 13 : 8. And all that dwell upon the earth shall worship him, whose names are not written in the book of life of the Lamb slain from the foundation of the world.

Intercede for others. *Continuance of the gospel in the land.*

Amos 8 : 11, 12. Behold, the days come, saith the Lord God, that I will send a famine in the land, not a famine of bread, nor a thirst for water, but of hearing the words of the Lord: and they shall wander from sea to sea, and from the north even to the east, they shall run to and fro to seek the word of the Lord, and shall not find it.

SECOND SAB. MORN.. FEBRUARY. LESSON, EZEK. 2.
Address to God. *Power.*

Job 42 : 2. I know that thou canst do every thing, and that no thought can be withholden from thee.

Ps. 62 : 11. God hath spoken once; twice have I heard this: that power belongeth unto God.

Lk. 1 : 37. For with God nothing shall be impossible.

Confess sin. *Carnal security.*

Amos 6 : 3. Ye that put far away the evil day, and cause the seat of violence to come near;

Ps. 30 : 6. And in my prosperity I said, I shall never be moved.

Is. 56 : 12. Come ye, say they, I will fetch wine, and we will fill ourselves with strong drink; and tomorrow shall be as this day, and much more abundant.

Ask for blessings. *Sense of reconciliation.*

Heb. 9 : 14. How much more shall the blood of Christ, who through the eternal Spirit offered himself without spot to God, purge your conscience from dead works to serve the living God?

Thank for mercies. *Old Testament church favored.*

Ps. 80 : 8, 9. Thou hast brought a vine out of Egypt: thou hast cast out the heathen, and planted it. Thou preparedst room before it, and didst cause it to take deep root, and it filled the land.

Intercede for others. *Continuance of peace in the land.*

Is. 60 : 17, 18. I will also make thy officers peace, and thine exactors righteousness. Violence shall no more be heard in thy land, wasting nor destruction within thy borders; but thou shalt call thy walls Salvation, and thy gates Praise.

Is. 62 : 4. Thou shalt no more be termed Forsaken; neither shall thy land any more be termed Desolate: but thou shalt be called Hephzibah, and thy land Beulah: for the Lord delighteth in thee, and thy land shall be married.

SECOND SAB. EVE., FEBRUARY. LESSON, 1 PET. 5.
Address to God. *Holiness.*
Ps. 22 : 3. But thou art holy, O thou that inhabitest the praises of Israel.
Ps. 111 : 9. He sent redemption unto his people: he hath commanded his covenant for ever: holy and reverend is his name.
Ps. 30 : 4. Sing unto the Lord, O ye saints of his, and give thanks at the remembrance of his holiness.

Confess sin. *Ingratitude.*
Prov. 19 : 3. The foolishness of man perverteth his way: and his heart fretteth against the Lord.
II Chron. 24 : 22. Thus Joash the king remembered not the kindness which Jehoiada his father had done to him, but slew his son. And when he died, he said, The Lord look upon it, and require it.

Ask for blessings. *Peace of conscience.*
I Pet. 2 : 3. If so be ye have tasted that the Lord is gracious.
Ps. 143 : 8. Cause me to hear thy lovingkindness in the morning; for in thee do I put my trust: cause me to know the way wherein I should walk; for I lift up my soul unto thee.

Thank for mercies. *Christ's incarnation.*
John 18 : 37. Pilate therefore said unto him, Art thou a king then? Jesus answered, Thou sayest that I am a king. To this end was I born, and for this cause came I into the world, that I should bear witness unto the truth. Every one that is of the truth heareth my voice.
John 6 : 69. and we believe and are sure that thou art that Christ, the Son of the living God.

Intercede for others. *Wickedness suppressed.*
Ps. 107 : 42. The righteous shall see it, and rejoice: and all iniquity shall stop her mouth.
P . 106 : 30. Then stood up Phinehas, and executed judgment: and so the plague was stayed.

THIRD SAB. MORN., FEBRUARY. LESSON, LAM. 2 : 1—19.
Address to God. *Justice.*
Jer. 12 : 1. Righteous art thou, O Lord, when I plead with thee: yet let me talk with thee of thy judgments: Wherefore doth the way of the wicked prosper? wherefore are all they happy that deal very treacherously.
Ps. 51 : 4. Against thee, thee only have I sinned, and done this evil in thy sight: that thou mightest be justified when thou speakest, and clear when thou judgest.

GUIDE TO PRAYER.

Confess sin. *Uncharitableness.*
Gen. 42 : 21. And they said one to another, We are verily guilty concerning our brother, in that we saw the anguish of his soul, when he besought us, and we would not hear: therefore is this distress come upon us.
Rom. 14 : 19. Let us therefore follow after the things that make for peace, and things wherewith one may edify another.
Ask for blessings. *Divine aid.*
Heb. 4 : 16. Let us therefore come boldly unto the throne of grace, that we may obtain mercy, and find grace to help in time of need.
Thank for mercies. *God's owning Christ's work.*
II Cor. 5 : 19. To wit, that God was in Christ, reconciling the world unto himself, not imputing their trespasses unto them; and hath committed unto us the word of reconciliation.
Intercede for others. *Heal divisions.*
Rom. 15 : 5, 6. Now the God of patience and consolation grant you to be likeminded one toward another according to Christ Jesus: that ye may with one mind and one mouth glorify God, even the Father of our Lord Jesus Christ.
Jude 3. Beloved, when I gave a dilligence to write unto you of the common salvation, it was needful for me to write unto you, and exhort you that ye should earnestly contend for the faith which was once delivered to the saints.

THIRD SAB. EVE., FEBRUARY. LESSON, HEB. 9 : 11—28.
Address to God. *Goodness.*
Ps. 136 : 1. O give thanks unto the Lord; for he is good: for his mercy endureth for ever.
Ps. 100 : 5. For the Lord is good; his mercy is everlasting; and his truth endureth to all generations.
Ps. 117 : 2. For his merciful kindness is great toward us: and the truth of the Lord endureth for ever. Praise ye the Lord.
Confess sin. *Sins of the tongue.*
Prov. 10 : 19. In the multitude of words there wanteth not sin : but he that refraineth his lips is wise.
Job 11 : 2. Should not the multitude of words be answered? and should a man full of talk be justified?
Ask for blessings. *Deliverance from sin.*
Rom. 6 : 6, 12, 13. Knowing this, that our old man is crucified with him, that the body of sin might be destroyed, that henceforth we should

not serve sin. * Let not sin therefore reign in your mortal body, that ye should obey it in the lusts thereof. Neither yield ye your members as instruments of unrighteousness unto sin: but yield yourselves unto God, as those that are alive from the dead, and your members as instruments of righteousness unto God.

Thank for mercies. *Christ's doctrine.*

Heb. 1 : 2. Hath in these last days spoken unto us by his Son, whom he hath appointed heir of all things, by whom also he made the worlds;

John 7 : 16. Jesus answered them, and said, My doctrine is not mine, but his that sent me.

Matt. 7 : 29. For he taught them as one having authority, and not as the scribes.

Matt. 11 : 29. Take my yoke upon you, and learn of me; for I am meek and lowly in heart: and ye shall find rest unto your souls.

Intercede for others. *Victory over enemies.*

Judg. 5 : 18. Zebulun and Naphtali were a people that jeoparded their lives unto the death in the high places of the field.

Ps. 18 : 34, 35. He teacheth my hands to war, so that a bow of steel is broken by my arms. Thou hast also given me the shield of thy salvation: and thy right hand hath holden me up, and thy gentleness hath made me great.

Ps. 140 : 7. O God the Lord, the strength of my salvation, thou hast covered my head in the day of battle.

FOURTH SAB. MORN., FEBRUARY. LESSON, EZRA 3.

Address to God. *Incomprehensible.*

Job 26 : 14. Lo, these are parts of his ways: but how little a portion is heard of him? but the thunder of his power who can understand?

Confess sin. *Spiritual decay.*

Rev. 3 : 2. Be watchful, and strengthen the things that remain, that are ready to die: for I have not found thy works perfect before God.

Ask for blessings. *Deliverance from sin.*

Matt. 26 : 41. Watch and pray, that ye enter not into temptation: the spirit indeed is willing, but the flesh is weak.

1 Cor. 10 : 13. There hath no temptation taken you but such as is common to man: but God is faithful, who will not suffer you to be tempted above that ye are able; but will with the temptation also make a way to escape, that ye may be able to bear it.

Thank for mercies. *Encouraged to seek the Saviour.*

Matt. 9 : 6, 13. But that ye may know that the Son of man hath power on earth to forgive sins, (then saith he to the sick of the palsy,)

Arise, take up thy bed, and go unto thine house. * But go ye and learn what that meaneth, I will have mercy and not sacrifice: for I am not come to call the righteous, but sinners to repentance.

Matt. 1 : 21. And she shall bring forth a son, and thou shalt call his name JESUS: for he shall save his people from their sins.

John 1 : 29. The next day John seeth Jesus coming unto him, and saith, Behold the Lamb of God, which taketh away the sin of the world!

Matt. 11 : 19. The Son of man came eating and drinking, and they say, Behold a man gluttonous, and a winebibber, a friend of publicans and sinners. But wisdom is justified of her children.

Intercede for others. *Godly civil rulers.*

Ps. 132 : 18. His enemies will I clothe with shame: but upon himself shall his crown flourish.

Is. 49 : 23. And kings shall be thy nursing fathers, and their queens thy nursing mothers: they shall bow down to thee with their faces toward the earth, and lick up the dust of thy feet; and thou shalt know that I am the Lord: for they shall not be ashamed that wait for me.

F**OURTH SAB., EVE.** FEBRUARY. LESSON, PHIL. 2.
Address to God. *Glory.*

Ps. 103 : 19. The Lord hath prepared his throne in the heavens; and his kingdom ruleth over all.

Is. 6 : 1, 2. In the year that king Uzziah died I saw also the Lord sitting upon a throne, high and lifted up, and his train filled the temple. Above it stood the seraphim: each one had six wings; with twain he covered his face, and with twain he covered his feet, and with twain he did fly.

Job 26 : 9. He holdeth back the face of his throne, and spreadeth his cloud upon it.

Confess sin. *Sinfulness of sin.*

Rom. 7 : 13. Was then that which is good made death unto me? God forbid. But sin, that it might appear sin, working death in me by that which is good; that sin by the commandment might become exceeding sinful.

1 John 3 : 4. Whosoever committeth sin transgresseth also the law: for sin is the transgression of the law.

Ask for blessings. *Christ's righteousness.*

1 Cor. 1 : 30. But of him are ye in Christ Jesus, who of God is made unto us wisdom, and righteousness, and sanctification, and redemption:

Thank for mercies. *Christ satisfying the law.*

Rom. 5 : 8. But God commendeth his love toward us, in that, while we were yet sinners, Christ died for us.

1 John 4 : 10. Herein is love, not that we loved God, but that he loved us, and sent his son to be the propitiation for our sins.

1 John 2 : 2. And he is the propitiation for our sins: and not for ours only, but also for the sins of the whole world.

Heb. 2 : 9, 14. But we see Jesus, who was made a little lower than the angels for the suffering of death, crowned with glory and honor; that he by the grace of God should taste death for every man. * Forasmuch then as the children are partakers of flesh and blood, he also himself likewise took part of the same; that through death he might destroy him that had the power of death, that is, the devil;

Intercede for others. *Continuance of godly rule.*

Num. 14 : 4. And they said one to another, Let us make a captain, and let us return into Egypt.

Rev. 13 : 11, 12, 13. And I beheld another beast coming up out of the earth; and he had two horns like a lamb, and he spake as a dragon. And he exerciseth all the power of the first beast before him, and causeth the earth and them which dwell therein to worship the first beast, whose deadly wound was healed. And he doeth great wonders, so that he maketh fire come down from heaven on the earth in the sight of men.

FIFTH SAB. MORN., FEBRUARY. LESSON, GEN., 42 : 1—24.

Address to God. *Glory.*

Rev. 4 : 11. Thou art worthy, O Lord, to receive glory and honor and power: for thou hast created all things, and for thy pleasure they are and were created.

Confess sin. *Folly of sin.*

Ps. 69 : 5. O God, thou knowest my foolishness; and my sins are not hid from thee.

Tit. 3 : 3. For we ourselves were sometime foolish, disobedient, deceived, serving divers lusts and pleasures, living in malice and envy, hateful, and hating one another.

1 Tim. 6 : 9. But they that will be rich fall into temptation and a snare, and into many foolish and hurtful lusts, which drown men in destruction and perdition.

Ask for blessings. *Converting grace.*

Ps. 51 : 13. Then will I teach transgressors thy ways; and sinners shall be converted unto thee.

Lk. 1 : 17. And he shall go before him in the spirit and power of Elias, to turn the hearts of the fathers to the children, and the disobedient to the wisdom of the just; to make ready a people prepared for the Lord.

GUIDE TO PRAYER.

Thank for mercies. *Christ's resurrection.*
Rom. 4 : 25. Who was delivered for our offences, and was raised again for our justification.
Rom. 1 : 4. And declared to be the Son of God with power, according to the Spirit of holiness, by the resurrection from the dead:
Intercede for others. *Wisdom to rulers.*
Ps. 82 : 1. God standeth in the congregation of the mighty; he judgeth among the gods.
Ps. 47 : 9. The princes of the people are gathered together, even the people of the God of Abraham: for the shields of the earth belong unto God: he is greatly exalted.

FIFTH SAB. EVE., FEBRUARY. LESSON, COL. 2.
Address to God. *Trinity.*
Matt. 11 : 25. At that time Jesus answered and said, I thank thee, O Father, Lord of heaven and earth, because thou hast hid these things from the wise and prudent and hast revealed them unto babes.
John 1 : 1, 2, 3, 14. In the beginning was the Word, and the Word was with God, and the Word was God. The same was in the beginning with God. All things were made by him; and without him was not anything made that was made. * And the word was made flesh, and dwelt among us, (and we beheld his glory, the glory as of the only begotten of the Father,) full of grace and truth.
Confess sin. *Unprofitableness of sin.*
Job 33 : 27. He looketh upon men, and if any say, I have sinned, and perverted that which was right, and it profited me not:
Ask for blessings. *Sustaining grace.*
II Cor. 12 : 9, 10. And he said unto me, My grace is sufficient for thee: for my strength is made perfect in weakness. Most gladly therefore will I rather glory in my infirmities, that the power of Christ may rest upon me. Therefore I take pleasure in infirmities, in reproaches, in necessities, in persecutions, in distresses for Christ's sake: for when I am weak, then am I strong.
Eph. 6 : 10. Finally, my brethren, be strong in the Lord, and in the power of his might.
Thank for mercies. *Christ's ascension.*
Heb. 6 : 20. Whither the forerunner is for us entered, even Jesus, made a high priest forever after the order of Melchisedec.
Heb. 9 : 24. For Christ is not entered into the holy places made with hands, which are the figures of the true: but into heaven itself, now to appear in the presence of God for us.

Rev. 5 : 6. And I beheld, and, lo, in the midst of the throne and of the four beasts, and in the midst of the elders, stood a Lamb as it had been slain, having seven horns and seven eyes, which are the seven Spirits of God sent forth into all the earth.

Intercede for others. *Judges.*

Ex. 18 : 21. Moreover thou shalt provide out of all the people able men, such as fear God, men of truth, hating covetousness; and place such over them, to be rulers of thousands, and rulers of hundreds, rulers of fifties, and rulers of tens:

Amos 5 : 24. But let judgment run down as waters, and righteousness as a mighty stream.

FIRST SAB. MORN., MARCH. LESSON, EZEK. 17 : 1—21.
Address to God. *Creator.*

Ps. 100 : 3. Know ye that the Lord he is God: it is he that hath made us, and not we ourselves; we are his people, and the sheep of his pasture.

Ps. 95 : 6. O come, let us worship and bow down: let us kneel before the Lord our maker.

Confess sin. *Deceitfulness of sin.*

Rom. 7 : 11. For sin, taking occasion by the commandment, deceived me, and by it slew me.

Heb. 3 : 13. But exhort one another daily, while it is called To-day; lest any of you be hardened through the deceitfulness of sin.

Jas. 1 : 14. But every man is tempted, when he is drawn away of his own lust, and enticed.

Ask for blessings. *Instructing grace.*

Heb. 8 : 11. And they shall not teach every man his neighbor, and every man his brother, saying, Know the Lord: for all shall know me, from the least to the greatest.

Hos. 6 : 3. Then shall we know, if we follow on to know the Lord: his going forth is prepared as the morning; and he shall come unto us as the rain, as the latter and former rain unto the earth.

John 17 : 3. And this is life eternal, that they might know thee the only true God, and Jesus Christ, whom thou hast sent.

Thank for mercies. *Christ's intercession.*

Is. 53 : 12. Therefore will I divide him a portion with the great, and he shall divide the spoil with the strong; because he hath poured out his soul unto death: and he was numbered with the transgressors; and he bear the sin of many, and made intercession for the transgressors.

John 17 : 20, 21. Neither pray I for these alone, but for them also which shall believe on me through their word; that they may also be one: as thou, Father, art in me, and I in thee, that they also may be one in us: that the world may believe that thou hast sent me.

Intercede for others. *Ministry.*
1 Tim. 4 : 13, 15, 16. Till I come, give attendance to reading, to exhortation, to doctrine. * Meditate upon these things; give thy self wholly to them; that thy profiting may appear to all. Take heed unto thyself, and unto the doctrine; continue in them: for in doing this thou shalt both save thyself, and them that hear thee.

Acts 6 : 4. But we will give ourselves continually to prayer, and to the ministry of the word.

FIRST SAB. EVE.,   MARCH.   LESSON, EPH. 5 : 6—33.
Address to God. *God as our God.*
Ps. 16 : 2. O my soul, thou hast said unto the Lord, Thou art my Lord : my goodness extendeth not to thee;

Job 35 : 7. If thou be righteous, what givest thou him? or what receiveth he of thine hand?

Confess sin. *Offense of sin.*
Rom. 2 : 23. Thou that makest thy boast of the law, through breaking the law dishonorest thou God?

Is. 1 : 3, 4. The ox knoweth his owner, and the ass his master's crib: but Israel doth not know, my people doth not consider. Ah sinful nation, a people laden with iniquity, a seed of evil doers, children that are corrupters: they have forsaken the Lord, they have provoked the Holy one of Israel unto anger, they are gone away backward.

Hos. 12 : 14. Ephraim provoked him to anger most bitterly: therefore shall he leave his blood upon him, and his reproach shall his Lord return unto him.

II Sam. 11 : 27. And when the mourning was past, David sent and fetched her to his house, and she became his wife, and bare him a son. But the thing that David had done displeased the Lord.

Ask for blessings. *Instructing grace.*
John 16 : 13. Howbeit when he, the Spirit of truth is come, he will guide you into all truth; for he shall not speak of himself; but whatsoever he shall hear, that shall he speak: and he will shew you things to come.

Job 6 : 24. Teach me, and I will hold my tongue: and cause me to understand wherein I have erred.

Thank for mercies. *Christ's exaltation.*
Matt. 28 : 18. And Jesus came and spake unto them, saying, All power is given unto me in heaven and in earth.

Heb. 2 : 7, 8, 9. Thou madest him a little lower than the angels;

thou crownedst him with glory and honor, and didst set him over the works of thy hands: thou hast put all things in subjection under his feet. For in that he put all in subjection under him, he left nothing that is not put under him. But now we see not yet all things put under him. But we see Jesus, who was made a little lower than the angels for the suffering of death, crowned with glory and honor; that he by the grace of God should taste death for every man.

Intercede for others. *Youth.*
Ps. 110 : 3. Thy people shall be willing in the day of thy power, in the beauties of holiness from the womb of the morning: thou hast the dew of thy youth.

Gal. 4 : 19. My little children, of whom I travail in birth again until Christ be formed in you.

Second Sab. Morn.,   MARCH.   Lesson, I Kin. 19.

Address to God. *Prayed to.*
Eph. 6 : 18. Praying always with all prayer and supplication in the Spirit, and watching thereunto with all perseverance and supplication for all saints;

Col. 4 : 2. Continue in prayer, and watch in the same with thanksgiving.

Phil. 4 : 6. Be careful for nothing; but in everything by prayer and supplication with thanksgiving let your requests be made known unto God.

Confess sin. *Damage of sin.*
Is. 50 : 1. Thus saith the Lord, Where is the bill of your mother's divorcement, whom I have put away? or which of my creditors is it to whom I have sold you? Behold, for your iniquities have ye sold yourselves, and for your transgressions is your mother put away.

Prov. 8 : 36. But he that sinneth against me wrongeth his own soul: and they that hate me love death.

Ask for blessings. *Remembering grace.*
John 14 : 26. But the Comforter, which is the Holy Ghost, whom the Father will send in my name, he shall teach you all things, and bring all things to your remembrance, whatsoever I have said unto you.

Col. 3 : 16. Let the word of Christ dwell in you richly in all wisdom; teaching and admonishing one another in psalms and hymns and spiritual songs, singing with grace in your hearts to the Lord.

Thank for mercies. *Second advent.*
II Thess. 1 : 7, 8, 10. And to you who are troubled rest with us, when the Lord Jesus shall be revealed from heaven with his mighty angels, in flaming fire taking vengeance on them that know not God, and that

obey not the gospel of our Lord Jesus Christ: * When he shall come to be glorified in his saints, and to be admired in all them that believe (because our testimony among you was believed) in that day.

1 Thess. 4 : 14. For if we believe that Jesus died and rose again, even so them also which sleep in Jesus will God bring with him.

Intercede for others.   *Aged christian.*

Ps. 71 : 17, 18. O God, thou hast taught me from my youth: and hitherto have I declared thy wondrous works. Now also when I am old and grayheaded, O God forsake me not; until I have shewed thy strength unto this generation, and thy power to every one that is to come.

Second Sab. Eve.,   MARCH.   Lesson, I John 5.
Address to God.   *Our unworthiness.*

II Chron. 6 : 18. But will God in very deed dwell with men on the earth? Behold, heaven and the heaven of heavens cannot contain thee; how much less this house which I have built!

Job 25 : 6. How much less man, that is a worm? and the son of man, which is a worm?

Confess sin.   *Secret sins.*

Lev. 16 : 21. And Aaron shall lay both his hands upon the head of the live goat, and confess over him all the iniquities of the children of Israel, and all their transgressions in all their sins, putting them upon the head of the goat, and shall send him away by the hand of a fit man into the wilderness.

Ask for blessings.   *Wisdom to do duty.*

I Kin. 3 : 9. Give therefore thy servant an understanding heart to judge thy people, that I may discern between good and bad: for who is able to judge this thy so great a people?

Ecc. 10 : 10. If the iron be blunt, and he do not whet the edge, then must he put to more strength: but wisdom is profitable to direct.

Prov. 14 : 8. The wisdom of the prudent is to understand his way: but the folly of fools is deceit.

Thank for mercies.   *Holy Spirit.*

John 14 : 16, 17. And I will pray the Father, and he shall give you another Comforter, that he may abide with you forever; even the Spirit of truth; whom the world cannot receive, because it seeth him not, neither knoweth him: but ye know him; for he dwelleth with you, and shall be in you.

John 16 : 14. He shall glorify me: for he shall receive of mine, and shall shew it unto you.

Intercede for others. *Afflicted.*

Ps. 34 : 19. Many are the afflictions of the righteous: but the Lord delivereth him out of them all.

Heb. 12 :11. Now no chastening for the present seemeth to be joyous, but grievous: nevertheless, afterward it yieldeth the peaceable fruit of righteousness unto them which are exercised thereby.

THIRD SAB. MORN., MARCH. LESSON, DAN. 3 : 1—18.
Address to God. *Desired.*

Ps. 73 : 25, 26. Whom have I in heaven but thee? and there is none upon earth that I desire beside thee. My flesh and my heart faileth: but God is the strength of my heart, and my portion forever.

Ps. 16 : 5, 6. The Lord is the portion of mine inheritance and of my cup: thou maintainest my lot. The lines are fallen unto me in pleasant places: yea I have a goodly heritage.

Confess sin. *Willfulness.*

Lk. 12 : 47. And that servant which knew his lord's will, and prepared not himself, neither did according to his will, shall be beaten with many stripes.

Ask for blessings. *Sanctification.*

Jer. 31 : 33. But this shall be the covenant that I will make with the house of Israel; After those days, saith the Lord, I will put my law in their inward parts, and write it in their hearts; and will be their God, and they shall be my people.

II Cor. 3 : 3. Forasmuch as ye are manifestly declared to be the epistles of Christ ministered by us, written not with ink, but with the Spirit of the living God; not in tables of stone, but in fleshly tables of the heart.

Ps. 37 : 31. The law of his God is in his heart; none of his steps shall slide.

Ps. 40 : 8. I delight to do thy will, O my God: yea, thy law is within my heart.

Rom. 7 : 22. For I delight in the law of God after the inward man:

Thank for mercies. *Covenant of grace.*

Is. 55 : 3. Incline your ear, and come unto me: hear and your soul shall live; and I will make an everlasting covenant with you, even the sure mercies of David.

Is. 54 : 10. For the mountains shall depart, and the hills be removed; but my kindness shall not depart from thee, neither shall the covenant of my peace be removed, saith the Lord that hath mercy on thee.

Intercede for others. *Enemies.*

Prov. 16 : 7. When a man's ways please the Lord, he maketh even his enemies to be at peace with him.

THIRD SAB. EVE.. MARCH. LESSON, MATT., 3.
Address to God. *Confidence.*
Ps. 31 : 1. In thee. O Lord. do I put my trust; let me never be ashamed: deliver me in thy righteousness.
Ps. 25 : 3. Yea. let none that wait on thee be ashamed: let them be ashamed which transgress without cause.
Ps. 62 : 1, 2. Truly my soul waiteth upon God: from him cometh my salvation. He only is my rock and my salvation; he is my defence; I shall not be greatly moved.
Ps. 89 : 17, 18. For thou art the glory of their strength: and in thy favor our horn shall be exalted. For the Lord is our defence; and the Holy One of Israel is our King.

Confess sin. *Inconsistency.*
Is. 48 : 1, 2. Hear ye this, O house of Jacob, which are called by the name of Israel. and are come forth out of the waters of Judah, and make mention of the God of Israel, but not in truth, nor in righteousness. For they call themselves of the holy city, and stay themselves upon the God of Israel: the Lord of hosts is his name.
Jas. 2 : 6. But ye have despised the poor. Do not rich men oppress you, and draw you before the judgment seats?
II Sam. 12 : 14. Howbeit, because by this deed thou hast given great occasion to the enemies of the Lord to blaspheme, the child also that is born unto thee shall surely die.

Ask for blessings. *Faith.*
Phil. 1 : 29. For unto you it is given in the behalf of Christ, not only to believe on him, but also to suffer for his sake:
Eph. 2 : 8. For by grace are ye saved through faith; and that not of yourselves: it is the gift of God:

Thank for mercies. *Scriptures.*
John 5 : 39. Search the scriptures: for in them ye think ye have eternal life: and they are they which testify of me.
II Tim. 3 : 16. All Scripture is given by inspiration of God, and is profitable for doctrine, for reproof, for correction, for instruction in righteousness.

Intercede for others. *Heathen.*
Ps. 2 : 8. Ask of me, and I shall give thee the heathen for thine inheritance, and the uttermost parts of the earth for thy possession.
Is. 49 : 6. And he said, It is a light thing that thou shouldest be my servant to raise up the tribes of Jacob, and to restore the preserved of

GUIDE TO PRAYER. 25

Israel: I will also give thee for a light to the Gentiles, that thou mayest be my salvation unto the end of the earth.

FOURTH SAB. MORN., MARCH. LESSON, EZEK. 33 : 1—16.
Address to God. *Accept services.*
Ps. 4 : 6, 7. There be many that say, Who will show us any good? Lord, lift thou up the light of thy countenance upon us. Thou hast put gladness in my heart, more than in the time that their corn and their wine increased.
Ps. 119 : 58. I entreated thy favor with my whole heart: be merciful unto me according to thy word.
II Cor. 5 : 9. Wherefore we labor, that, whether present or absent, we may be accepted of him.

Confess sin. *Ingratitude.*
Is. 1 : 2. Hear, O heavens, and give ear, O earth: for the Lord hath spoken; I have nourished and brought up children, and they have rebelled against me.

Ask for blessings. *Fear God.*
Prov. 1 : 7. The fear of the Lord is the beginning of knowledge: but fools despise wisdom and instruction.
Prov. 15 : 33. The fear of the Lord is the instruction of wisdom; and before honor is humility.
Prov. 14 : 27. The fear of the Lord is a fountain of life, to depart from the snares of death.

Thank for mercies. *Ordinances.*
Ps. 147 : 19, 20. He sheweth his word unto Jacob, his statutes and his judgments unto Israel. He hath not dealt so with any nation: and as for his judgments, they have not known them. Praise ye the Lord.

Intercede for others. *Propagation of the gospel.*
Mal. 1 : 11. For, from the rising of the sun even unto the going down of the same, my name shall be great among the Gentiles; and in every place incense shall be offered unto my name, and a pure offering: for my name shall be great among the heathen, saith the Lord of hosts.
Rom. 15 : 16. That I should be the minister of Jesus Christ to the Gentiles, ministering the gospel of God, that the offering up of the Gentiles might be acceptable, being sanctified by the Holy Ghost.

FOURTH SAB., EVE. MARCH. LESSON, ACTS 21 : 17—39.
Address to God. *Aid in prayer.*
Rom. 8 : 26. Likewise the Spirit also helpeth our infirmities: for we know not what we should pray for as we ought: but the Spirit itself maketh intercession for us with groanings which cannot be uttered.

Confess sin. *Perverseness.*

Prov. 29 : 1. He, that being often reproved hardeneth his neck, shall suddenly be destroyed, and that without remedy.

Is. 57 : 17. For the iniquity of his covetousness was I wroth, and smote him: I hid me, and was wroth and he went on frowardly in the way of his heart.

Ask for blessings. *Love to God.*

Matt. 22 : 37. Jesus said unto him, Thou shalt love the Lord thy God with all thy heart, and with all thy soul, and with all thy mind.

Ps. 91 : 14. Because he hath set his love upon me, therefore will I deliver him: I will set him on high, because he hath known my name.

Ps. 37 : 4. Delight thyself also in the Lord: and he shall give thee the desires of thine heart.

Thank for mercies. *Advance of the gospel.*

Rom. 16 : 25, 26. Now to him that is of power to stablish you according to my gospel, and the preaching of Jesus Christ, according to the revelation of the mystery, which was kept secret since the world began, but now is made manifest, and by the Scriptures of the prophets, according to the commandment of the everlasting God, made known to all nations for the obedience of faith:

II Cor. 10 : 4. (For the weapons of our warfare are not carnal, but mighty through God to the pulling down of strong holds:)

Mk. 16 : 20. And they went forth, and preached every where, the Lord working with them, and confirming the word with signs following.

Lk. 10 : 18. And he said unto them, I beheld Satan as lightning fall from heaven.

Intercede for others. *Church universal.*

Eph. 6 : 24. Grace be with all them that love our Lord Jesus Christ in sincerity.

II Tim. 2 : 19. Nevertheless the foundation of God standeth sure, having this seal. The Lord knoweth them that are his. And, Let every one that nameth the name of Christ depart from iniquity.

FIFTH SAB· MORN., MARCH. LESSON, GEN. 22 : 1—19.

Address to God. *Glorified.*

Lev. 10 : 3. Then Moses said unto Aaron, this is it that the Lord spake, saying, I will be sanctified in them that come nigh me, and before all the people I will be glorified.

Ps. 86 : 9. All nations whom thou hast made shall come and worship before thee, O Lord; and shall glorify thy name.

Ps. 50 : 15. And call upon me in the day of trouble: I will deliver thee, and thou shalt glorify me.

Confess sin. *Stubbornness.*
Jer. 5 : 3. O Lord, are not thine eyes upon the truth? thou hast stricken them, but they have not grieved; thou hast consumed them, but they have refused to receive correction: they have made their faces harder than a rock; they have refused to return.
Prov. 22 : 15. Foolishness is bound in the heart of a child; but the rod of correction shall drive it far from him.

Ask for blessings. *Tender conscience.*
I Thess. 5 : 22. Abstain from all appearance of evil.
II Cor. 2 : 11. Lest Satan should get an advantage of us: for we are not ignorant of his devices.

Thank for mercies. *Helpful examples.*
II Cor. 6 : 4. But in all things approving ourselves as the ministers of God, in much patience, in afflictions in necessities, in distresses.
Lk. 21 : 12—15. But before all these, they shall lay their hands on you, and persecute you, delivering you up to the synagogues, and into prisons, being brought before kings and rulers for my name's sake. And it shall turn to you for a testimony. Settle it therefore in your hearts, not to meditate before what ye shall answer: for I will give you a mouth and wisdom, which all your adversaries shall not be able to gainsay nor resist.

Intercede for others. *Defeat church's enemies.*
II Thess. 2 : 2, 3, 8, 10, 11. That ye be not soon shaken in mind, or be troubled, neither by spirit, nor by word, nor by letter as from us, as that the day of Christ is at hand. Let no man deceive you by any means: for that day shall not come, except there come a falling away first, and that man of sin be revealed the son of perdition: * And then shall that Wicked be revealed, whom the Lord shall consume with the spirit of his mouth, and shall destroy with the brightness of his coming: * And with all deceivableness of unrighteousness in them that perish; because they received not the love of the truth, that they might be saved. And for this cause God shall send them strong delusion, that they should believe a lie:

FIFTH SAB. EVE., MARCH. LESSON, JOHN 3 : 14—36.
Address to God. *Reliance on Christ.*
Dan. 9 : 18. O my God, incline thine ear, and hear; open thine eyes, and behold our desolations, and the city which is called by thy name: for we do not present our supplications before thee for our righteousnesses, but for thy great mercies.
Ezra 9 : 15. O Lord God of Israel, thou art righteous; for we remain yet escaped, as it is this day: behold, we are before thee in our tres-

passes; for we cannot stand before thee because of this. Ps. 130 : 3. If thou, Lord, shouldest mark iniquities, O Lord who shall stand?

Jer. 23 : 6. In his days Judah shall be saved, and Israel shall dwell safely: and this is the name whereby he shall be called, THE LORD OUR RIGHTEOUSNESS.

Confess sin. *Treachery.*

Jer. 34 : 18. And I will give the men that have transgressed my covenant, which have not performed the words of the covenant which they had made before me, when they cut the calf in twain, and passed between the parts thereof.

Is. 24 : 16. From the uttermost part of the earth have we heard songs, even glory to the righteous. But I said, My leanness, my leanness, woe unto me! the treacherous dealers have dealt treacherously; yea, the treacherous dealers have dealt very treacherously.

Ask for blessings. *Brotherly love.*

I Thess. 4 : 9, 10. But as touching brotherly love ye need not that I write unto you: for ye yourselves are taught of God to love one another. And indeed ye do it toward all the brethren which are in all Macedonia: but we beseech you, brethren, that ye increase more and more:

Gal. 6 : 10. As we have therefore opportunity, let us do good unto all men, especially unto them who are of the household of faith.

Rom. 12 : 18. If it be possible, as much as lieth in you, live peaceably with all men.

Rom. 14 : 19. Let us therefore follow after the things which make for peace, and things wherewith one may edify another.

Thank for mercies. *Communion of saints.*

I John 1 : 7. But if we walk in the light, as he is in the light, we have fellowship one with another, and the blood of Jesus Christ his Son cleanseth us from all sin.

I Cor. 1 : 2. Unto the church of God which is at Corinth, to them that are sanctified in Christ Jesus, called to be saints, with all that in every place call upon the name of Jesus Christ our Lord, both theirs and ours:

Intercede for others. *Deliver from persecution.*

Ps. 102 : 13, 16, 17. Thou shalt arise, and have mercy upon Zion: for the time to favor her, yea, the set time, is come. * When the Lord shall build up Zion, he shall appear in his glory. He will regard the prayer of the destitute, and will not despise their prayer.

FIRST SAB. MORN., APRIL. LESSON, DAN. 5 : 1—16.
Address to God. *To be worshipped.*

Lam. 3 : 41. Let us lift up our heart with our hands unto God in the heavens.

John 17 : 1. These words spake Jesus, and lifted up his eyes to heaven, and said, Father the hour is come; glorify thy Son, that thy Son also may glorify thee.

Confess sin. *Self condemnation.*

Ezra. 9 : 10. And now, O our God, what shall we say after this? for we have forsaken thy commandments.

Job 7 : 20. I have sinned; what shall I do unto thee, O thou preserver of men? why hast thou set me as a mark against thee, so that I am a burden to myself?

Ask for blessings. *Self denial.*

Matt. 16 : 24. Then said Jesus unto his disciples, If any man will come after me, let him deny himself, and take up his cross, and follow me.

I Cor. 9 : 27. But I keep under my body, and bring it into subjection: lest that by any means, when I have preached to others, I myself should be a castaway.

Thank for mercies. *Hope of eternal life.*

Jas. 1 : 12. Blessed is the man that endureth temptation: for when he is tried, he shall receive the crown of life, which the Lord hath promised to them that love him.

Intercede for others. *Our own land.*

I Kin. 4 : 25. And Judah and Israel dwelt safely, every man under his vine and under his fig tree, from Dan even to Beer-sheba, all the days of Solomon.

II Chron. 15 : 5. And in those times there was no peace to him that went out, nor to him that came in, but great vexations were upon all the inhabitants of the countries.

FIRST SAB. EVE., APRIL. LESSON, JAS. 1.
Address to God. *To be desired.*

Ps. 63 : 1. O God, thou art my God; early will I seek thee: my soul thirsteth for thee, my flesh longeth for thee in a dry and thirsty land, where no water is;

Ex. 15 : 2. The Lord is my strength and song, and he is become my salvation: he is my God, and I will prepare him a habitation; my father's God, and I will exalt him.

Confess sin. *Tried God's patience.*

Rom. 2 : 4. Or despisest thou the riches of his goodness and forbearance and longsuffering; not knowing that the goodness of God leadeth thee to repentance?

II Pet. 3 : 9. The Lord is not slack concerning his promise, as some men count slackness; but is longsuffering to us-ward, not willing that any should perish, but that all should come to repentance.

Ask for blessings. *Humility.*
Job 33 : 17. That he may Withdraw man from his purpose, and hide pride from man.

I Pet. 5 : 5. Likewise, ye younger, submit yourselves unto the elder. Yea, all of you be subject one to another, and be clothed with humility: for God resisteth the proud, and giveth grace to the humble.

I Pet. 3 : 5. For after this manner in the old time the holy women also, who trusted in God, adorned themselves, being in subjection unto their own husbands:

Thank for mercies. *Regeneration.*
1 Thess. 1 : 2, 5. We give thanks to God always for you all, making mention of you in our prayers: * For our gospel came not unto you in word only, but also in power, and in the Holy Ghost, and in much assurance; as ye know what manner of men we were among you for your sake.

Intercede for others. *Continuance of gospel in the land.*
Is. 33 : 6. And wisdom and knowledge shall be the stability of thy times, and strength of salvation; the fear of the Lord is his treasure.

Ps. 72 : 5, 7. They shall fear thee as long as the sun and moon endure, throughout all generations. * In his days shall the righteous flourish; and abundance of peace so long as the moon endureth.

Ps. 102 : 18. This shall be written for the generation to come: and the people which shall be created shall praise the Lord.

SECOND SAB. MORN., APRIL. LESSON, Is. 63.
Address to God. *Perfection.*
I John 1 : 5. This then is the message which we have heard of him, and declare unto you, that God is light, and in him is no darkness at all.

I John 4 : 16. And we have known and believed the love that God hath to us. God is love; and he that dwelleth in love dwelleth in God, and God in him.

Confess sin. *Unrepentant.*
Matt. 3 : 2. And saying, Repent ye: for the kingdom of heaven is at hand.

Acts 5 : 31. Him hath God exalted with his right hand to be a Prince and a Saviour, for to give repentance to Israel, and forgiveness of sins.

Ask for blessings. *Contentment.*
Phil. 4 : 12. I know both how to be abased, and I know how to

GUIDE TO PRAYER. 31

abound: everywhere and in all things I am instructed both to be full and to be hungry, both to abound and to suffer need.

Prov. 15 : 16, 17. Better is little with the fear of the Lord, than great treasure and trouble therewith. Better is a dinner of herbs where love is, than a stalled ox and hatred therewith.

I Tim. 6 : 6. But godliness with contentment is great gain.

Thank for mercies. *Remission of sins.*

Eph. 1 : 7. In whom we have redemption through his blood, the forgiveness of sins, according to the riches of his grace;

Intercede for others. *National peace and righteousness.*

Is. 48 : 18. O that thou hadst hearkened to my commandments! then had thy peace been as a river, and thy righteousness as the waves of the sea:

Prov. 14 : 34. Righteousness exalteth a nation: but sin is a reproach to any people.

SECOND SAB. EVE., APRIL. LESSON, Lk. 2 : 39—52.
Address to God. *Being recognized.*

Heb. 11 : 6. But without faith it is impossible to please him: for he that cometh to God must believe that he is, and that he is a rewarder of them that diligently seek him.

Confess sin. *Polluted.*

Job 11 : 4. For thou hast said, My doctrine is pure, and I am clean in thine eyes.

Lam. 3 : 29. He putteth his mouth in the dust; if so be there may be hope.

Lev. 13 : 45. And the leper in whom the plague is, his clothes shall be rent, and his head bare, and he shall put a covering upon his upper lip, and shall cry, Unclean, unclean.

Ask for blessings. *Resignation.*

Heb. 13 : 5. Let your conversation be without covetousness; and be content with such things as ye have: for he hath said, I will never leave thee, nor forsake thee.

Acts 21 : 4. And when he would not be persuaded, we ceased, saying, The will of the Lord be done.

Thank for mercies. *Preserving grace.*

Matt. 12 : 20. A bruised reed shall he not break, and smoking flax shall he not quench, till he send forth judgment unto victory.

Zech. 4 : 10. For who hath despised the day of small things? for they shall rejoice, and shall see the plummet in the hand of Zerubbabel with those seven; they are the eyes of the Lord, which run to and fro through the whole earth.

Acts 26 : 22. Having therefore obtained help of God, I continue unto this day, witnessing both to small and great, saying none other things than those which the prophets and Moses did say should come:
Intercede for others. *Wickedness suppressed.*
Heb. 12 : 3, 4. For consider him that endured such contradiction of sinners against himself, lest ye be wearied and faint in your minds. Ye have not yet resisted unto blood, striving against sin.

THIRD SAB. MORN., APRIL. LESSON, DAN. 12.
Address to God. *Incomprehensible.*
Ps. 145 : 3. Great is the Lord, and greatly to be praised; and his greatness is unsearchable.
Confess sin. *Lack of contrition.*
Ps. 51 : 17. The sacrifices of God are a broken spirit: a broken and a contrite heart, O God, thou wilt not despise.
Is. 57 : 15. For thus saith the high and lofty One that inhabiteth eternity, whose name is holy; I dwell in the high and holy place, with him also that is of a contrite and humble spirit, to revive the spirit of the humble, and to revive the heart of the contrite ones.
Is. 66 : 1, 2. Thus saith the Lord, The heaven is my throne, and the earth is my footstool: where is the house that ye build unto me? and where is the place of my rest? For all those things hath mine hand made, and all those things have been, saith the Lord: but to this man will I look, even to him that is poor and of a contrite spirit, and trembleth at my word.
Ask for blessings. *Hope.*
Rom. 5 : 4, 5. And patience, experience; and experience, hope: and hope maketh not ashamed; because the love of God is shed abroad in our hearts by the Holy Ghost which is given unto us.
Rom. 15 : 4. For whatsoever things were written aforetime were written for our learning, that we through patience and comfort of the Scriptures might have hope.
Rom. 8 : 24. For we are saved by hope: but hope that is seen is not hope: for what a men seeth, why doth he yet hope for.
Thank for mercies. *Ordinances.*
Is. 56 : 7. Even them will I bring to my holy mountain, and make them joyful in my house of prayer: their burnt offerings and their sacrifices shall be accepted upon mine altar; for mine house shall be called a house of prayer for all people.
Ps. 73 : 28. But it is good for me to draw near to God: I have put my trust in the Lord God, that I may declare all thy works.

GUIDE TO PRAYER. 33

Intercede for others. *Heal divisions.*
Rom. 14 : 3, 19. Let not him that eateth despise him that eateth not; and let not him which eateth not judge him that eateth: for God hath received him. * Let us therefore follow after the things which make for peace, and things wherewith one may edify another.
II Cor. 13 : 11. Finally, brethren, farewell. Be perfect, be of good comfort, be of one mind, live in peace; and the God of love and peace shall be with you.

THIRD SAB. EVE., APRIL. LESSON, I PET. 4.
Address to God. *Perfections matchless.*
Ps. 89. 6, 8. For who in the heaven can be compared unto the Lord? who among the sons of the mighty can be likened unto the Lord? O Lord God of hosts, who is a strong Lord like unto thee? or to thy faithfulness round about thee?
Confess sin. *Corruption of nature.*
Is. 1 : 4. Ah sinful nation, a people laden with iniquity, a seed of evil doers, children that are corrupters: they have forsaken the Lord, they have provoked the Holy One of Israel unto anger, they are gone away backward.
Ezek. 16 : 2, 3. Son of man, cause Jerusalem to know her abominations, and say, Thus saith the Lord God unto Jerusalem; thy birth and thy nativity is of the land of Canaan; thy father was an Amorite, and thy mother a Hittite.
Is. 48 : 8. Yea, thou heardest not; yea, thou knewest not; yea, from that time that thine ear was not opened: for I knew that thou wouldest deal very treacherously, and wast called a transgressor from the womb.
Ask for blessings. *Preserve from sin.*
Ps. 119 : 11. Thy word have I hid in mine heart, that I might not sin against thee.
II Cor. 12 : 9. And he said unto me, My grace is sufficient for thee: for my strength is made perfect in weakness. Most gladly therefore will I rather glory in my infirmities, that the power of Christ may rest upon me.
Ps. 81 : 12. So I gave them up unto their own heart's lust: and they walked in their own counsels.
Thank for mercies. *Answer to prayer.*
Ps. 130 : 1, 2. Out of the depths have I cried unto thee, O Lord. Lord, hear my voice: let thine ears be attentive to the voice of my supplications.
Ps. 61 : 5. For thou, O God, hast heard my vows: thou hast given me the heritage of those that fear thy name.

Intercede for others. *Godly rule continued.*

Is. 33 : 20—22. Look upon Zion, the city of our solemnities: thine eyes shall see Jerusalem a quiet habitation, a tabernacle that shall not be taken down; not one of the stakes thereof shall ever be removed, neither shall any of the cords thereof be broken. But there the glorious Lord will be unto us a place of broad rivers and streams: wherein shall go no galley with oars, neither shall gallant ship pass thereby. For the Lord is our judge, the Lord is our lawgiver, and the Lord is our King; he will save us.

FOURTH SAB. MORN., APRIL. LESSON, JER. 23 : 5—22.

Address to God. *Supreme.*

Hos. 11 : 9. I will not execute the fierceness of mine anger, I will not return to destroy Ephraim: for I am God and not man; the Holy One in the midst of thee: and I will not enter into the city.

Job 10 : 4, 5. Hast thou eyes of flesh? or seest thou as man seeth? Are thy days as the days of man? or thy years as man's days?

Confess sin. *Depravity.*

Jer. 4 : 22. For my people is foolish, they have not known me; they are sottish children, and they have none understanding: they are wise to do evil, but to do good they have no knowledge.

Ps. 82 : 5. They know not, neither will they understand; they walk on in darkness: all the foundations of the earth are out of course.

Ask for blessings. *Govern tongue.*

Ecc. 5 : 2. Be not rash with thy mouth, and let not thine heart be hasty to utter anything before God: for God is in heaven, and thou upon earth: therefore let thy words be few.

Ps. 39 : 1. I said, I will take heed to my ways, that I sin not with my tongue: I will keep my mouth with a bridle, while the wicked is before me.

Thank for mercies. *Aid in affliction.*

Heb. 12 : 10, 11. For they verily for a few days chastened us after their own pleasure; but he for our profit, that we might be partakers of his holiness. Now no chastening for the present seemeth to be joyous, but grievous: nevertheless, afterward it yieldeth the peaceable fruit of righteousness unto them which are exercised thereby.

Intercede for others. *Wisdom to rulers.*

Is. 58 : 12. And they that shall be of thee shall build the old waste places: thou shalt raise up the foundations of many generations; and thou shalt be called, The repairer of the breach, The restorer of paths to dwell in.

Fourth Sab., Eve. APRIL. LESSON, JOHN 14.
Address to God. *Eternity.*

Heb. 13 : 8. Jesus Christ the same yesterday, and to day, and for ever.

Ps. 90 : 2. Before the mountains were brought forth, or ever thou hadst formed the earth and the world, even from everlasting to everlasting, thou art God.

Confess sin. *Forgetfulness of God.*

Ps. 10 : 4. The wicked, through the pride of his countenance, will not seek after God: God is not in all his thoughts.

Deut. 32 : 18. Of the Rock that begat thee thou art unmindful, and hast forgotten God that formed thee.

Jer. 2 : 32. Can a maid forget her ornaments, or a bride her attire? yet my people have forgotten me days without number.

Ps. 49 : 11, 13. Their inward thought is, that their houses shall continue for ever, and their dwellingplaces to all generations; they call their lands after their own names. * This their way is their folly: yet their posterity approve their sayings. Selah.

Ask for blessings. *Govern tongue.*

Col. 4 : 6. Let your speech be always with grace, seasoned with salt, that ye may know how ye ought to answer every man.

Matt. 12 : 35. A good man out of the good treasure of the heart bringeth forth good things: and an evil man out of the evil treasure bringeth forth evil things.

Ps. 37 : 30. The mouth of the righteous speaketh wisdom, and his tongue talketh of judgment.

Is. 59 : 21. As for me, this is my covenant with them, saith the Lord; My Spirit that is upon thee, and my words which I have put in thy mouth, shall not depart out of thy mouth, nor out of the mouth of thy seed, nor out of the mouth of thy seed's seed, saith the Lord, from henceforth and for ever.

Thank for mercies. *Performance of God's promises.*

Ps. 119 : 65. Thou hast dealt well with thy servant, O Lord, according unto thy word.

Ps. 105 : 8. He hath remembered his covenant forever, the word which he commanded to a thousand generations.

Intercede for others. *Judges.*

Ps. 10 : 18. To judge the fatherless and the oppressed, that the man of the earth may no more oppress.

Rom. 13 : 4. For he is the minister of God to thee for good. But if thou do that which is evil, be afraid; for he beareth not the sword in vain: for he is the minister of God, a revenger to execute wrath upon him that doeth evil.

I Pet. 2 : 14. Or unto governors, as unto them that are sent by him for the punishment of evil doers, and for the praise of them that do well.

FIFTH SAB' MORN.,   APRIL.   LESSON, EZEK. 43 : 1—12.
Address to God.   *Omnipresence.*

Acts 17 : 27. That they should seek the Lord, if haply they might feel after him, and find him, though he be not far from every one of us:

Confess sin.   *Affections misplaced.*

Jer. 2 : 13. For my people have committed two evils; they have forsaken me the fountain of living waters, and hewed them out cisterns, broken cisterns, that can hold no water.

Jonah 2 : 8. They that observe lying vanities forsake their own mercy.

Ask for blessings.   *Grace to help.*

Tit. 2 : 11—14. For the grace of God that bringeth salvation hath appeared to all men, teaching us that, denying ungodliness and worldly lusts, we should live soberly, righteously, and godly, in this present world; looking for that blessed hope, and the glorious appearing of the great God and our Saviour Jesus Christ; who gave himself for us, that he might redeem us from all iniquity, and purify unto himself a peculiar people, zealous of good works.

Thank for mercies.   *Spirit of praise.*

Heb. 13 : 15. By him therefore let us offer the sacrifice of praise to God continually, that is, the fruit of our lips, giving thanks to his name.

Ps. 50 : 23. Whoso offereth praise glorifieth me: and to him that ordereth his conversation aright will I show the salvation of God.

Ps. 69 : 31. This also shall please the Lord better than an ox or bullock that hath horns and hoofs.

Intercede for others.   *Ministry.*

Eph. 6 : 19, 20. And for me, that utterance may be given unto me, that I may open my mouth boldly, to make known the mystery of the gospel, for which I am an embassador in bonds; that therein I may speak boldly, as I ought to speak.

II Cor. 3 : 6. Who also hath made us able ministers of the new testament; not of the letter, but of the spirit: for the letter killeth, but the spirit giveth life.

I Cor. 7 : 25. Now concerning virgins I have no commandment of the Lord: yet I give my judgment, as one that hath obtained mercy of the Lord to be faithful.

F**IFTH SAB. EVE.,** APRIL. LESSON, ACTS 9 : 1—22.
Address to God. *Omnipresence.*

Prov. 15 : 3. The eyes of the Lord are in every place, beholding the evil and the good.

II Chron. 16 : 9. For the eyes of the Lord run to and fro throughout the whole earth, to shew himself strong in the behalf of them whose heart is perfect toward him. Herein thou hast done foolishly: therefore from henceforth thou shalt have wars.

Confess sin. *Misplaced affections.*

Matt. 6 : 31, 32. Therefore take no thought, saying, What shall we eat? or, What shall we drink? or, Wherewithal shall we be clothed? (For after all these things do the Gentiles seek:) for your heavenly Father knoweth that ye have need of all these things.

Ask for blessings. *Wisdom.*

Jas. 1 : 5. If any of you lack wisdom, let him ask of God, that giveth to all men liberally, and upbraideth not; and it shall be given him.

Matt. 10 : 16. Behold, I send you forth as sheep in the midst of wolves: be ye therefore wise as serpents, and harmless as doves.

Ecc. 8 : 1, 18. Who is as the wise man? and who knoweth the interpretation of a thing? a man's wisdom maketh his face to shine, and the boldness of his face shall be changed. * Wisdom is better than weapons of war;

Thank for mercies. *God's goodness.*

Ps. 145 : 8. The Lord is gracious, and full of compassion; slow to anger, and of great mercy.

Lam. 3 : 32, 33. But though he cause grief, yet will he have compassion according to the multitude of his mercies. For he doth not afflict willingly, nor grieve the children of men.

Intercede for others. *Assurance of faith.*

II Pet. 1 : 4. Whereby are given unto us exceeding great and precious promises; that by these ye might be partakers of the divine nature, having escaped the corruption that is in the world through lust.

II Tim. 1 : 12. For the which cause I also suffer these things: nevertheless I am not ashamed; for I know whom I have believed, and am persuaded that he is able to keep that which I have committed unto him against that day.

F**IRST SAB. MORN.,** MAY. LESSON, I Kin., 8 : 1—21.
Address to God. *Wisdom.*

Is. 28 : 29. This also cometh forht from the Lord of hosts, which is wonderful in counsel, and excellent in working.

GUIDE TO PRAYER.

Job 9 : 4. He is wise in heart, and mighty in strength: who hath hardened himself against him, and hath prospered?
Confess sin. *Corrupt nature.*
Rom. 7 : 21—23. I find then a law, that, when I would do good, evil is present with me. For I delight in the law of God after the inward man: but I see another law in my members, warring against the law of my mind, and bringing me into captivity to the law of sin which is in my members.
Ask for blessings. *Diligence.*
John 9 : 4. I must work the works of him that sent me, while it is day: the night cometh, when no man can work.
Ecc. 9 : 10. Whatsoever thy hand findeth to do, do it with thy might; for there is no work, nor device, nor knowledge, nor wisdom, in the grave, whither thou goest.
Thank for mercies. *God's goodness.*
Ps. 104 : 27—31. These wait all upon thee; that thou mayest give them their meat in due season. That thou givest them they gather: thou openest thine hand, they are filled with good. Thou hidest thy face, they are troubled: thou takest away their breath, they die, and return to their dust. Thou sendest forth thy spirit, they are created; and thou renewest the face of the earth. The glory of the Lord shall endure forever: the Lord shall rejoice in his works.
Intercede for others. *Guide of life.*
II Tim. 3 : 14. But continue thou in the things which thou hast learned and hast been assured of, knowing of whom thou hast learned them.
Prov. 16 : 31. The hoary head is a crown of glory, if it be found in the way of righteousness.

FIRST SAB. EVE., MAY. LESSON, MATT. 20 : 1—16.
Address to God. *Sovereignty.*
Job 12 : 10. In whose hand is the soul of every living thing, and the breath of all mankind.
Confess sin. *Unfaithfulness.*
Jas. 4 : 17. Therefore to him that knoweth to do good, and doeth it not, to him it is sin.
Matt. 25 : 18, 25. But he that had received one went and digged in the earth, and hid his lord's money. * And I was afraid, and went and hid thy talent in the earth: lo, there thou hast that is thine.
Ask for blessings. *Courage.*
II Tim. 2 : 3. Thou therefore endure hardness, as a good soldier of Jesus Christ.

Is. 51 : 7. Hearken unto me, ye that know righteousness, the people in whose heart is my law; fear ye not the reproach of men, neither be ye afraid of their revilings.
Mk. 8 : 38. Whosoever therefore shall be ashamed of me and of my words, in this adulterous and sinful generation, of him also shall the Son of man be ashamed, when he cometh in the glory of his Father with the holy angels.

Thank for mercies. *Man made a rational creature.*
Ps. 8 : 5. For thou hast made him a little lower than the angels, and hast crowned him with glory and honor.
Job 32 : 8. But there is a spirit in man: and the inspiration of the Almighty giveth them understanding.
Prov. 20 : 27. The spirit of man is the candle of the Lord, searching all the inward parts of the belly.
I Cor. 6 : 19. What! know ye not that your body is the temple of the Holy Ghost which is in you, which ye have of God, and ye are not your own?

Intercede for others. *Enemies.*
Is. 11 : 6, 9, 13. The wolf also shall dwell with the lamb, and the leopard shall lie down with the kid; and the calf and the young lion and the fatling together, and a little child shall lead them. * They shall not hurt nor destroy in all my holy mountain: for the earth shall be full of the knowledge of the Lord, as the waters cover the sea. * The envy also of Ephraim shall depart, and the adversaries of Judah shall be cut off: Ephraim shall not envy Judah, and Judah shall not vex Ephraim.

SECOND SAB. MORN., MAY. LESSON, EZEK. 37 : 1—19.
Address to God. *Power.*
Matt. 28 : 18. And Jesus came and spake unto them, saying, all power is given unto me in heaven and in earth.

Confess sin. *Disobedient.*
Ps. 51 : 4. Against thee, thee only, have I sinned, and done this evil in thy sight: that thou mightest be justified when thou speakest, and be clear when thou judgest.
Dan. 9 : 10. Neither have we obeyed the voice of the Lord our God, to walk in his laws, which he set before us by his servants the prophets.
Rom. 7 : 12. Wherefore the law is holy, and the commandment holy, and just, and good.

Ask for blessings. *Joyousness.*
I Thess. 5 : 16. Rejoice evermore.
Phil. 4 : 4. Rejoice in the Lord always: and again I say, Rejoice.

Acts 8 : 39. And when they were come up out of the water, the Spirit of the Lord caught away Philip, that the eunuch saw him no more: and he went on his way rejoicing.

Ecc. 9 : 7. Go thy way, eat thy bread with joy, and drink thy wine with a merry heart; for God now accepteth thy works.

Thank for mercies. *Preserving care.*

Ps. 3 : 5. I laid me down and slept: I awaked; for the Lord sustained me.

Intercede for others. *Church universal.*

John 17 : 20, 21. Neither pray I for these alone, but for them also which shall believe on me through their word; that they all may be one; as thou, Father, art in me, and I in thee, that they also may be one in us: that the world may believe that thou hast sent me.

Eph. 4 : 4—6. There is one body, and one Spirit, even as ye are called in one hope of your calling; one Lord, one faith, one baptism, one God and Father of all, who is above all, and through all, and in you all.

Jer. 32 : 39. And I will give them one heart, and one way, that they may fear me for ever, for the good of them, and of their children after them.

SECOND SAB. EVE., MAY. LESSON, ROM. 13.

Address to God. *Holiness.*

Hab. 1 : 13. Thou art of purer eyes than to behold evil, and canst not look on iniquity: wherefore lookest thou upon them that deal treacherously, and holdest thy tongue when the wicked devoureth the man that is more righteous than he?

Ps. 5 : 4. For thou art not a God that hath pleasure in wickedness: neither shall evil dwell with thee.

Confess sin. *Trusting in self.*

Prov. 3 : 5. Trust in the Lord with all thine heart; and lean not unto thine own understanding.

Prov. 28 : 26. He that trusteth in his own heart is a fool: but whoso walketh wisely, he shall be delivered.

Hab. 1 : 16. Therefore they sacrifice unto their net, and burn incense unto their drag; because by them their portion is fat, and their meat plenteous.

Ask for blessings. *Christian fellowship.*

Ps. 133 : 1, 3. Behold how good and how pleasant it is for brethren to dwell together in unity! As the dew of Hermon, and as the dew that descended upon the mountains of Zion: for there the Lord commanded the blessing, even life for evermore.

I Pet. 3 : 7. Likewise, ye husbands, dwell with them according to knowledge, giving honor unto the wife, as unto the weaker vessel, and as being heirs together of the grace of life; that your prayers be not hindered.

Thank for mercies. *Deliverance in peril.*

1 Sam. 20 : 3. And David sware moreover, and said, Thy father certainly knoweth that I have found grace in thine eyes; and he saith, Let not Jonathan know this, lest he be grieved: but truly, as the Lord liveth, and as thy soul liveth, there is but a step between me and death.

II Cor. 1 : 9. But we had the sentence of death in ourselves, that we should not trust in ourselves, but in God which raiseth the dead.

Is. 38 : 10, 17. I said in the cutting off of my days, I shall go to the gates of the grave: I am deprived of the residue of my years. * Behold, for peace I had great bitterness; but thou hast in love to my soul delivered it from the pit of corruption: for thou hast cast all my sins behind thy back.

Intercede for others. *Defeat of Church's enemies.*

Rev. 18 : 2, 21. And he cried mightily with a strong voice, saying, Babylon the great is fallen, is fallen, and is become the habitation of devils, and the hold of every foul spirit, and a cage of every unclean and hateful bird. * And a mighty angel took up a stone like a great millstone, and cast it into the sea, saying, Thus with violence shall that great city Babylon be thrown down, and shall be found no more at all.

Rev. 17 : 13. These have one mind, and shall give their power and strength unto the beast.

Rev. 21 : 24. And the nations of them which are saved shall walk in the light of it: and the kings of the earth do bring their glory and honor into it.

THIRD SAB. MORN., MAY. LESSON, EX. 3 : 1—18.
Address to God. *Justice.*

Ps. 36 : 6. Thy righteousness is like the great mountains; thy judgments are a great deep: O Lord, thou preservest man and beast.

Ps. 97 : 1, 2. The Lord reigneth; let the earth rejoice; let the multitude of isles be glad thereof. Clouds and darkness are round about him; righteousness and judgment are the habitation of his throne.

Confess sin. *Covetousness.*

Heb. 13 : 5. Let your conversation be without covetousness; and be content with such things as ye have: for he hath said, I will never leave thee nor forsake thee.

Phil. 4 : 11. Not that I speak in respect of want: for I have learned, in whatsoever state I am, therewith to be content.

Ask for blessings. *Submission.*

II Cor. 5 : 14, 15. For the love of Christ constraineth us; because we thus judge, that if one died for all, then were all dead: and that he died for all, that they which live should not henceforth live unto themselves, but unto him which died for them, and rose again.

Thank for mercies. *Warned of false security.*

1 Tim. 6 : 17. Charge them that are rich in this world, that they be not high minded, nor trust in uncertain riches, but in the living God, who giveth us richly all things to enjoy;

Job 12 : 6. The tabernacles of robbers prosper, and they that provoke God are secure: into whose hand God bringeth abundantly.

Intercede for others. *Afflicted.*

Amos 7 : 5. Then said I, O Lord God, cease, I beseech thee: by whom shall Jacob arise? for he is small.

Dan. 9 : 17. Now therefore, O our God, hear the prayer of thy servant, and his supplications, and cause thy face to shine upon thy sanctuary that is desolate, for the Lord's sake.

THIRD SAB. EVE., MAY. LESSON, JOHN 13 : 1—26.

Address to God. *Goodness.*

Ex. 34 : 6, 7. And the Lord passed by before him, and proclaimed, The Lord, The Lord God, merciful and gracious, longsuffering, and abundant in goodness and truth, keeping mercy for thousands, forgiving iniquity and transgression and sin, and that will by no means clear the guilty; visiting the iniquity of the fathers upon the children, and upon the children's children, unto the third and to the fourth generation.

Prov. 18 : 10. The name of the Lord is a strong tower: the righteous runneth into it, and is safe.

Confess sin. *Carnal security.*

Lk. 12 : 19, 20. And I will say to my soul, Soul, thou hast much goods laid up for many years; take thine ease, eat, drink, and be merry. But God said unto him, Thou fool, this night thy soul shall be required of thee: then whose shall those things be, which thou hast provided?

Ask for blessings *Grace.*

Col. 2 : 19. And not holding the Head, from which all the body by joints and bands having nourishment ministered, and knit together, increaseth with the increase of God.

II Pet. 3 : 18. But grow in grace, and in the knowledge of our Lord and Saviour Jesus Christ. To him be glory both now and for ever.

Job 17 : 9. The righteous also shall hold on his way, and he that hath clean hands shall be stronger and stronger.

Thank for mercies. *Temporal Blessings.*
Gen. 32 : 10. I am not worthy of the least of all the mercies, and of all the truth, which thou hast shewed unto thy servant; for with my staff I passed over this Jordan; and now I am become two bands.
Ps. 68 : 6. God setteth the solitary in families: he bringeth out those which are bound with chains: but the rebellious dwell in a dry land.
Intercede for others. *Own land.*
I Kin. 10 : 9. Blessed be the Lord thy God, which delighted in thee to set thee on the throne of Israel: because the Lord loved Israel for ever, therefore made he thee king, to do judgment and justice.
Rom. 13 : 3. For rulers are not a terror to good works, but to the evil. Wilt thou then not be afraid of the power? do that which is good, and thou shalt have praise of the same.

FOURTH SAB. MORN., MAY. LESSON, HOS. 10.
Address to God. *Incomprehensible.*
Job 37 : 23. Touching the Almighty, we cannot find him out: he is excellent in power, and in judgment, and in plenty of justice: he will not afflict.
Neh. 9 : 5. Then the Levites, Jeshua, and Kadmiel, Bani, Hashabniah, Sherebiah, Hodijah, Shebaniah, and Pethahiah, said, Stand up and bless the Lord your God for ever and ever: and blessed be thy glorious name, which is exalted above all blessing and praise.
Confess sin. *Impatience.*
Prov. 3 : 11. My son, despise not the chastening of the Lord; neither be weary of his correction:
Prov. 24 : 10. If thou faint in the day of adversity, thy strength is small.
Ask for blessings. *Sustaining power.*
Deut. 33 : 27. The eternal God is thy refuge, and underneath are the everlasting arms: and he shall thrust out the enemy from before thee; and shal say, Destroy them.
Is. 57 : 16. For I will not contend for ever, neither will I be always wroth: for the spirit should fail before me, and the souls which I have made.
Thank for mercies. *Blessings to land.*
Ps. 147 : 14. He maketh peace in thy borders, and filleth thee with the finest of the wheat.
Judg. 5 : 11. They that are delivered from the noise of archers in the places of drawing water, there shall they rehearse the righteous acts of the Lord, even the righteous acts toward the inhabitants of his villages in Israel: then shall the people of the Lord go down to the gates.

Intercede for others. *Country's peace, plenty, and righteousness.*

Deut. 28 : 23. And thy heaven that is over thy head shall be brass, and the earth that is under thee shall be iron.

Hos. 2 : 9. Therefore will I return, and take away my corn in the time thereof, and my wine in the season thereof, and will recover my wool and my flax given to cover her nakedness.

Joel 2 : 23. Be glad then, ye children of Zion, and rejoice in the Lord your God: for he hath given you the former rain moderately, and he will cause to come down for you the rain, the former rain, and the latter rain in the first month.

Jer. 5 : 24. Neither say they in their heart, Let us now fear the Lord our God, that giveth rain, both the former and the latter, in his season: he reserveth unto us the appointed weeks of the harvest.

Lev. 26 : 4, 5. Then I will give you rain in due season, and the land shall yield her increase, and the trees of the field shall yield their fruit. And your threshing shall reach unto the vintage, and the vintage shall reach unto the sowing time: and ye shall eat your bread to the full, and dwell in your land safely.

FOURTH SAB., EVE.   MAY.   LESSON, COL., 3.
Address to God.   *Glory.*

Ps. 104 : 4. Who maketh his angels spirits; his ministers a flaming fire:

Dan. 7 : 10. A fiery stream issued and came forth from before him: thousand thousands ministered unto him, and ten thousand times ten thousand stood before him: the judgment was set, and the books were opened.

Ps. 103 : 20, 21. Bless the Lord, ye his angels, that excel in strength, that do his commandments, hearkening unto the voice of his word. Bless the Lord, all ye his hosts; ye ministers of his, that do his pleasure.

Heb. 12 : 22, 23. But ye are come unto mount Sion, and unto the city of the living God, the heavenly Jerusalem, and to an innumerable company of angels, to the general assembly and church of the firstborn, which are written in heaven, and to God the Judge of all, and to the spirits of just men made perfect.

Confess sin.   *Uncharitableness.*

I Cor. 13 : 4, 5. Charity suffereth long, and is kind; charity envieth not; charity vaunteth not itself, is not puffed up, doth not behave itself unseemly, seeketh not her own, is not easily provoked, thinketh no evil;

Prov. 17 : 5. Whoso mocketh the poor reproacheth his Maker: and he that is glad at calamities shall not be unpunished.

GUIDE TO PRAYER. 45

Ask for blessings. *Preserving grace.*
II Tim. 4 : 18. And the Lord shall deliver me from every evil work, and will preserve me unto his heavenly kingdom: to whom be glory for ever and ever. Amen.
Jude 1 : 24. Now unto him that is able to keep you from falling, and to present you faultless before the presence of his glory with exceeding joy,

Thank for mercies. *Spiritual blessings.*
Ps. 49 : 7. None of them can by any means redeem his brother, nor give to God a ransom for him:
Job 33 : 24. Then he is gracious unto him, and saith, Deliver him from going down to the pit: I have found a ransom.

Intercede for others. *Wickedness suppressed.*
Zech. 13 : 2. And it shall come to pass in that day, saith the Lord of hosts, that I will cut off the names of the idols out of the land, and they shall no more be remembered: and also I will cause the prophets and the unclean spirit to pass out of the land.
Zeph. 3 : 9. For then will I turn to the people a pure language, that they may all call upon the name of the Lord, to serve him with one consent.

FIFTH SAB. MORN., MAY. LESSON, I KIN. 6 : 1—22.
Address to God. *Creator.*
Rev. 14 : 7. Saying with a loud voice, Fear God, and give glory to him: for the hour of his judgment is come: and worship him that made heaven, and earth and the sea, and the fountains of waters.
Ps. 33 : 9. For he spake, and it was done; he commanded, and it stood fast.
Gen. 1 : 3, 6, 7. And God said, Let there be light: and there was light. * And God said, Let there be a firmament in the midst of the waters, and let it divide the waters from the waters. And God made the firmament, and divided the waters which were under the firmament from the waters which were above the firmament: and it was so.
Ps. 119 : 91. They continue this day according to thine ordinances: for all are thy servants.

Confess sin. *Tongue.*
Prov. 10 : 21, 32. The lips of the righteous feed many: but fools die for want of wisdom. * The lips of the righteous know what is acceptable: but the mouth of the wicked speaketh frowardness.
Eph. 4 : 29. Let no corrupt communication proceed out of your mouth, but that which is good to the use of edifying, that it may minister grace unto the hearers.

Eph. 5 : 4. Neither filthiness, nor foolish talking, nor jesting, which are not convenient: but rather giving of thanks.

Ask for blessings. *Dying grace.*

Ps. 39 : 4, 5. Behold, thou hast made my days as a handbreadth; and mine age is as nothing before thee: verily every man at his best state is altogether vanity.. Selah. Lord, make me to know mine end, and the measure of my days, what it is; that I may know how frail I am.

I Chron. 29 : 15. For we are strangers before thee, and sojourners, as were all our fathers: our days on the earth are as a shadow, and there is none abiding.

Thank for mercies. *Predestination.*

II Thess. 2 : 13. But we are bound to give thanks always to God for you, brethren beloved of the Lord, because God hath from the beginning chosen you to salvation through sanctification of the Spirit and belief of the truth:

Rom. 11 : 5. Even so then at this present time, also there is a remnant according to the election of grace.

Eph. 1 : 4—6. According as he hath chosen us in him before the foundation of the world, that we should be holy and without blame before him in love: having predestinated us unto the adoption of children by Jesus Christ to himself, according to the good pleasure of his will, to the praise of the glory of his grace, wherein he hath made us accepted in the beloved.

Intercede for others. *Heal divisions.*

Phil. 2 : 3. Let nothing be done through strife or vainglory; but in lowliness of mind let each esteem other better than themselves.

Phil. 4 : 5. Let your moderation be known unto all men. The Lord is at hand.

FIFTH SAB. EVE., MAY. LESSON, LK. 15 : 11—32.
Address to God. *Trinity.*

John 5 : 23. That all men should honor the Son, even as they honor the Father. He that honoreth not the Son honoreth not the Father which hath sent him.

Heb. 1 : 3, 6. Who being the brightness of his glory, and the express image of his person, and upholding all things by the word of his power, when he had by himself purged our sins, sat down on the right hand of the Majesty on high; * And again, when he bringeth in the firstbegotten into the world, he saith, And let all the angels of God worship him.

Confess sin. *Slothfulness.*

Ecc. 11 : 4. He that observeth the wind shall not sow; and he that regardeth the clouds shall not reap.
Prov. 26 : 14. As the door turneth upon his hinges, so doth the slothful upon his bed.
Prov. 6 : 10. Yet a little sleep, a little slumber, a little folding of the hands to sleep:

Ask for blessings. *Fit for heaven.*
Col. 1 : 12. Giving thanks unto the Father, which hath made us meet to be partakers of the inheritance of the saints in light:
II Cor. 5 : 5. Now he that hath wrought us for the selfsame thing is God, who also hath given unto us the earnest of the Spirit.

Thank for mercies. *Redeemer provided.*
John 5 : 22, 26, 27. For the Father judgeth no man, but hath committed all judgment unto the Son: * For as the Father hath life in himself; so hath he given to the Son to have life in himself: and hath given him authority to execute judgment also, because he is the Son of man.
John 3 : 35. The Father loveth the Son, and hath given all things into his hand.
Zech. 6 : 13. Even he shall build the temple of the Lord; and he shall bear the glory, and shall sit and rule upon his throne; and he shall be a priest upon his throne; and the counsel of peace shall be between them both.

Intercede for others. *Ministry.*
Gen. 49 : 24. But his bow abode in strength, and the arms of his hands were made strong by the hands of the mighty God of Jacob; (from thence is the shepherd, the stone of Israel;)
Micah 3 : 8. But truly I am full of power by the Spirit of the Lord, and of judgment, and of might, to declare unto Jacob his transgression, and to Israel his sin.
Is. 58 : 1. Cry aloud, spare not, lift up thy voice like a trumpet, and shew my people their transgression, and the house of Jacob their sins.

FIRST SAB. MORN., JUNE. LESSON, NUM. 24.
Address to God. *Creator.*
Ps. 139 : 14—16. I will praise thee; for I am fearfully and wonderfully made: marvelous are thy works; and that my soul knoweth right well. My substance was not hid from thee, when I was made in secret, and curiously wrought in the lowest parts of the earth. Thine eyes did see my substance, yet being unperfect; and in thy book all my members were written, which in continuance were fashioned, when as yet there was none of them.

Confess sin. *Presumptuous sin.*

Lk. 19 : 14. But his citizens hated him, and sent a message after him, saying, We will not have this man to reign over us.

Ex. 5 : 2. And Pharaoh said, Who is the Lord, that I should obey his voice to let Israel go? I know not the Lord, neither will I let Israel go.

Num. 15 : 30. But the soul that doeth aught presumptuously, whether he be born in the land, or a stranger, the same reproacheth the Lord; and that soul shall be cut off from among his people.

Neh. 9 : 26. Nevertheless they were disobedient, and rebelled against thee, and cast thy law behind their backs, and slew thy prophets which testified against them to turn them to thee, and they wrought great provocations.

Ask for blessings. *Temporal blessings.*

I Tim. 4 : 8. For bodily exercise profiteth little: but godliness is profitable unto all things, having promise of the life that now is, and of that which is to come.

Matt. 6 : 32, 33. (For after all these things do the Gentiles seek:) for your heavenly Father knoweth that ye have need of all these things. But seek ye first the kingdom of God, and his righteousness; and all these things shall be added unto you.

I Pet. 5 : 7. Casting all your care upon him: for he careth for you.

Thank for mercies. *Salvation in earliest days.*

Heb. 11 : 2, 4, 39. For by it the elders obtained a good report. * By faith Abel offered unto God a more excellent sacrifice than Cain, by which he obtained witness that he was righteous, God testifying of his gifts: and by it he being dead yet speaketh. * And these all, having obtained a good report through faith, received not the promise:

Intercede for others. *Country's plenty.*

Ps. 132 : 15. I will abundantly bless her provision: I will satisfy her poor with bread.

Is. 62 : 9. But they that have gathered it shall eat it, and praise the Lord; and they that have brought it together shall drink it in the courts of my holiness.

Hag. 1 : 9. Ye looked for much, and, lo, it came to little: and when ye brought it home, I did blow upon it. Why? saith the Lord of hosts. Because of mine house that is waste, and ye run every man unto his own house.

Mal. 3 : 10, 12. Bring ye all the tithes into the storehouse, that there may be meat in mine house, and prove me now herewith, saith the Lord of hosts, if I will not open you the windows of heaven, and pour you out a blessing, that there shall not be room enough to receive it. * And all nations shall call you blessed: for ye shall be a delightsome land, saith the Lord of hosts.

FIRST SAB. EVE.,   JUNE.   LESSON, ACTS 6.
Address to God.   *God as our God.*
Ps. 44 : 4. Thou art my King, O God: command deliverances for Jacob.
Is. 26 : 13. O Lord our God, other lords besides thee have had dominion over us; but by thee only will we make mention of thy name.
Confess sin.   *Folly of sin.*
Prov. 22 : 15. Foolishness is bound in the heart of a child; but the rod of correction shall drive it far from him.
Job 11 : 12. For vain man would be wise, though man be born like a wild ass's colt.
Ask for blessings.   *Preserve from calamities.*
Ps. 91 : 2, 4. 9, 10. I will say of the Lord, He is my refuge and my fortress: my God; in him will I trust. * He shall cover thee with his feathers, and under his wings shalt thou trust: his truth shall be thy shield and buckler. * Because thou hast made the Lord, which is my refuge, even the Most High, thy habitation; there shall no evil befall thee, neither shall any plague come nigh thy dwelling.
Thank for mercies.   *O. T. church favored.*
Rom. 3 : 2. Much every way: chiefly, because that unto them were committed the oracles of God.
Rom. 9 : 4. Who are Israelites; to whom pertaineth the adoption, and the glory, and the covenants, and the giving of the law, and the service of God, and the promises:
I Kin. 8 : 56. Blessed be the Lord, that hath given rest unto his people Israel, according to all that he promised: there hath not failed one word of all his good promise, which he promised by the hand of Moses his servant.
Intercede for others.   *Wickedness suppressed.*
Deut. 26 : 19. And to make thee high above all nations which he hath made, in praise, and in name, and in honor; and that thou mayest be a holy people unto the Lord thy God, as he hath spoken.

SECOND SAB. MORN.,   JUNE.   LESSON, EZEK. 10.
Address to God.   *Prayed to.*
Matt. 7 : 7. Ask, and it shall be given you; seek, and ye shall find: knock, and it shall be opened unto you.
Confess sin.   *Unprofitableness of sin.*

GUIDE TO PRAYER.

Rom. 6 : 21. What fruit had ye then in those things whereof ye are now ashamed? for the end of those things is death.

Matt. 16 : 26. For what is a man profited, if he shall gain the whole world, and lose his own soul; or what shall a man give in exchange for his soul?

Ask for blessings. *Supply needs.*

Ps. 90 : 17. And let the beauty of the Lord our God be upon us: and establish thou the work of our hands upon us; yea, the work of our hands establish thou it.

Ps. 118 : 25. Save now, I beseech thee, O Lord: O Lord, I beseech thee, send now prosperity.

Thank for mercies *Incarnation.*

Lk. 19 : 10. For the Son of man is come to seek and to save that which was lost.

John 10 : 10. The thief cometh not, but for to steal, and to kill, and to destroy: I am come that they might have life, and that they might have it more abundantly.

1 John 3 : 8. He that committeth sin is of the devil; for the devil sinneth from the beginning. For this purpose the Son of God was manifested, that he might destroy the works of the devil.

Intercede for others. *Ministry.*

Tit. 1 : 13. This witness is true. Wherefore rebuke them sharply, that they may be sound in the faith:

Tit. 2 : 1. But speak thou the things which become sound doctrine:

II Tim. 2 : 24, 25. And the servant of the Lord must not strive; but be gentle unto all men, apt to teach, patient; in meekness instructing those that oppose themselves; if God peradventure will give them repentance to the acknowledging of the truth;

Second Sab. Eve., JUNE. Lesson. John 3 : 1—24.

Address to God. *Unworthiness.*

II Sam. 7 : 18, 19. Then went king David in, and sat before the Lord, and he said, Who am I, O Lord God? and what is my house, that thou hast brought me hitherto? And this was yet a small thing in thy sight, O Lord God: but thou hast spoken also of thy servant's house for a great while to come. And is this the manner of man, O Lord God?

Eph. 2 : 18. For through him we both have access by one Spirit unto the Father.

Confess sin. *Deceitfulness of sin.*

II Pet. 2 : 19. While they promise them liberty, they themselves are the servants of corruption: for of whom a man is overcome, of the same is he brought in bondage.

GUIDE TO PRAYER. 51

Prov. 29 : 5. A man that flattereth his neighbor spreadeth a net for his feet.

Ask for blessings. *Fulfill promises.*

II Pet. 1 : 4. Whereby are given unto us exceeding great and precious promises; that by these ye might be partakers of the divine nature, having escaped the corruption that is in the world through lust.

II Cor. 1 : 20. For all the promises of God in him are yea, and in him Amen, unto the glory of God by us.

Lk. 1 : 38. And Mary said, Behold the handmaid of the Lord; be it unto me according to thy word. And the angel departed from her.

Thank for mercies. *Owning Christ's work.*

I John 4 : 9. In this was manifested the love of God toward us, because that God sent His only begotten Son into the world, that we might live through him.

Intercede for others. *Ministry.*

I Tim. 4 : 12. Let no man despise thy youth; but be thou an example of the believers, in word, in conversation, in charity, in spirit, in faith, in purity.

Is. 52 : 11. Depart ye, depart ye, go ye out from thence, touch no unclean thing; go ye out of the midst of her; be ye clean, that bear the vessels of the Lord.

Ex. 28 : 36. And thou shalt make a plate of pure gold, and grave upon it, like the engravings of a signet, HOLINESS TO THE LORD.

THIRD SAB. MORN., JUNE. LESSON, JER. 28.

Address to God. *Desired.*

Is. 26 : 8, 9. Yea, in the way of thy judgments, O Lord have we waited for thee; the desire of our soul is to thy name, and to the remembrance of thee. With my soul have I desired thee in the night; yea, with my spirit within me will I seek thee early: for when thy judgments are in the earth, the inhabitants of the world will learn righteousness.

Confess sin. *Offense of sin.*

Ezek. 6 : 9. And they that escape of you shall remember me among the nations whither they shall be carried captives, because I am broken with their whorish heart, which hath departed from me, and with their eyes, which go a whoring after their idols: and they shall loathe themselves for the evils which they have committed in all their abominations.

Ask for blessings. *Encourage to pray.*

Matt. 6 : 7, 8. But when ye pray, use not vain repetitions, as the heathen do; for they think that they shall be heard for their much speaking. Be not ye therefore like unto them: for your Father knoweth what things ye have need of, before ye ask him.

John 16 : 23, 24. And in that day ye shall ask me nothing. Verily, verily, I say unto you, Whatsoever ye shall ask the Father in my name, he will give it you. Hitherto have ye asked nothing in my name: ask, and ye shall receive, that your joy may be full.

Thank for mercies. *Christ's holy life.*

I Pet. 2 : 21—23. For even hereunto were ye called: because Christ also suffered for us, leaving us an example, that ye should follow his steps: who did no sin, neither was guile found in his mouth: who, when he was reviled, reviled not again: when he suffered, he threatened not: but committed himself to him that judgeth righteously:

John 4 : 34. Jesus saith unto them, My meat is to do the will of him that sent me, and to finish his work.

Heb. 7 : 26. For such a high priest became us, who is holy, harmless, undefiled, separate from sinners, and made higher than the heavens;

I Pet. 4 : 1. For as much then as Christ hath suffered for us in the flesh, arm yourselves likewise with the same mind: for he that hath suffered in the flesh hath ceased from sin:

I John 4 : 17. Herein is our love made perfect, that we may have boldness in the day of judgment: because as he is, so are we in this world.

Intercede for others. *Ministry.*

Is. 49 : 4. Then I said, I have labored in vain, I have spent my strength for nought, and in vain: yet surely my judgment is with the Lord, and my work with my God.

Acts 11 : 21. And the hand of the Lord was with them: and a great number believed, and turned unto the Lord.

Philemon, 25. The grace of our Lord Jesus Christ be with your spirit. Amen.

THIRD SAB. EVE., JUNE. LESSON, I COR. 9 : 11—27.

Address to God. *Confidence in God.*

Ps. 142 : 4, 5. I looked on my right hand, and beheld, but there was no man that would know me: refuge failed me; no man cared for my soul. I cried unto thee, O Lord: I said, Thou art my refuge and my portion in the land of the living.

Confess sin. *Danger of sin.*

Is. 59 : 2. But your iniquities have separated between you and your God, and your sins have hid his face from you, that he will not hear.

Tit. 1 : 15. Unto the pure all things are pure: but unto them that are defiled and unbelieving is nothing pure; but even their mind and conscience is defiled.

Ask for blessings. *Justification.*

Rom. 3 : 24. Being justified freely by his grace through the redemption that is in Christ Jesus:

Acts 13 : 39. And by him all that believe are justified from all things, from which ye could not be justified by the law of Moses.

Thank for mercies. *Encouragement to seek Christ.*

Matt. 11 : 28. Come unto me, all ye that labor and are heavy laden, and I will give you rest.

John 6 : 37. All that the Father giveth me shall come to me; and him that cometh to me I will in no wise cast out.

Intercede for others. *Enemies.*

Lk. 23 : 34. Then said Jesus, Father, forgive them; for they know not what they do. And they parted his raiment, and cast lots.

Acts 7 : 60. And he kneeled down, and cried with a loud voice, Lord, lay not this sin to their charge. And when he had said this, he fell asleep.

Col. 3 : 13. Forbearing one another, and forgiving one another, if any man have a quarrel against any: even as Christ forgave you, so also do ye.

Mark 11 : 25. And when ye stand praying, forgive, if ye have aught against any; that your Father also which is in heaven may forgive you your trespasses.

FOURTH SAB. MORN., JUNE. LESSON, GEN. 12.

Address to God. *Accept services.*

Ps. 143 : 1. Hear my prayer, O Lord, give ear to my supplications: in thy faithfulness answer me, and in thy righteousness.

Deut. 4 : 7. For what nation is there so great, who hath God so nigh unto them, as the Lord our God is in all things that we call upon him for?

Is. 45 : 19. I have not spoken in secret, in a dark place of the earth: I said not unto the seed of Jacob, seek ye me in vain: I the Lord speak righteousness, I declare things that are right.

Confess sin. *Willfulness of sin.*

Jer. 5 : 4, 5. Therefore I said, Surely these are poor; they are foolish: for they know not the way of the Lord, nor the judgment of their God. I will get me unto the great men, and will speak unto them; for they have known the way of the Lord, and the judgment of their God: but these have altogether broken the yoke, and burst the bonds.

Ask for blessings. *Mercy.*

Mic. 7 : 18, 19. Who is a God like unto thee, that pardoneth iniquity, and passeth by the transgression of the remnant of his heritage? he retaineth not his anger for ever, because he delighteth in mercy. He will turn again, he will have compassion upon us; he will subdue our iniquities; and thou wilt cast all their sins into the depths of the sea.

Thank for mercies. *Christ satisfying the law.*

Dan. 9 : 24. Seventy weeks are determined upon thy people and upon thy holy city, to finish the transgression, and to make an end of sins, and to make reconciliation for iniquity, and to bring in everlasting righteousness, and to seal up the vision and prophecy, and to anoint the Most Holy.

Intercede for others. *Poor.*

Zech. 11 : 11. And it was broken in that day; and so the poor of the flock that waited upon me knew that it was the word of the Lord.

FOURTH SAB., EVE.   JUNE.   LESSON, MATT. 4.
Address to God. *Aid in prayer.*

Zech. 12 : 10. And I will pour upon the house of David, and upon the inhabitants of Jerusalem, the spirit of grace and of supplications: and they shall look upon me whom they have pierced, and they shall mourn for him, as one mourneth for his only son, and shall be in bitterness for him, as one that is in bitterness for his firstborn.

Rom. 8 : 15. For ye have not received the spirit of bondage again to fear; but ye have received the Spirit of adoption, whereby we cry, Abba, Father.

Confess sin. *Inconsistency in profession.*

II Tim. 2 : 19. Nevertheless the foundation of God standeth sure, having this seal, The Lord knoweth them that are his. And, Let every one that nameth the name of Christ depart from iniquity.

Ask for blessings. *Christ's righteousness.*

Heb. 12 : 18, 19, 24. For ye are not come unto the mount that might be touched, and that burned with fire, nor unto blackness, and darkness, and tempest, and the sound of a trumpet, and the voice of words: which voice they that heard entreated that the word should not be spoken to them any more: * And to Jesus the mediator of the new covenant, and to the blood of sprinkling, that speaketh better things than that of Abel.

Thank for mercies. *Our Lord's resurrection.*

Rev. 1 : 18. I am he that liveth and was dead; and, behold, I am alive forevermore, Amen: and have the keys of hell and of death.

GUIDE TO PRAYER. 55

Rom. 6 : 9. Knowing that Christ being raised from the dead dieth no more; death hath no more dominion over him.
Intercede for others. *Rich.*
Matt. 19 : 23, 26. Then said Jesus unto his disciples, Verily I say unto you, That a rich man shall hardly enter into the kingdom of heaven. * But Jesus beheld them, and said unto them, With men this is impossible; but with God all things are possible.

FIFTH SAB. MORN.   JUNE.   LESSON, AMOS 5.
Address to God. *Glory.*
Rom. 11 : 36. For of him, and through him, and to him, are all things: to whom be glory for ever. Amen.
Confess sin. *Ingratitude.*
Deut. 32 : 5, 6. They have corrupted themselves, their spot is not the spot of his children: they are a perverse and crooked generation. Do ye thus requite the Lord, O foolish people and unwise? is not he thy father that hath bought thee? hath he not made thee, and established thee?
Ask for blessings. *Pardon.*
Lev. 16 : 22. And the goat shall bear upon him all their iniquities unto a land not inhabited: and he shall let go the goat in the wilderness.
Ps. 103 : 12. As far as the east is from the west, so far hath he removed our transgressions from us.
Thank for mercies. *Our Lord's ascension.*
Heb. 8 : 1. Now of the things which we have spoken this is the sum: We have such a high priest, who is set on the right hand of the throne of the Majesty in the heavens;
I Pet. 3 : 22. Who is gone into heaven, and is on the right hand of God; angels and authorities and powers being made subject unto him.
Intercede for others. *Aged christian.*
Is. 46 : 4. And even to your old age I am he; and even to hoar hairs will I carry you: I have made and I will bear; even I will carry, and will deliver you.

FIFTH SAB. EVE.,   JUNE.   LESSON, REV. 8.
Address to God. *Reliance upon Christ.*
I Pet. 2 : 5. Ye also, as lively stones, are built up a spiritual house, a holy priesthood, to offer up spiritual sacrifices, acceptable to God by Jesus Christ.
John 16 : 23. And in that day ye shall ask me nothing. Verily, ver-

ily, I say unto you. Whatsoever ye shall ask the Father in my name, he will give it you.

Eph. 1 : 6. To the praise of the glory of his grace, wherein he hath made us accepted in the beloved:

Rev. 8 : 4. And the smoke of the incense which came with the prayers of the saints, ascended up before God out of the angel's hand.

Confess sin. *Perverseness.*

Jer. 44 : 4, 5. Howbeit I sent unto you all my servants the prophets, rising early and sending them, saying, Oh, do not this abominable thing that I hate. But they hearkened not, nor inclined their ear to turn from their wickedness, to burn no incense unto other gods.

Ask for blessings. *Mercy.*

Ps. 79 : 8, 9. O remember not against us former iniquities: let thy tender mercies speedily prevent us; for we are brought very low. Help us, O God of our salvation, for the glory of thy name: and deliver us, and purge away our sins, for thy name's sake.

Thank for mercies. *Intercession of Christ.*

I John 2 : 1. My little children these things write I unto you,-that ye sin not. And if any man sin, we have an advocate with the Father, Jesus Christ the righteous:

Heb. 7 : 25. Wherefore he is able also to save them to the uttermost that come unto God by him, seeing he ever liveth to make intercession for them.

Intercede for others. *Youth.*

Tit. 2 : 6. Young men likewise exhort to be soberminded.

I John 2 : 14. I have written unto you, fathers, because ye have known him that is from the beginning. I have written unto you, young men, because ye are strong, and the word of God abideth in you, and ye have overcome the wicked one.

FIRST SAB. MORN., JULY. LESSON, II SAM. 17 : 1—24.
Address to God. *Worshipped.*

Is. 64 : 7. And there is none that calleth upon thy name, that stirreth up himself to take hold of thee; for thou hast hid thy face from us, and hast consumed us, because of our iniquities.

Ps. 27 : 8. When thou saidest, Seek ye my face; my heart said unto thee. Thy face, Lord, will I seek.

Ps. 29 : 2. Give unto the Lord the glory due unto his name; worship the Lord in the beauty of holiness.

Confess sin. *Stubbornness.*

II Sam. 7 : 14. I will be his father, and he shall be my son. If he

commit iniquity, I will chasten him with the rod of men, and with the stripes of the children of men:
Is. 9 : 13. For the people turneth not unto him that smiteth them, neither do they seek the Lord of hosts.

Ask for blessings. *Pardon.*
Lk. 7 : 47, 50. Wherefore I say unto thee, Her sins, which are many, are forgiven; for she loved much: but to whom little is forgiven, the same loveth little. * And he said to the woman, Thy faith hath saved thee; go in peace.
Is. 33 : 24. And the inhabitant shall not say, I am sick: the people that dwell therein shall be forgiven their iniquity.

Thank for mercies. *Christ's exaltation.*
Rev. 19 : 16. And he hath on his vesture and on his thigh a name written, KING OF KINGS, AND LORD OF LORDS.
Dan. 7 : 14. And there was given him dominion, and glory, and a kingdom, that all people, nations, and languages, should serve him: his dominion is an everlasting dominion, which shall not pass away, and his kingdom that which shall not be destroyed.

Intercede for others. *Common people.*
Acts 10 : 35. But in every nation he that feareth him, and worketh righteousness, is accepted with him.
Ps. 35 : 27. Let them shout for joy, and be glad, that favor my righteous cause: yea, let them say continually, Let the Lord be magnified, which hath pleasure in the prosperity of his servant.

FIRST SAB. EVE., JULY. LESSON, JOHN, 6 : 1—21.
Address to God. *True God.*
Jer. 10 : 10. But the Lord is the true God, he is the living God, and an everlasting King: at his wrath the earth shall tremble, and the nations shall not be able to abide his indignation.
Deut. 6 : 4. Hear, O Israel: the Lord our God is one Lord:

Confess sin. *Under condemnation.*
Gal. 3 : 10. For as many as are of the works of the law are under the curse: for it is written, Cursed is every one that continueth not in all things which are written in the book of the law to do them.
Rom. 6 : 23. For the wages of sin is death; but the gift of God is eternal life through Jesus Christ our Lord.
Eph. 5 : 6. Let no man deceive you with vain words: for because of these things cometh the wrath of God upon the children of disobedience.

Ask for blessings. *Favor.*
Ps. 30 : 5. For his anger endureth but a moment; in his favor is life:

weeping may endure for a night, but joy cometh in the morning.
Ps. 63 : 3. Because thy lovingkindness is better than life, my lips shall praise thee.
Ps. 85 : 5, 6. Wilt thou be angry with us for ever? wilt thou draw out thine anger to all generations? Wilt thou not revive us again: that thy people may rejoice in thee.
Jer. 17 : 14. Heal me, O Lord: and I shall be healed: save me, and I shall be saved: for thou art my praise.

Thank for mercies. *Second advent.*
Matt. 13 : 41, 43. The Son of man shall send forth his angels, and they shall gather out of his kingdom all things that offend, and them which do iniquity: * Then shall the righteous shine forth as the sun in the kingdom of their Father. Who hath ears to hear, let him hear.

Intercede for others. *Schools.*
II Kin. 2 : 21. And he went forth unto the spring of the waters, and cast the salt in there, and said, thus saith the Lord, I have healed these waters; there shall not be from thence any more death or barren land.
Ps. 46 : 4. There is a river, the streams whereof shall make glad the city of God, the holy place of the tabernacles of the Most High.

SECOND SAB. MORN., JULY. LESSON, Gen. 1,
Address to God. *Immutable.*
Jas. 1 : 17. Every good gift and every perfect gift is from above, and cometh down from the Father of lights, with whom is no variableness, neither shadow of turning.

Confess sin. *Tried divine patience.*
Ps. 103 : 10. He hath not dealt with us after our sins; nor rewarded us according to our iniquities.
Is. 30 : 18. And therefore will the Lord wait, that he may be gracious unto you, and therefore will he be exalted, that he may have mercy upon you: for the Lord is a God of judgment: blessed are all they that wait for him.

Ask for blessings. *Converting grace.*
Lk. 15 : 19. And am no more worthy to be called thy son: make me as one of thy hired servants.
Jer. 3 : 19. But I said, How shall I put thee among the children, and give thee a pleasant land, a goodly heritage of the hosts of nations? and I said, Thou shalt call me, My father; and shalt not turn away from me.
Jer. 3 : 4. Wilt thou not from this time cry unto me, My father, thou art the guide of my youth?

GUIDE TO PRAYER. 59

Thank for mercies. *Holy Spirit.*
Acts 2 : 33. Therefore being by the right hand of God exalted, and having received of the Father the promise of the Holy Ghost, he hath shed forth this, which ye now see and hear.
John 7 : 38. He that believeth on me, as the Scripture hath said, out of his belly shall flow rivers of living water.

Intercede for others. *Ministry.*
Acts 18 : 24. And a certain Jew named Apollos, born at Alexandria, an eloquent man, and mighty in the Scriptures, came to Ephesus.
II Tim. 3 : 17. That the man of God may be perfect, thoroughly furnished unto all good works.
Tit. 2 : 7. In all things showing thyself a pattern of good works: in doctrine showing uncorruptness, gravity, sincerity,

SECOND SAB. EVE.,   JULY.   LESSON, ROM. 12.
Address to God. *Incomprehensible.*
Ps. 106 : 2. Who can utter the mighty acts of the Lord? who can show forth all his praise?

Confess sin. *Unrepentant.*
Job. 42 : 5, 6. I have heard of thee by the hearing of the ear; but now mine eye seeth thee: wherefore I abhor myself, and repent in dust and ashes.
Ezek. 7 : 16. But they that escape of them shall escape, and shall be on the mountains like doves of the valleys, all of them mourning, every one for his iniquity.

Ask for blessings. *Divine favor.*
Num. 6 : 24—26. The Lord bless thee, and keep thee: the Lord make his face shine upon thee, and be gracious unto thee: the Lord lift up his countenance upon thee, and give thee peace.

Thank for mercies. *Covenant of grace.*
II Pet. 1 : 4. Whereby are given unto us exceeding great and precious promises; that by these ye might be partakers of the divine nature, having escaped the corruption that is in the world through lust.
Heb. 8 : 6. But now hath he obtained a more excellent ministry, by how much also he is the mediator of a better covenant, which was established upon better promises.

Intercede for others. *Judges.*
II Chron. 19 : 6, 7. And said to the judges, Take heed what ye do: for ye judge not for man, but for the Lord, who is with you in the judgment. Wherefore now let the fear of the Lord be upon you; take heed

and do it: for there is no iniquity with the Lord our God, nor respect of persons, nor taking of gifts.

THIRD SAB. MORN., JULY. LESSON, MAL. 3.
Address to God. *Matchless perfection.*
Ps. 86 : 8, 10. Among the gods there is none like unto thee, O Lord; neither are there any works like unto thy works. * For thou art great, and doest wondrous things: thou art God alone.
Confess sin. *Defiled.*
Job 15 : 15, 16. Behold, he putteth no trust in his saints; yea, the heavens are not clean in his sight. How much more abominable and filthy is man, which drinketh iniquity like water?
Ask for blessings. *Fatherly blessing.*
Gen. 27 : 38. And Esau said unto his father, Hast thou but one blessing, my father? bless me, even me also, O my father. And Esau lifted up his voice and wept.
Gal. 3 : 14. That the blessing of Abraham might come on the Gentiles through Jesus Christ; that we might receive the promise of the Spirit through faith.
Gen. 32 : 26. And he said let me go, for the day breaketh. And he said, I will not let thee go, except thou bless me.
Thank for mercies. *Scriptures.*
Rom. 15 : 4. For whatsoever things were written aforetime were written for our learning, that we through patience and comfort of the Scriptures might have hope.
II Pet. 1 : 19. We have also a more sure word of prophecy; whereunto ye do well that ye take heed, as unto a light that shineth in a dark place, until the day dawn, and the daystar arise in your hearts:
Intercede for others. *Wisdom to rulers.*
Job 12 : 20. He removeth away the speech of the trusty, and taketh away the understanding of the aged.
Lk. 19 : 42. Saying, If thou hadst known, even thou, at least in this thy day, the things which belong unto thy peace! but now they are hid from thine eyes.

THIRD SAB. EVE., JULY. LESSON, I PET. 2.
Address to God. *Above other beings.*
Is. 55 : 9. For as the heavens are higher than the earth, so are my ways higher than your ways, and my thoughts than your thoughts.
Confess sin. *Slow to confess.*
Prov. 28 : 13. He that covereth his sins shall not prosper: but whoso confesseth and forsaketh them shall have mercy.

Ps. 32 : 5, 6. I acknowledged my sin unto thee, and mine iniquity have I not hid. I said, I will confess my transgressions unto the Lord; and thou forgavest the iniquity of my sin. Selah. For this shall every one that is godly pray unto thee in a time when thou mayest be found: surely in the floods of great waters they shall not come nigh unto him.

1 John 1 : 8, 9. If we say that we have no sin, we deceive ourselves, and the truth is not in us. If we confess our sins, he is faithful and just to forgive us our sins, and to cleanse us from all unrighteousness.

Ask for blessings. *Sanctification.*

Ps. 51 : 10—12. Create in me a clean heart, O God; and renew a right spirit within me. Cast me not away from thy presence; and take not thy Holy Spirit from me. Restore unto me the joy of thy salvation; and uphold me with thy free Spirit.

Ps. 140 : 13. Surely the righteous shall give thanks unto thy name: the upright shall dwell in thy presence.

Thank for mercies. *Ordinances.*

Rev. 21 : 3. And I heard a great voice out of heaven saying, Behold, the tabernacle of God is with men, and he will dwell with them, and they shall be his people, and God himself shall be with them, and be their God.

Ezek. 37 : 26. Moreover I will make a covenant of peace with them; it shall be an everlasting covenant with them: and I will place them, and multiply them, and will set my sanctuary in the midst of them for evermore.

Ex. 29 : 43. And there I will meet with the children of Israel, and the tabrnacle shall be sanctified by my glory.

Intercede for others. *Continuance of godly rule.*

Ps. 61 : 7, 8. He shall abide before God for ever: O prepare mercy and truth, which may preserve him. So will I sing praise unto thy name for ever, that I may daily perform my vows.

Ps. 69 : 35, 36. For God will save Zion, and will build the cities of Judah: that they may dwell there, and have it in possession. The seed also of his servants shall inherit it: and they that love his name shall dwell therein.

FOURTH SAB. MORN., JULY. LESSON, EX. 16 : 1—21.
Address to God. *Immutability.*

Ps. 102 : 25—27. Of old hast thou laid the foundation of the earth: and the heavens are the work of thy hands. They shall perish, but thou shalt endure: yea, all of them shall wax old like a garment; as a vesture shalt thou change them, and they shall be changed: but thou art the same, and thy years shall have no end.

Confess sin. *Degeneracy through original sin.*
Jer. 2 : 21. Yet I had planted thee a noble vine, wholly a right seed; how then art thou turned into the degenerate plant of a strange vine unto me?

Deut. 32 : 32. For their vine is of the vine of Sodom, and of the fields of Gomorrah: their grapes are grapes of gall, their clusters are bitter:

Lam. 4 : 1. How is the gold become dim! how is the most fine gold changed?

Ask for blessings. *Adoption.*
Rom. 8 : 16, 17. The Spirit itself beareth witness with our spirit, that we are the children of God: and if children, then heirs; heirs of God, and joint heirs with Christ;

Thank for mercies. *Advance of the gospel.*
1 Thess. 2 : 2. But even after that we had suffered before, and were shamefully entreated, as ye know, at Philippi, we were bold in our God to speak unto you the gospel of God with much contention.

Acts 19 : 20. So mightily grew the word of God and prevailed.

1 Thess. 1 : 9. For they themselves shew of us what manner of entering in we had unto you, and how ye turned to God from idols to serve the living and true God:

Intercede for others. *Chief magistrate.*
Prov. 20 : 28. Mercy and truth preserve the king: and his throne is upholden by mercy.

Prov. 25 : 5. Take away the wicked from before the king, and his throne shall be established in righteousness.

Ps. 21 : 4—7. He asked life of thee, and thou gavest it him, even length of days for ever and ever. His glory is great in thy salvation: honor and majesty hast thou laid upon him. For thou hast made him most blessed for ever: thou hast made him exceeding glad with thy countenance. For the king trusteth in the Lord, and through the mercy of the Most High he shall not be moved.

FOURTH SAB., EVE. JULY. LESSON, LK. 17 : 1—19.
Address to God. *Omnipresence.*
Prov. 15 : 3. The eyes of the Lord are in every place, beholding the evil and the good.

Ps. 139 : 7—10. Whither shall I go from thy Spirit? or whither shall I flee from thy presence? If I ascend up into heaven, thou art there: if I make my bed in hell, behold, thou art there. If I take the wings of the morning, and dwell in the uttermost parts of the sea; even there shall thy hand lead me, and thy right hand shall hold me.

Confess sin. *Depravity.*
Job 33 : 14. For God speaketh once, yea twice, yet man perceiveth it not.

Matt. 13 : 14. And in them is fulfilled the prophecy of Esaias, which saith, By hearing ye shall hear, and shall not understand; and seeing ye shall see, and shall not perceive:

Mark. 8 : 24. And he looked up, and said, I see men as trees, walking.

Ask for blessings. *Peace of conscience.*
Phil. 4 : 7. And the peace of God, which passeth all understanding, shall keep your hearts and minds through Christ Jesus.

Col. 3 : 15. And let the peace of God rule in your hearts, to the which also ye are called in one body; and be ye thankful.

Thank for mercies. *Helpful examples.*
Rom. 8 : 36, 37., As it is written, For thy sake we are killed all the day long; we are accounted as sheep for the slaughter. Nay, in all these things we are more than conquerors through him that loved us.

Intercede for others. *Victory over external enemies.*
Deut. 33 : 29. Happy art thou, O Israel: who is like unto thee, O people saved by the Lord, the shield of thy help, and who is the sword of thy excellency! and thine enemies shall be found liars unto thee; and thou shalt tread upon their high places.

Ex. 14 : 25. And took off their chariot wheels, that they drave them heavily: so that the Egyptians said, Let us flee from the face of Israel: for the Lord fighteth for them against the Egyptians.

FIFTH SAB. MORN., JULY. LESSON, ZECH. 12.
Address to God. *Omniscience.*
Jer. 17 : 10. I the Lord search the heart, I try the reins, even to give every man according to his ways, and according to the fruit of his doings.

Confess sin. *Misplaced affections.*
Ps. 24 : 4. He that hath clean hands, and a pure heart; who hath not lifted his soul unto vanity, nor sworn deceitfully.

Prov. 23 : 5. Wilt thou set thine eyes upon that which is not? for riches certainly make themselves wings; they fly away as an eagle toward heaven.

II Cor. 4 : 18. While we look not at the things which are seen, but at the things which are not seen: for the things which are seen are temporal; but the things which are not seen are eternal.

Ask for blessings. *Divine aid.*

John 1 : 16. And of his fulness have all we received, and grace for grace.

Col. 1 : 19. For it pleased the Father that in him should all fulness dwell.

Thank for mercies. *Communion of saints.*

1 Cor. 10 : 17. For we being many are one bread, and one body: for we are all partakers of that one bread.

1 Cor. 12 : 4—6. Now there are diversities of gifts, but the same Spirit. And there are differences of administration, but the same Lord. And there are diversities of operations, but it is the same God which worketh all in all.

Intercede for others. *Heal divisions.*

1 Cor. 1 : 10. Now I beseech you brethren, by the name of our Lord Jesus Christ, that ye all speak the same thing, and that there be no divisions among you; but that ye be perfectly joined together in the same mind and in the same judgment.

FIFTH SAB. EVE., JULY. LESSON, ACTS 4 : 32—5 : 11.
Address to God. *Wisdom.*

Ps. 104 : 24. O Lord, how manifold are thy works! in wisdom hast thou made them all: the earth is full of thy riches.

Eph. 1 : 11. In whom also we have obtained an inheritance, being predestinated according to the purpose of him who worketh all things after the counsel of his own will:

Confess sin. *Corrupt nature.*

Hos. 11 : 7. And my people are bent to backsliding from me: though they called them to the Most High, none at all would exalt him.

Jer. 17 : 9. The heart is deceitful above all things, and desperately wicked: who can know it?

Hos. 7 : 16. They return, but not to the Most High: they are like a deceitful bow: their princes shall fall by the sword for the rage of their tongue: this shall be their derision in the land of Egypt.

Ask for blessings. *Deliverance from sin.*

Gal. 6 : 14. But God forbid that I should glory, save in the cross of our Lord Jesus Christ, by whom the world is crucified unto me, and I unto the world.

Thank for mercies. *Hope of eternal life.*

Heb. 13 : 14. For here have we no continuing city, but we seek one to come.

Heb. 11 : 10, 16. For he looked for a city which hath foundations, whose builder and maker is God. * But now they desire a better coun-

try, that is, a heavenly: wherefore God is not ashamed to be called their God: for he hath prepared for them a city.
Intercede for others. *Wickedness suppressed.*
Rom. 11 : 26. And so all Israel shall be saved: as it is written, there shall come out of Sion the Deliverer, and shall turn away ungodliness from Jacob:

Is. 4 : 4. When the Lord shall have washed away the filth of the daughter of Zion, and shall have purged the blood of Jerusalem from the midst thereof by the spirit of judgment, and by the spirit of burning.

FIRST SAB. MORN., AUGUST. LESSON, LEV. 25 : 1—24.

Address to God. *Sovereignty.*
Dan. 4 : 34, 35. And at the end of the days I Nebuchadnezzar lifted up mine eyes unto heaven, and mine understanding returned unto me, and I blessed the Most High, and I praised and honored him that liveth forever, whose dominion is an everlasting dominion, and his kingdom is from generation to generation: and all the inhabitants of the earth are reputed as nothing: and he doeth according to his will in the army of heaven, and among the inhabitants of the earth: and none can stay his hand, or say unto him, What doest thou?

Confess sin. *Unfaithfulness.*
Lk. 16 : 1. And he said also unto his disciples, There was a certain rich man, which had a steward; and the same was accused unto him that he had wasted his goods.

Ecc. 9 : 18. Wisdom is better than weapons of war: but one sinner destroyeth much good.

Prov. 17 : 16. Wherefore is there a price in the hand of a fool to get wisdom, seeing he hath no heart to it.

Ask for blessings. *Resist temptation.*
Jas. 4 : 7. Submit yourselves therefore to God. Resist the devil, and he will flee from you.

1 Pet. 5 : 9. Whom resist steadfast in the faith, knowing that the same afflictions are accomplished in your brethren that are in the world.

Rom. 16 : 20. And the God of peace shall bruise Satan under your feet shortly. The grace of our Lord Jesus Christ be with you. Amen.

Thank for mercies. *Spiritual mercies.*
Rom. 2 : 15. Which shew the work of the law written in their hearts, their conscience also bearing witness, and their thoughts the meanwhile accusing or else excusing one another;

Intercede for others. *Continuance of peace in the land.*

GUIDE TO PRAYER.

Ps. 122 : 7. Peace be within thy walls, and prosperity within thy palaces.

Deut. 33 : 18. And of Zebulun he said, Rejoice Zebulun, in thy going out; and, Issachar, in thy tents.

FIRST SAB. EVE.,   AUGUST.   LESSON, JOHN, 9 : 1—38.
Address to God.   *Power.*

Deut. 32 : 39. See now that I, even I, am he, and there is no god with me: I kill, and I make alive; I wound, and I heal: neither is there any that can deliver out of my hand.

Confess sin.   *Word and deed.*

Jas. 3 : 2. For in many things we offend all. If any man offend not in word, the same is a perfect man, and able also to bridle the whole body.

Ps. 40 : 12. For innumerable evils have compassed me about: mine iniquities have taken hold upon me, so that I am not able to look up; they are more than the hairs of mine head: therefore my heart faileth me.

Ask for blessings.   *Grace to help.*

Rom. 6 : 4. Therefore we are buried with him by baptism into death: that like as Christ was raised up from the dead by the glory of the Father, even so we also should walk in newness of life.

Thank for mercies.   *Regeneration.*

Jer. 31 : 3. The Lord hath appeared of old unto me, saying, Yea, I have loved thee with an everlasting love: therefore with lovingkindness have I drawn thee.

Hos. 11 : 4. I drew them with the cords of a man, with bands of love: and I was to them as they that take off the yoke on their jaws, and I laid meat unto them.

Intercede for others.   *Continuance of the gospel in the land.*

Rev. 2 : 4, 5. Nevertheless I have somewhat against thee, because thou hast left thy first love. Remember therefore from whence thou art fallen, and repent, and do the first works; or else I will come unto thee quickly, and will remove thy candlestick out of his place, except thou repent.

Jer. 7 : 12. But go ye now unto my place which was in Shiloh, where I set my name at the first, and see what I did to it for the wickedness of my people Israel.

SECOND SAB. MORN.,   AUGUST.   LESSON, ZEPH. 2.
Address to God.   *Righteous.*

Deut. 32 : 4. He is the Rock, his work is perfect: for all his ways are

GUIDE TO PRAYER. 67

judgment: a God of truth and without iniquity, just and right is he.
Ps. 92 : 15. To shew that the Lord is upright: he is my rock, and there is no unrighteousness in him:

Confess sin. *Pride.*
John 7 : 18. He that speaketh of himself seeketh his own glory: but he that seeketh his glory that sent him, the same is true, and no unrighteousness is in him.
I Cor. 5 : 2. And ye are puffed up, and have not rather mourned, that he that hath done this deed might be taken away from among you.

Ask for blessings. *Renewing grace.*
Eph. 2 : 1. And you hath he quickened, who were dead in trespasses and sins;
Ezek. 16 : 8. Now when I passed by thee, and looked upon thee, behold, thy time was the time of love; and I spread my skirt over thee, and covered thy nakedness: yea, I sware unto thee, and entered into a covenant with thee, saith the Lord God, and thou becamest mine.

Thank for mercies. *Remission of sins.*
Ps. 103 : 3, 4. Who forgiveth all thine iniquities; who healeth all thy diseases; who redeemeth thy life from destruction; who crowneth thee with lovingkindness and tender mercies.
Is. 38 : 17. Behold, for peace I had great bitterness; but thou hast in love to my soul delivered it from the pit of corruption: for thou hast cast all my sins behind thy back.

Intercede for others. *National mercies.*
Ps. 80 : 2, 3. Before Ephraim and Benjamin and Manasseh stir up thy strength, and come and save us. Turn us again, O God, and cause thy face to shine; and we shall be saved.

SECOND SAB. EVE., AUGUST. LESSON, II COR. 6.
Address to God. *Goodness.*
Ps. 119 : 68. Thou art good, and doest good: teach me thy statutes.
Ps. 73 : 1. Truly God is good to Israel, even to such as are of a clean heart.
Ps. 145 : 9. The Lord is good to all: and his tender mercies are over all his works.

Confess sin. *Sensuality.*
Rom. 8 : 5. For they that are after the flesh do mind the things of the flesh; but they that are after the Spirit, the things of the Spirit.
Jas. 5 : 5. Ye have lived in pleasure on the earth, and been wanton; ye have nourished your hearts, as in a day of slaughter.

Ask for blessings. *Preserving grace.*

Phil. 1 : 6. Being confident of this very thing, that he which hath begun a good work in you will perform it unil the day of Jesus Christ:
Thank for mercies. *Sustaining grace.*
Ps. 73 : 2, 3. But as for me, my feet were almost gone: my steps had well nigh slipped, for I was envious at the foolish, when I saw the prosperity of the wicked.
Intercede for others. *Humility for national sins.*
Matt. 24 12. And because iniquity shall abound, the love of many shall wax cold.

THIRD SAB. MORN., AUGUST. LESSON, GEN. 8.

Address to God. *Creator.*
Ps. 74 : 16, 17. The day is thine, the night also is thine: thou hast prepared the light and the sun. Thou hast set all the borders of the earth: thou hast made summer and winter.
Confess sin. *Carnal security.*
I Tim. 6 : 17. Charge them that are rich in this world, that they be not high minded, nor trust in uncertain riches, but in the living God, who giveth us richly all things to enjoy.
Job 31 : 24. If I have made gold my hope, or have said to the fine gold, Thou art my confidence;
Ask for blessings. *Instructing grace.*
Ps. 119 : 124, 125, 169. Deal with thy servant according unto thy mercy, and teach me thy statutes. I am thy servant; give me understanding, that I may know thy testimonies. * Let my cry come near before thee, O Lord; give me understanding according unto thy word.
Ps. 111 : 10. The fear of the Lord is the beginning of wisdom: a good understanding have all they that do his commandments: his praise endureth for ever.
Thank for mercies. *Ordinances.*
Ps. 84 : 10—12. For a day in thy courts is better than a thousand. I had rather be a doorkeeper in the house of my God, than to dwell in the tents of wickedness. For the Lord God is a sun and shield: the Lord will give grace and glory: no good thing will he withhold from them that walk uprightly. O Lord of hosts, blessed is the man that trusteth in thee.
Intercede for others. *Own land.*
Ps. 85 : 1. Lord thou hast been favorable unto thy land: thou hast brought back the captivity of Jacob.
Ps. 44 : 1. We have heard with our ears, O God, our fathers have told us, what work thou didst in their days, in the times of old.

GUIDE TO PRAYER.   69

Ps. 48 : 8, 9. As we have heard, so have we seen in the city of the Lord of hosts, in the city of our God: God will establish it for ever. Selah. We have thought of thy lovingkindness, O God, in the midst of thy temple.

THIRD SAB. EVE.,   AUGUST.   LESSON, MATT. 24 : 23—42.
Address to God.   *Trinity.*
Rev. 19 : 1, 5. And after these things I heard a great voice of much people in heaven, saying, Alleluia; Salvation, and glory, and honor, and power, unto the Lord our God: * And a voice came out of the throne, saying, Praise our God, all ye his servants, and ye that fear him, both small and great.
Phil. 2 : 11. And that every tongue should confess that Jesus Christ is Lord, to the glory of God the Father.
Confess sin.   *Impatience.*
Ps. 31 : 22. For I said in my haste, I am cut off from before thine eyes: nevertheless thou heardest the voice of my supplications when I cried unto thee.
Is. 49 : 14. But Zion said, The Lord hath forsaken me, and my Lord hath forgotten me.
Ps. 77 : 7, 8, 10. Will the Lord cast off for ever? and will he be favorable no more? is his mercy clean gone for ever? doth his promise fail for evermore? And I said, This is my infirmity: but I will remember the years of the right hand of the Most High.
Ask for blessings.   *Divine enlightenment.*
John 7 : 17. If any man will do his will, he shall know of the doctrine, whether it be of God, or whether I speak of myself.
John 8 : 32, 36. And ye shall know the truth, and the truth shall make you free. * If the Son therefore shall make you free, ye shall be free indeed.
Thank for mercies.   *Answer to prayer.*
Is. 65 : 24. And it shall come to pass, that before they call, I will answer; and while they are yet speaking, I will hear.
Is. 58 : 9. Then shalt thou call, and the Lord shall answer; thou shalt cry, and he shall say, Here I am. If thou take away from the midst of thee the yoke, the putting forth of the finger, and speaking vanity;
Deut. 4 : 7. For what nation is there so great, who hath God so nigh unto them, as the Lord our God is in all things that we call upon him for?
Intercede for others.   *For own and other nations.*
Ps. 46 : 9. He maketh wars to cease unto the end of the earth; he

breaketh the bow, and cutteth the spear in sunder; he burneth the chariot in the fire.

Is. 2 : 4. And he shall judge among the nations, and shall rebuke many people: and they shall beat their swords into ploughshares, and their spears into pruninghooks: nation shall not lift up sword against nation, neither shall they learn war any more.

FOURTH SAB. MORN., AUGUST. LESSON, MICAH 7.
Address to God. *Creator.*

Heb. 12 : 9. Furthermore we have had fathers of our flesh which corrected us, and we gave them reverence: shall we not much rather be in subjection unto the Father of spirits, and live?

Zech. 12 : 1. The burden of the word of the Lord for Israel, saith the Lord, which stretcheth forth the heavens, and layeth the foundation of the earth, and formeth the spirit of man within him.

Jer. 38 : 16. So Zedekiah the king sware secretly unto Jeremiah, saying, As the Lord liveth, that made us this soul, I will not put thee to death, neither will I give thee into the hand of these men that seek thy life.

Job 33 : 4. The Spirit of God hath made me, and the breath of the Almighty hath given me life.

Job 38 : 6. Who hath put wisdom in the inward parts? or who hath given understanding to the heart?

Confess sin. *Quarrelsome.*

Gal. 5 : 26. Let us not be desirous of vain-glory, provoking one another, envying one another.

Heb. 10 : 24. And let us consider one another to provoke unto love and to good works:

Ask for blessings. *Remembering grace.*

Acts 18 : 24. And a certain Jew named Apollos, born at Alexandria, an eloquent man, and mighty in the Scriptures, came to Ephesus.

II Tim. 3 : 17. That the man of God may be perfect, thoroughly furnished unto all good works.

Thank for mercies. *Aid in affliction.*

Ps. 119 : 67, 71. Before I was afflicted I went astray: but now have I kept thy word. * It is good for me that I have been afflicted; that I might learn thy statutes.

Intercede for others. *Deliverance from persecution.*

Rev. 13 : 10. He that leadeth into captivity shall go into captivity: he that killeth with the sword must be killed with the sword. Here is the patience and the faith of the saints.

Lam. 3 : 26. It is good that a man should both hope and quietly wait for the salvation of the Lord.

FOURTH SAB., EVE.   AUGUST.   LESSON, ACTS 1.
Address to God.   *God as our God.*
Deut. 26 : 17—19. Thou hast avouched the Lord this day to be thy God, and to walk in his ways, and to keep his statutes, and his commandments, and his judgments, and to hearken unto his voice: and the Lord hath avouched thee this day to be his peculiar people, as he hath promised thee, and that thou shouldest keep all his commandments; and to make thee high above all nations which he hath made, in praise, and in name, and in honor; and that thou mayest be a holy people unto the Lord thy God, as he hath spoken.
Jer. 13 : 11. For as the girdle cleaveth to the loins of a man, so have I caused to cleave unto me the whole house of Israel and the whole house of Judah, saith the Lord; that they might be unto me for a people, and for a name, and for a praise, and for a glory: but they would not hear.

Confess sin.   *Sins of tongue.*
Matt. 12 : 36, 37. But I say unto you, That every idle word that men shall speak, they shall give account thereof in the day of judgment. For by thy words thou shalt be justified, and by thy words thou shalt be condemned.
Is. 6 : 5. Then said I, Woe is me! for I am undone; because I am a man of unclean lips, and I dwell in the midst of a people of unclean lips: for mine eyes have seen the King, the Lord of hosts.

Ask for blessings.   *Direction in duty.*
II Chron. 20 : 12. O our God, wilt thou not judge them? for we have no might against this great company that cometh against us; neither know we what to do: but our eyes are upon thee.
Is. 30 : 21. And thine ears shall hear a word behind thee saying, This is the way, walk ye in it, when ye turn to the right hand, and when ye turn to the left.

Thank for mercies.   *Fulfillment of God's promises.*
Ps. 116 : 7, 12, 13. Return unto thy rest, O my soul; for the Lord hath dealt bountifully with thee. * What shall I render unto the Lord for all his benefits toward me? I will take the cup of salvation, and call upon the name of the Lord.
Ps. 100 : 5. For the Lord is good; his mercy is everlasting; and his truth endureth to all generations.

Intercede for others.   *Defeat church's enemies.*

Ps. 9 : 20. Put them in fear, O Lord: that the nations may know themselves to be but men. Selah.
Ex. 18 : 11. Now I know that the Lord is greater than all gods: for in the thing wherein they dealt proudly he was above them.

FIFTH SAB. MORN.,	AUGUST.	LESSON, NUM. 16 : 12—35.
Address to God.	*Prayed to.*
Heb. 4 : 16. Let us therefore come boldly unto the throne of grace, that we may obtain mercy, and find grace to help in time of need.
Confess sin.	*Spiritual sloth.*
Rev. 2 : 4. Nevertheless I have somewhat against thee, because thou hast left thy first love.
Gal. 4 : 15. Where is then the blessedness ye spake of? for I bear you record, that, if it had been possible, ye would have plucked out your own eyes, and have given them to me.
Ask for blessings.	*Sanctification.*
Rom. 6 : 17. But God be thanked, that ye were the servants of sin, but ye have obeyed from the heart that form of doctrine which was delivered you.
Rom. 12 : 2. And be not conformed to this world: but be ye transformed by the renewing of your mind, that ye may prove what is that good and acceptable, and perfect will of God.
I Pet. 1 : 14. As obedient children, not fashioning yourselves according to the former lusts in your ignorance:
Thank for mercies.	*God's lovingkindness.*
Is. 63 : 7. I will mention the lovingkindnesses of the Lord, and the praises of the Lord, according to all that the Lord hath bestowed on us, and the great goodness toward the house of Israel, which he hath bestowed on them according to his mercies, and according to the multitude of his lovingkindnesses.
Intercede for others.	*Reviving church.*
Tit. 1 : 5. For this cause left I thee in Crete, that thou shouldest set in order the things that are wanting, and ordain elders in every city, as I had appointed thee:
Matt. 15 : 3. But he answered and said unto them, Why do ye also transgress the commandment of God by your tradition?

FIFTH SAB. EVE.,	AUGUST.	LESSON, LK. 14 : 1—24.
Address to God.	*Unworthy suppliants.*
Ps. 8 : 4. What is man, that thou art mindful of him? and the son of man, that thou visitest him?
Confess sin.	*Folly of sin.*

Ps. 49 : 13. This their way is their folly: yet their posterity approve their sayings. Selah.
II Sam. 24 : 10. And David's heart smote him after that he had numbered the people. And David said unto the Lord, I have sinned greatly in that I have done; and now, I beseech thee, O Lord, take away the iniquity of thy servant; for I have done very foolishly.

Ask for blessings. *Faith.*
Heb. 4 : 2. For unto us was the gospel preached, as well as unto them; but the word preached did not profit them, not being mixed with faith in them that heard it.
John 3 : 33. He that hath received his testimony hath set to his seal that God is true.

Thank for mercies. *God's goodness.*
Ps. 147 : 11. The Lord taketh pleasure in them that fear him, in those that hope in his mercy.

Intercede for others. *Conversion of unbelievers.*
Is. 8 : 20. To the law and to the testimony: if they speak not according to this word, it is because there is no light in them.
Ps. 138 : 2. I will worship toward thy holy temple, and praise thy name for thy lovingkindness and for thy truth: for thou hast magnified thy word above all thy name.
Is. 42 : 21. The Lord is well pleased for his righteousness' sake; he will magnify the law and make it honorable.

FIRST SAB. MORN., SEPTEMBER. LESSON, JER. 35.
Address to God. *Desired.*
Ps. 42 : 1, 2, 8. As the hart panteth after the water brooks, so panteth my soul after thee, O God. My soul thirsteth for God, for the living God: when shall I come and appear before God? * Yet the Lord will command his lovingkindness in the daytime, and in the night his song shall be with me, and my prayer unto the God of my life.

Confess sin. *Deceitfulness of sin.*
Obad. 3. The pride of thine heart hath deceived thee, thou that dwellest in the clefts of the rock, whose habitation is high; that saith in his heart, Who shall bring me down to the ground?

Ask for blessings. *Fear of God.*
Ps. 86 : 11. Teach me thy way, O Lord; I will walk in thy truth: unite my heart to fear thy name.
Ecc. 12 : 13. Let us hear the conclusion of the whole matter: Fear God and keep his commandments: for this is the whole duty of man.

Thank for mercies. *Man a rational being.*

Is. 43 : 21. This people have I formed for myself; they shall show forth my praise.

Intercede for others. *Universal church.*

Ps. 128 : 5, 6. The Lord shall bless thee out of Zion: and thou shalt see the good of Jerusalem all the days of thy life. Yea, thou shalt see thy children's children, and peace upon Israel.

Is. 14 : 32. What shall one then answer the messengers of the nation? That the Lord hath founded Zion, and the poor of his people shall trust in it.

FIRST SAB. EVE., SEPTEMBER. LESSON, JOHN, 8 : 33—59.
Address to God. *Confidence.*

Ps. 20 : 7. Some trust in chariots, and some in horses: but we will remember the name of the Lord our God.

Ps. 52 : 8, 9. But I am like a green olive tree in the house of God: I trust in the mercy of God for ever and ever. I will praise thee for ever, because thou hast done it: and I will wait on thy name; for it is good before thy saints.

Confess sin. *Offense of sin.*

Ps. 95 : 9, 10. When your fathers tempted me, proved me, and saw my work. Forty years long was I grieved with this generation, and said, It is a people that do err in their heart, and they have not known my ways:

Is. 63 : 10. But they rebelled, and vexed his Holy Spirit: therefore he was turned to be their enemy, and he fought against them.

Amos 2 : 13. Behold I am pressed under you as a cart is pressed that is full of sheaves.

Ask for blessings. *Love to Christ.*

I Pet. 2 : 7. Unto you therefore which believe he is precious: but unto them which be disobedient, the stone which the builders disallowed, the same is made the head of the corner.

Cant. 5 : 10, 16. My beloved is white and ruddy, the chiefest among tenthousand. * His mouth is most sweet: yea, he is altogether lovely. This is my beloved, and this is my friend, O daughters of Jerusalem.

I Pet. 1 : 8. Whom having not seen, ye love; in whom, though now ye see him not, yet believing, ye rejoice with joy unspeakable and full of glory:

Thank for mercies. *God's goodness.*

Ecc. 1 : 4. One generation passeth away, and another generation cometh: but the earth abideth forever.

Deut. 29 : 20. The Lord will not spare him, but then the anger of the Lord and his jealousy shall smoke against that man, and all the curses that are written in this book sholl lie upon him, and the Lord shall blot out his name from under heaven.

Intercede for others. *Church in ends of world.*
Ps. 65 : 5. By terrible things in righteousness wilt thou answer us, O God of our salvation; who art the confidence of all the ends of the earth, and of them that are afar off upon the sea:

Gen. 49 : 26. The blessings of thy father have prevailed above the blessings of my progenitors unto the utmost bound of the everlasting hills: they shall be on the head of Joseph, and on the crown of the head of him that was separate from his brethren.

SECOND SAB. MORN., SEPTEMBER. LESSON, EX. 20.
Address to God. *Faithful.*
Ps. 147 : 9. He giveth to the beast his food, and to the young ravens which cry.

Ps. 28 : 1. Unto thee will I cry, O Lord my rock; be not silent to me: lest, if thou be silent to me, I become like them that go down into the pit.

Confess sin. *Danger of sin.*
Jer. 2 : 19. Thine own wickedness shall correct thee, and thy backslidings shall reprove thee: know therefore and see that it is an evil thing and bitter, that thou hast forsaken the Lord thy God, and that my fear is not in thee, saith the Lord God of hosts.

Ask for blessings. *Tender conscience.*
I Cor. 10 : 12. Wherefore let him that thinketh he standeth take heed lest he fall.

Thank for mercies. *God's preserving care.*
Ps. 91 : 12, 13. They shall bear thee up in their hands, lest thou dash thy foot against a stone. Thou shalt tread upon the lion and adder: the young lion and the dragon shalt thou trample under feet.

Heb. 1 : 14. Are they not all ministering spirits, sent forth to minister for them who shall be heirs of salvation?

Intercede for others. *Heal apostasy.*
Is. 1 : 25, 26. And I will turn my hand upon thee, and purely purge away thy dross, and take away all thy tin: and I will restore thy judges as at the first, and thy counsellors as at the beginning: afterward thou shalt be called, The city of righteousness, the faithful city.

Ps. 126 : 4. Turn again our captivity, O Lord, as the streams in the south.

SECOND SAB. EVE., SEPTEMBER. LESSON, MARK 16.
Address to God. *Aid in prayer.*

Ps. 43 : 3. O send out thy light and thy truth: let them lead me; let them bring me unto thy holy hill, and to thy tabernacles.

Confess sin. *Deplorableness of sin.*

Rom. 1 : 32. Who, knowing the judgment of God, that they which commit such things are worthy of death, not only do the same, but have pleasure in them that do them.

Ask for blessings. *Brotherly love.*

Matt. 5 : 44. But I say unto you, Love your enemies, bless them that curse you, do good to them that hate you, and pray for them which despitefully use you, and persecute you;

Col. 3 : 13. Forbearing one another, and forgiving one another, if any man have a quarrel against any; even as Christ forgave you, so also do ye.

Thank for mercies. *Deliverance from sickness.*

Ps. 116 : 3—9. The sorrows of death compassed me, and the pains of hell gat hold upon me: I found trouble and sorrow. Then called I upon the name of the Lord; O Lord, I beseech thee, deliver my soul. Gracious is the Lord, and righteous; yea, our God is merciful. The Lord preserveth the simple: I was brought low and he helped me. Return unto thy rest, O my soul; for the Lord hath dealt bountifully with thee. For thou hast delivered my soul from death, mine eyes from tears, and my feet from falling. I will walk before the Lord in the land of the living.

Intercede for others. *Jews.*

Zech. 12 : 10. And I will pour upon the house of David, and upon the inhabitants of Jerusalem, the spirit of grace and supplications: and they shall look upon me whom they have pierced, and they shall mourn for him, as one mourneth for his only son, and shall be in bitterness for him, as one that is in bitterness for his firstborn.

II Cor. 3 : 16. Nevertheless, when it shall turn to the Lord, the vail shall be taken away.

THIRD SAB. MORN., SEPTEMBER. LESSON, Is. 14 : 1—20.
Address to God. *Rely on Christ.*

Heb. 4 : 14. Seeing then that we have a great high priest, that is passed into the heavens, Jesus the Son of God, let us hold fast our profession.

Heb. 7 : 25. Wherefore he is able also to save them to the uttermost that come unto God by him, seeing he ever liveth to make intercession for them.

Confess sin. *Ingratitude*

II Chron. 32 : 25. But Hezekiah rendered not again according to the benefit done unto him; for his heart was lifted up: therefore there was wrath upon him, and upon Judah and Jerusalem.

Ask for blessings. *Self denial.*
II Tim. 3 : 2. For men shall be lovers of their own selves, covetous, boasters, proud, blasphemers, disobedient to parents, unthankful, unholy.

Prov. 3 : 5, 7. Trust in the Lord with all thine heart; and lean not unto thine own understanding. * Be not wise in thine own eyes: fear the Lord, and depart from evil.

Thank for mercies. *Divine guidance.*
Deut. 8 : 2. And thou shalt remember all the way which the Lord thy God led thee these forty years in the wilderness, to humble thee, and to prove thee, to know what was in thine heart, whether thou wouldest keep his commandments, or no.

I Sam. 7 : 12. Then Samuel took a stone, and set it between Mizpeh and Shen, and called the name of it Eben-ezer, saying, Hitherto hath the Lord helped us.

Intercede for others. *Propagation of the gospel.*
Acts 2 : 47. Praising God, and having favor with all the people. And the Lord added to the church daily such as should be saved.

Is. 54 : 2. Enlarge the place of thy tent, and let them stretch forth the curtains of thine habitations: spare not, lengthen thy cords, and strengthen thy stakes:

THIRD SAB. EVE.,   SEPTEMBER.   LESSON, I JOHN 4.
Address to God. *Worshiped.*
Heb. 10 : 19. Having therefore, brethren, boldness to enter into the holiest by the blood of Jesus,

I Cor. 7 : 35. And this I speak for your own profit; not that I may cast a snare upon you, but for that which is comely, and that ye may attend upon the Lord without distraction.

Confess sin. *Perverseness.*
Is. 28 : 13. But the word of the Lord was unto them precept upon precept, precept upon precept; line upon line, line upon line; here a little, and there a little; that they might go, and fall backward, and be broken, and snared, and taken.

Jas. 1 : 23, 24. For if any be a hearer of the word, and not a doer, he is like unto a man beholding his natural face in a glass: for he beholdeth himself, and goeth his way, and straightway forgetteth what manner of man he was.

Ask for blessings. *Grant promised blessings.*

Is. 12 : 3. Therefore with joy shall ye draw water out of the wells of salvation.

Is. 66 : 11. That ye may suck and be satisfied with the breasts of her consolation; that ye may milk out, and be delighted with the abundance of her glory.

II Sam. 7 : 25. And now, O Lord God, the word that thou hast spoken concerning thy servant, and concerning his house, establish it for ever, and do as thou hast said.

II Sam. 23 : 5. Although my house be not so with God; yet he hath made with me an everlasting covenant, ordered in all things and sure: for this is all my salvation, and all my desire, although he make it not to grow.

Thank for mercies. *Temporal blessings.*

Ecc. 9 : 9. Live joyfully with the wife whom thou lovest all the days of the life of thy vanity, which he hath given thee under the sun, all the days of thy vanity: for that is thy portion in this life, and in thy labor which thou takest under the sun.

Prov. 5 : 19. Let her be as the loving hind and pleasant roe; let her breasts satisfy thee at all times; and be thou ravished always with her love.

Intercede for others. *All men.*

Ps. 67 : 2. That thy way may be known upon earth, thy saving health among all nations.

Eph. 2 : 12. That at that time ye were without Christ, being aliens from the commonwealth of Israel, and strangers from the covenants of promise, having no hope, and without God in the world:

Ps. 67 : 3, 4. Let the people praise thee, O God; let all the people praise thee. O let the nations be glad and sing for joy: for thou shalt judge the people righteously, and govern the nations upon earth. Selah.

FOURTH SAB. MORN., SEPTEMBER. LESSON, II SAM. 6 : 1—19.
Address to God. *True God.*

Jer. 10 : 15, 16. They are vanity, and the work of errors: in the time of their visitation they shall perish. The portion of Jacob is not like them: for he is the former of all things; and Israel is the rod of his inheritance: the Lord of hosts is his name.

Rom. 9 : 5. Whose are the fathers, and of whom as concerning the flesh Christ came, who is over all, God blessed for ever. Amen.

Confess sin. *Self condemnation.*

Rom. 3 : 19. Now we know that what things soever the law saith, it saith to them who are under the law: that every mouth may be stopped, and all the world may become guilty before God.

GUIDE TO PRAYER. 79

Gal. 3 : 22. But the Scripture hath concluded all under sin, that the promise by faith of Jesus Christ might be given to them that believe.

Ezra 9 : 14. Should we again break thy commandments, and join in affinity with the people of these abominations? wouldest not thou be angry with us till thou hadst consumed us, so that there should be no remnant nor escaping.

Ask for blessings. *Supply needs.*

Rom. 8 : 28. And we know that all things work together for good to them that love God, to them who are the called according to his purpose.

Thank for mercies. *Blessings to land.*

Rom. 13 : 4. For he is the minister of God to thee for good. But if thou do that which is evil, be afraid; for he beareth not the sword in vain: for he is the minister of God, a revenger to execute wrath upon him that doeth evil.

Esther 10 : 3. For Mordecai the Jew was next unto king Ahasuerus, and great among the Jews, and accepted of the multitude of his brethren, seeking the wealth of his people, and speaking peace to all his seed.

Intercede for others. *Divine panoply.*

Eph. 6 : 13. Wherefore take unto you the whole armor of God, that ye may be able to withstand in the evil day, and having done all, to stand.

FOURTH SAB., EVE. SEPTEMBER. LESSON, JOHN 20 : 19—31.
Address to God. *Only potentate.*

I Tim. 6 : 15, 16. Which in his times he shall shew, who is the blessed and only Potentate, the King of kings, and Lord of lords; who only hath immortality, dwelling in the light which no man can approach unto, whom no man hath seen, nor can see: to whom be honor and power everlasting. Amen.

Confess sin. *Trying God's patience.*

Ecc. 8 : 11. Because sentence against an evil work is not executed speedily, therefore the heart of the sons of men is fully set in them to do evil.

Rev. 2 : 21. And I gave her space to repent of her fornication; and she repented not.

Jer. 3 : 22. Return, ye backsliding children, and I will heal your backslidings. Behold, we come unto thee; for thou art the Lord our God.

Ask for blessings. *Preserve from calamity.*

Ps. 121 : 4—8. Behold, he that keepeth Israel shall neither slumber nor sleep. The Lord is thy keeper: the Lord is thy shade upon thy right hand. The sun shall not smite thee by day, nor the moon by night. The Lord shall preserve thee from all evil: he shall preserve thy soul. The Lord shall preserve thy going out and thy coming in from this time forth, and even for evermore.

Thank for mercies. *Spiritual blessings.*
Eph. 1 : 3. Blessed be the God and Father of our Lord Jesus Christ, who hath blessed us with all spiritual blessings in heavenly places in Christ:

Intercede for others. *All men.*
1 John 5 : 19. And we know that we are of God, and the whole world lieth in wickedness.

John 12 : 31. Now is the judgment of this world: now shall the prince of this world be cast out.

II Cor. 4 : 4. In whom the god of this world hath blinded the minds of them which believe not, lest the light of the glorious gospel of Christ, who is the image of God, should shine unto them.

FIFTH SAB. MORN., SEPTEMBER. LESSON, GEN. 3.
Address to God. *Above other beings.*
Is. 40 : 15, 17. Behold, the nations are as a drop of a bucket, and are counted as the small dust of the balance: behold he taketh up the isles as a very little thing. * All nations before him are as nothing; and they are counted to him less than nothing, and vanity.

Confess sin. *Unrepentant.*
Jer. 9 : 1. Oh that my head were waters, and mine eyes a fountain of tears, that I might weep day and night for the slain of the daughter of my people!

Ps. 126 : 5, 6. They that sow in tears shall reap in joy. He that goeth forth and weepeth, bearing precious seed, shall doubtless come again with rejoicing, bringing his sheaves with him.

Ask for blessings. *Fit for heaven.*
Phil. 3 : 20, 21. For our conversation is in heaven; from whence also we look for the Saviour, the Lord Jesus Christ; who shall change our vile body, that it may be fashioned like unto his glorious body, according to the working whereby he is able even to subdue all things unto himself.

Thank for mercies. *Predestination.*
John 17 : 6. I have manifested thy name unto the men which thou gavest me out of the world: thine they were, and thou gavest them me; and they have kept thy word.

GUIDE TO PRAYER. 81

John 6 : 39. And this is the Father's will which hath sent me, that of all which he hath given me I should lose nothing, but should raise it up again at the last day.

Intercede for others. *Propagation of the gospel.*
Mark 16 : 16. He that believeth and is baptized shall be saved; but he that believeth not shall be damned.

Matt. 9 : 38. Pray ye therefore the Lord of the harvest, that he will send forth laborers into his harvest.

FIFTH SAB. EVE., SEPTEMBER. LESSON, ACTS 2 : 14—36.
Address to God. *Immutable.*
Heb. 1 : 12. And as a vesture shalt thou fold them up, and they shall be changed: but thou art the same, and thy years shall not fail.

Is. 40 : 28. Hast thou not known? hast thou not heard, that the everlasting God, the Lord, the Creator of the ends of the earth, fainteth not, neither is weary? there is no searching of his understanding.

Confess sin. *Ignored danger.*
Ps. 76 : 7. Thou, even thou, art to be feared: and who may stand in thy sight when once thou art angry?

Heb. 12 : 29. For our God is a consuming fire.

Ps. 90 : 11. Who knoweth the power of thine anger? even according to thy fear, so is thy wrath.

Ask for blessings. *Dying grace.*
Ps. 23 : 6. Surely goodness and mercy shall follow me all the days of my life: and I will dwell in the house of the Lord for ever.

II Sam. 15 : 20. Whereas thou camest but yesterday, should I this day make thee go up and down with us? seeing I go whither I may, return thou, and take back thy brethren: mercy and truth be with thee.

Thank for mercies. *Spiritual blessings.*
II Pet. 2 : 4. For if God spared not the angels that sinned, but cast them down to hell, and delivered them into chains of darkness, to be reserved unto judgment;

Is. 65 : 8. Thus saith the Lord, As the new wine is found in the cluster, and one saith, Destroy it not; for a blessing is in it: so will I do for my servants' sake, that I may not destroy them all.

Intercede for others. *Jews.*
Rom. 11 : 23—26. And they also, if they abide not still in unbelief, shall be graffed in: for God is able to graff them in again. For if thou wert cut out of the olive tree which is wild by nature, and wert graffed contrary to nature into a good olive tree; how much more shall these, which be the natural branches, be graffed into their own olive tree? For I would not, brethren, that ye should be ignorant of this mystery,

lest ye should be wise in your own conceits, that blindness in part is happened to Israel, until the fulness of the Gentiles be come in. And so all Israel shall be saved: as it is written, There shall come out of Sion the Deliverer, and shall turn away ungodliness from Jacob:

FIRST SAB. MORN.,   OCTOBER.   LESSON, JUDG. 2.
Address to God.   *Wisdom unsearchable.*
Rom. 11 : 33. O the depth of the riches both of the wisdom and knowledge of God! how unsearchable are his judgments, and his ways past finding out?

Confess sin.   *Depravity.*
Ps. 51 : 5. Behold, I was shapen in iniquity; and in sin did my mother conceive me.
Job 14 : 4. Who can bring a clean thing out of an unclean? not one.
Eph. 2 : 2, 3. Wherein in time past ye walked according to the course of this world, according to the prince of the power of the air, the spirit that now worketh in the children of disobedience: among whom also we all had our conversation in times past in the lusts of our flesh, fulfilling the desires of the flesh and of the mind; and were by nature the children of wrath, even as others.

Ask for blessings.   *Preserving grace.*
John 17 : 15, 17. I pray not that thou shouldest take them out of the world, but that thou shouldest keep them from the evil. * Sanctify them through thy truth: thy word is truth.

Thank for mercies.   *Redeemer provided.*
Is. 42 : 1. Behold my servant, whom I uphold; mine elect, in whom my soul delighteth; I have put my Spirit upon him: he shall bring forth judgment to the Gentiles.
Is. 49 : 8. Thus saith the Lord, In an acceptable time have I heard thee, and in a day of salvation have I helped thee: and I will preserve thee, and give thee for a covenant of the people, to establish the earth, to cause to inherit the desolate heritages;
Rom. 6 : 14. For sin shall not have dominion over you: for ye are not under the law, but under grace.

Intercede for others.   *Mohammedans.*
Rev. 1 : 11, 12. Saying, I am Alpha and Omega, the first and the last: and, What thou seest, write in a book, and send it unto the seven churches which are in Asia; unto Ephesus, and unto Smyrna, and unto Pergamos, and unto Thyatira, and unto Sardis, and unto Philadelphia, and unto Laodicea. And I turned to see the voice that spake with me. And being turned, I saw seven golden candlesticks;
Rev. 2 : 1. Unto the angel of the church of Ephesus write; These

GUIDE TO PRAYER. 83

things saith he that holdeth the seven stars in his right hand, who walketh in the midst of the seven golden candlesticks:

FIRST SAB. EVE.,   OCTOBER.   LESSON, MATT. 8 : 1—13.
Address to God.   *Holiness.*

Ps. 145 : 17. The Lord is righteous in all his ways, and holy in all his works.

Ps. 93 : 5. Thy testimonies are very sure: holiness becometh thine house, O Lord, forever.

Confess sin.   *Perverseness.*

Rom. 8 : 7. Because the carnal mind is enmity against God: for it is not subject to the law of God, neither indeed can be.

Ask for blessings.   *God's sustaining power.*

II Cor. 4 : 8. We are troubled on every side, yet not distressed; we are perplexed, but not in despair;

II Cor. 6 : 10. As sorrowful, yet always rejoicing; as poor, yet making many rich; as having nothing, and yet possessing all things.

Thank for mercies.   *Early indications of mercy.*

Gen. 12 : 3. And I will bless them that bless thee, and curse him that curseth thee: and in thee shall all families of the earth be blessed.

Gen. 49 : 10. The sceptre shall not depart from Judah, nor a lawgiver from between his feet, until Shiloh come; and unto him shall the gathering of the people be.

John 8 : 56. Your father Abraham rejoiced to see my day: and he saw it, and was glad.

Intercede for others.   *Universal church.*

Ps. 51 : 18. Do good in thy good pleasure unto Zion: build thou the walls of Jerusalem.

Ps. 122 : 7, 8. Peace be within thy walls, and prosperity within thy palaces. For my brethren and companions' sakes, I will now say, Peace be within thee.

SECOND SAB. MORN.,   OCTOBER.   LESSON, DEUT. 6.
Address to God.   *Goodness.*

Ex. 33 : 19. And he said, I will make all my goodness pass before thee, and I will proclaim the name of the Lord before thee; and will be gracious to whom I will be gracious, and will show mercy on whom I will show mercy.

Ps. 34 : 8. O taste and see that the Lord is good: blessed is the man that trusteth in him.

Ps. 26 : 3. For thy lovengkindness is before mine eyes: and I have walked in thy truth.

Confess sin. *Unfaithfulness.*
Ecc. 11 :10. Therefore remove sorrow from thy heart, and put away evil from thy flesh: for childhood and youth are vanity.
Ps. 90 : 9. For all our days are passed away in thy wrath: we spend our years as a tale that is told.

Ask for blessings. *Grace.*
Hos. 14 : 5, 6. I will be as the dew unto Israel: he shall grow as the lily, and cast forth his roots as Lebanon. His branches shall spread, and his beauty shall be as the olive tree, and his smell as Lebanon.
Mal. 4 : 2. But unto you that fear my name shall the Sun of righteousness arise with healing in his wings; and ye shall go forth, and grow up as calves of the stall.

Thank for mercies. *O. T. church favored.*
II Pet. 1 : 21. For the prophecy came not in old time by the will of man: but holy men of God spake as they were moved by the Holy Ghost.
I Pet. 1 : 10—12. Of which salvation the prophets have inquired and searched diligently, who prophesied of the grace that should come unto you: searching what, or what manner of time the Spirit of Christ which was in them did signify, when it testified beforehand the sufferings of Christ, and the glory that should follow. Unto whom it was revealed, that not unto themselves, but unto us they did minister the things, which are now reported unto you by them that have preached the gospel unto you with the Holy Ghost sent down from heaven; which things the angels desired to look into.

Intercede for others. *Conversion of unbelievers.*
II Tim. 2 : 25, 26. In meekness instructing those that oppose themselves; if God peradventure will give them repentance to the acknowledging of the truth; and that they may recover themselves out of the snare of the devil, who are taken captive by him at his will.
Eph. 4 : 21. If so be that ye have heard him, and have been taught by him, as the truth is in Jesus:
Tit. 1 : 1. Paul, a servant of God, and an apostle of Jesus Christ, according to the faith of God's elect, and the acknowledging of the truth which is after godliness:

SECOND SAB. EVE., OCTOBER. LESSON, JOHN 20 : 1—18.
Address to God. *Preserver.*
Heb. 1 : 3. Who being the brightness of his glory, and the express image of his person, and upholding all things by the word of his power, when he had by himself purged our sins, sat down on the right hand of the Majesty on high;

Col. 1 : 17. And he is before all things, and by him all things consist:
Confess sin. *Disobedience.*
Jer. 6 : 7. As a fountain casteth out her waters, so she casteth out her wickedness: violence and spoil is heard in her; before me continually is grief and wounds.
Jer. 22 : 21. I spake unto thee in thy prosperity; but thou saidst, I will not hear. This hath been thy manner from thy youth, that thou obeyedst not my voice.
Ask for blessings. *Submission.*
Ps. 119 : 33—36. Teach me, O Lord, the way of thy statutes; and I shall keep it unto the end. Give me understanding, and I shall keep thy law; yea, I shall observe it with my whole heart. Make me to go in the path of thy commandments; for therein do I delight. Incline my heart unto thy testimonies, and not to covetousness.
Thank for mercies. *Incarnation.*
Heb. 2 : 11, 14, 16, 17. For both he that sanctifieth and they who are sanctified are all of one: for which cause he is not ashamed to call them brethren. * Forasmuch then as the children are partakers of flesh and blood, he also himself likewise took part of the same; that through death he might destroy him that had the power of death, that is, the devil; * For verily he took not on him the nature of angels; but he took on him the seed of Abraham. Wherefore in all things it behooved him to be made like unto his brethren, that he might be a merciful and faithful high priest in things pertaining to God, to make reconciliation for the sins of the people.
Intercede for others. *Reviving church.*
Is. 32 : 15. But Judgment shall return unto righteousness: and all the upright in heart shall follow it.
Ps. 94 : 15. Until the Spirit be poured upon us from on high, and the wilderness be a fruitful field, and the fruitful field be counted for a forest.

THIRD SAB. MORN., OCTOBER. LESSON, I SAM. 13 : 5—23.
Address to God. *Holy Spirit.*
John 15 : 26. But when the Comforter is come, whom I will send unto you from the Father, even the Spirit of truth, which proceedeth from the Father, he shall testify of me:
John 14 : 26. But the Comforter, which is the Holy Ghost, whom the Father will send in my name, he shall teach you all things, and bring all things to your remembrance, whatsoever I have said unto you.
I Pet. 1 : 21. For the prophecy came not in old time by the will of

man: but holy men of God spake as they were moved by the Holy Ghost.

Confess sin. *Sensuality.*

Rom. 13 : 14. But put ye on the Lord Jesus Christ, and make not provision for the flesh, to fulfill the lusts thereof.

I Pet. 2 : 11. Dearly beloved, I beseech you as strangers and pilgrims, abstain from fleshly lusts, which war against the soul;

II Tim. 3 : 4. Traitors, heady, highminded, lovers of pleasures more than lovers of God:

Ask for blessings. *Submission.*

I Pet. 2 : 17. Honor all men. Love the brotherhood. Fear God. Honor the king.

Rom. 13 : 1, 5. Let every soul be subject unto the higher powers For there is no power but of God: the powers that be are ordained of God. * Wherefore ye must needs be subject, not only for wrath, but also for conscience sake.

Thank for mercies. *Christ's work owned.*

John 17 : 2. As thou hast given him power over all flesh, that he should give eternal life to as many as thou hast given him.

Intercede for others. *Defeat of church's enemies.*

Ps. 2 : 1—5. Why do the heathen rage, and the people imagine a vain thing? The kings of the earth set themselves, and the rulers take counsel together, against the Lord, and against his anointed, saying, Let us break their bands asunder, and cast away their cords from us. He that sitteth in the heavens shall laugh: the Lord shall have them in derision. Then shall he speak unto them in his wrath, and vex them in his sore displeasure.

THIRD SAB. EVE., OCTOBER. LESSON. LUKE 11 : 1—26.

Address to God. *Creator.*

Job 35 : 10, 11. But none saith, Where is God my maker, who giveth songs in the night; who teacheth us more than the beasts of the earth, and maketh us wiser than the fowls of heaven?

Confess sin. *Uncharitableness.*

I John 3 : 17. But whoso hath this world's good, and seeth his brother have need, and shutteth up his bowels of compassion from him, how dwelleth the love of God in him?

Is. 58 : 7. Is it not to deal thy bread to the hungry, and that thou bring the poor that are cast out to thy house? when thou seest the naked, that thou cover him; and that thou hide not thyself from thine own flesh?

Deut. 15 : 19. Beware that there be not a thought in thy wicked heart, saying, The seventh year, the year of release, is at hand; and thine eye be evil against thy poor brother, and thou givest him nought; and he cry unto the Lord against thee, and it be sin unto thee.

Jas. 2 : 7. Do not they blaspheme that worthy name by the which ye are called?

Ask for blessings. *Cheerfulness.*

Prov. 17 : 22. Heaviness in the heart of man maketh it stoop: but a good word maketh it glad.

Prov. 12 : 25. A merry heart doeth good like a medicine: but a broken spirit drieth the bones.

II Cor. 7 : 10. For godly sorrow worketh repentance to salvation not to be repented of: but the sorrow of the world worketh death.

Thank for mercies. *Miracles.*

John 5 : 36. But I have greater witness than that of John: for the works which the Father hath given me to finish, the same works that I do, bear witness of me, that the Father hath sent me.

Matt. 11 : 5. The blind receive their sight, and the lame walk, the lepers are cleansed, and the deaf hear, the dead are raised up, and the poor have the gospel preached to them.

Matt. 8 : 27. But the men marvelled, saying, What manner of man is this, that even the winds and the sea obey him!

Intercede for others. *Persecuted.*

Heb. 13 : 3. Remember them that are in bonds, as bound with them; and them which suffer adversity, as being yourselves also in the body.

Ps. 18 : 16, 17, 19. He sent from above, he took me, he drew me out of many waters. He delivered me from my strong enemy, and from them which hated me: for they were too strong for me. * He brought me forth also into a large place; he delivered me, because he delighted in me.

FOURTH SAB. MORN., OCTOBER. LESSON, EX. 32 : 15—35.
Address to God. *God as our God.*

Ps. 116 : 16. O Lord, truly I am thy servant; I am thy servant, and the son of thine handmaid: thou hast loosed my bonds.

I Cor. 6 : 19. What! know ye not that your body is the temple of the Holy Ghost which is in you, which ye have of God, and ye are not your own?

II Chron. 30 : 8. Now be ye not stiffnecked, as your fathers were, but yield yourselves unto the Lord, and enter into his sanctuary, which he hath sanctified for ever: and serve the Lord your God, that the fierceness of his wrath may turn away from you.

Jer. 50 : 5. They shall ask the way to Zion with their faces thitherward, saying. Come, and let us join ourselves to the Lord in a perpetual covenant that shall not be forgotten.

Confess sin. *Spiritual decay.*
Hos. 6 : 4. O Ephraim, what shall I do unto thee? O Judah, what shall I do unto thee? for your goodness is as a morning cloud, and as the early dew it goeth away.

Ask for blessings. *Courage.*
II Cor. 6 : 4, 7, 8. But in all things approving ourselves as the ministers of God, in much patience, in afflictions, in necessities, in distresses. * By the word of truth, by the power of God, by the armor of righteousness on the right hand and on the left, by honor and dishonor, by evil report and good report: as deceivers and yet true;

I Cor. 4 : 3, 4. But with me it is a very small thing that I should be judged of you, or of man's judgment: yea, I judge not mine own self. For I know nothing by myself; yet am I not hereby justified: but he that judgeth me is the Lord.

Thank for mercies. *Encouraged to seek Christ.*
John 7 : 37. In the last day, that great day of the feast, Jesus stood and cried, saying, If any man thirst, let him come unto me, and drink.

Intercede for others. *Other nations.*
Ps. 22 : 28. For the kingdom is the Lord's: and he is the governor among the nations.

Jer. 10 : 7. Who would not fear thee, O King of nations? for to thee doth it appertain: forasmuch as among all the wise men of the nations, and in all their kingdoms, there is none like unto thee.

Is. 9 : 4, 8. For thou hast maintained my right and my cause; thou satest in the throne judging right. * And he shall judge the world in righteousness, he shall minister judgment to the people in uprightness.

FOURTH SAB., EVE. OCTOBER. LESSON, JOHN 10 : 1—30.
Address to God. *Prayed to.*
Prov. 15 : 8. The sacrifice of the wicked is an abomination to the Lord: but the prayer of the upright is his delight.

Ps. 50 : 23. Whoso offereth praise glorifieth me: and to him that ordereth his conversation aright will I show the salvation of God.

Ps. 69 : 31. This also shall please the Lord better than an ox or bullock that hath horns and hoofs.

Confess sin. *Hypocrisy.*
Rom. 2 : 21. Thou therefore which teachest another, teachest thou not thyself? thou that preachest a man should not steal, dost thou steal?

Tit. 1 : 16. They profess that they know God; but in works they deny him, being abominable, and disobedient, and unto every good work reprobate.

Ask for blessings. *Diligence.*

Gal. 4 : 18. But it is good to be zealously affected always in a good thing, and not only when I am present with you.

Col. 3 : 23. And whatsoever ye do, do it heartily, as to the Lord, and not unto men;

Thank for mercies. *Christ satisfying the law.*

Eph. 3 : 18, 19. May be able to comprehend with all saints what is the breadth, and length, and depth, and height; and to know the love of Christ, which passeth knowledge, that ye might be filled with all the fulness of God.

Eph. 2 : 4. But God, who is rich in mercy, for his great love wherewith he loved us,

Intercede for others. *Own land.*

Is. 5 : 1. Now will I sing to my well beloved a song of my beloved touching his vineyard. My well beloved hath a vineyard in a very fruitful hill.

Job 39 : 6. Whose house I have made the wilderness, and the barren land his dwellings.

Ps. 85 : 12. Yea, the Lord shall give that which is good; and our land shall yield her increase.

FIFTH SAB. MORN., OCTOBER. LESSON, Is. 25.
Address to God. *Unworthy suppliants.*

Gen. 32 : 10. I am not worthy of the least of all the mercies, and of all the truth, which thou hast shewed unto thy servant; for with my staff I passed over this Jordan; and now I am become two bands.

Matt. 15 : 26, 27. But he answered and said, It is not meet to take the children's bread, and to cast it to dogs. And she said, Truth, Lord; yet the dogs eat of the crumbs which fall from their masters' table.

Rom. 10 : 12. For there is no difference between the Jew and the Greek: for the same Lord over all is rich unto all that call upon him.

Confess sin. *Condemnation.*

Deut. 29 : 20. The Lord will not spare him, but then the anger of the Lord and his jealousy shall smoke against that man, and all the curses that are written in this book shall lie upon him, and the Lord shall blot out his name from under heaven.

Is. 28 : 17. Judgment also will I lay to the line, and righteousness to the plummet: and the hail shall sweep away the refuge of lies, and the waters shall overflow the hiding place.

Ask for blessings. *Integrity.*
Ps. 41 : 12. And as for me, thou upholdest me in mine integrity, and settest me before thy face for ever.
Ps. 25 : 24. Judge me, O Lord my God, according to thy righteousness; and let them not rejoice over me.
Thank for mercies. *Christ's resurrection.*
Rom. 14 : 9. For to this end Christ both died, and rose, and revived, that he might be Lord both of the dead and living.
I Thess. 5 : 10. Who died for us, that, whether we wake or sleep, we should live together with him.
Intercede for others. *Humiliation for national sins.*
Is. 1 : 4. Ah sinful nation, a people laden with iniquity, a seed of evil doers, children that are corrupters: they have forsaken the Lord, they have provoked the Holy One of Israel unto anger, they are gone away backward:
Ezek. 9 : 4. And the Lord said unto him, Go through the midst of the city, through the midst of Jerusalem, and set a mark upon the foreheads of the men that sigh and that cry for all the abominations that be done in the midst thereof.

FIFTH SAB. EVE., OCTOBER. LESSON, MATT. 10 : 1—24.
Address to God. *Desired.*
Matt. 5 : 6. Blessed are they which do hunger and thirst after righteousness: for they shall be filled.
Lk. 1 : 53. He hath filled the hungry with good things; and the rich he hath sent empty away.
Confess sin. *Despising God's longsuffering.*
II Pet. 3 : 15. And account that the longsuffering of our Lord is salvation; even as our beloved brother Paul also according to the wisdom given unto him hath written unto you;
Judg. 13 : 23. But his wife said unto him, If the Lord were pleased to kill us, he would not have received a burnt offering and a meat offering at our hands, neither would he have shewed us all these things, nor would as at this time have told us such things as these.
Ask for blessings. *Govern tongue.*
Prov. 31 : 26. She openeth her mouth with wisdom; and in her tongue is the law of kindness.
Prov. 10 : 32. The lips of the righteous know what is acceptable: but the mouth of the wicked speaketh frowardness.
Prov. 10 : 20, 21. The tongue of the just is as choice silver: the heart of the wicked is little worth. The lips of the righteous feed many: but fools die for want of wisdom.

Thank for mercies. *Christ's ascension.*
John 14 : 2, 3. In my Father's house are many mansions: if it were not so, I would have told you. I go to prepare a place for you. And if I go and prepare a place for you, I will come again, and receive you unto myself; that where I am, there ye may be also.

John 13 : 36. Simon Peter said unto him, Lord, whither goest thou? Jesus answered him, whither I go, thou canst not follow me now; but thou shalt follow me afterwards.

Intercede for others. *National mercies.*
Jer. 14 : 7—9. O Lord, though our iniquities testify against us, do thou it for thy name's sake: for our backslidings are many; we have sinned against thee. O the hope of Israel, the Saviour thereof in time of trouble, why shouldest thou be as a stranger in the land, and as a wayfaring man that turneth aside to tarry for a night? Why shouldest thou be as a man astonished, as a mighty man that cannot save? yet thou, O Lord, art in the midst of us, and we are called by thy name; leave us not.

FIRST SAB. MORN., NOVEMBER. LESSON, IIKIN. 5 : 1—19.
Address to God. *Confidence in God.*
Ps. 119 : 43, 74. And take not the word of truth utterly out of my mouth; for I have hoped in thy judgments. * They that fear thee will be glad when they see me; because I have hoped in thy word.

Confess sin. *Need of repentance.*
Ps. 38 : 4. For mine iniquities have gone over mine head: as a heavy burden they are too heavy for me.

Matt. 11 : 28. Come unto me, all ye that labor and are heavy laden, and I will give you rest.

Ask for blessings. *Preserve from sin.*
Eph. 5 : 15. See then that ye walk circumspectly, not as fools, but as wise.

II Cor. 11 : 12. But what I do, that I will do, that I may cut off occasion from them which desire occasion; that wherein they glory, they may be found even as we.

I Pet. 2 : 15. For so is the will of God, that with well doing ye may put to silence the ignorance of foolish men:

Tit. 2 : 10. Therefore I endure all things for the elect's sake, that they may also obtain the salvation which is in Christ Jesus with eternal glory.

Thank for mercies. *Christ's intercession.*
Heb. 5 : 1, 2, 9. For every high priest taken from among men is ordained for men in things pertaining to God, that he may offer both

gifts and sacrifices for sins: who can have compassion on the ignorant, and on them that are out of the way; for that he himself also is compassed with infirmity. * And being made perfect, he became the author of eternal salvation unto all them that obey him;

Intercede for others. *Continuance of gospel.*
Ps. 45 : 6. Thy throne, O God, is for ever and ever: the sceptre of thy kingdom is a right sceptre.
Jer. 17 : 12. A glorious high throne from the beginning is the place of our sanctuary.

FIRST SAB. EVE., NOVEMBER. LESSON, JOHN 16 : 1—20.

Address to God. *Accept services.*
Ps. 141 : 2. Let my prayer be set forth before thee as incense; and the lifting up of my hands as the evening sacrifice.

Confess sin. *Sinful ignorance.*
1 Cor. 4 : 4. For I know nothing by myself; yet am I not hereby justified: but he that judgeth me is the Lord.
1 John 3 : 20. For if our heart condemn us, God is greater than our heart, and knoweth all things.
Lk. 15 : 21. And the son said unto him, Father, I have sinned against heaven, and in thy sight, and am no more worthy to be called thy son.

Ask for blessings. *Hope.*
1 Pet. 1 : 3. Blessed be the God and Father of our Lord Jesus Christ, which according to his abundant mercy hath begotten us again unto a lively hope by the resurrection of Jesus Christ from the dead.
Heb. 6 : 19, 20. Which hope we have as an anchor of the soul, both sure and steadfast, and which entereth into that within the vail: whither the forerunner is for us entered, even Jesus, made a high priest for ever after the order of Melchisedec.

Thank for mercies. *Christ's exaltation.*
1 Cor. 15 : 24, 25, 28. Then cometh the end, when he shall have delivered up the kingdom to God, even the Father; when he shall have put down all rule, and all authority and power. For he must reign, till he hath put all enemies under his feet. * And when all things shall be subdued unto him, then shall the Son also himself be subject unto him that put all things under him, that God may be all in all.
Ps. 2 : 6. Yet have I set my King upon my holy hill of Zion.
Lk. 1 : 33. And he shall reign over the house of Jacob for ever; and of his kingdom there shall be no end.

Intercede for others. *Continuance of peace.*
Zech. 2 : 5. For I, saith the Lord, will be unto her a wall of fire round about, and will be the glory in the midst of her.

GUIDE TO PRAYER.

Is. 4 : 5. And the Lord will create upon every dwellingplace of mount Zion, and upon her assemblies, a cloud and smoke by day, and the shining of a flaming fire by night: for upon all the glory shall be a defence.

SECOND SAB. MORN., NOVEMBER. LESSON, IS. 35.
Address to God. *Aid in prayer.*
Ps. 51 : 15. O Lord, open thou my lips; and my mouth shall shew forth thy praise.
Confess sin. *Depravity.*
Gen. 6 : 12. And God looked upon the earth, and, behold, it was corrupt; for all flesh had corrupted his way upon the earth.
Ps. 14 : 3. They are all gone aside, they are all together become filthy; there is none that doeth good, no, not one.
Ask for blessings. *Patience.*
Lk. 29 : 19. In your patience possess ye your souls.
Jas. 1 : 4. But let patience have her perfect work, that ye may be perfect and entire, wanting nothing.
Thank for mercies. *Second advent.*
II Pet. 3 : 13, 14. Nevertheless we, according to his promise, look for new heavens and a new earth, wherein dwelleth righteousness. Wherefore, beloved, seeing that ye look for such things, be diligent that ye may be found of him in peace, without spot, and blameless.
Rev. 22 : 20. He which testifieth these things saith, Surely I come quickly: Amen. Even so, come, Lord Jesus.
Intercede for others. *Wickedness suppressed.*
Ps. 7 : 9. Oh let the wickedness of the wicked come to an end; but establish the just: for the righteous God trieth the hearts and reins.
Ps. 94 : 16. Who will rise up for me against the evil doers? or who will stand up for me against the workers of iniquity?

SECOND SAB. EVE., NOVEMBER. LESSON, LK.16 : 19—31.
Address to God. *Reliance on the Saviour.*
Ps. 84 : 9. Behold, O God our shield, and look upon the face of thine anointed.
Matt. 3 : 17. And lo a voice from heaven, saying, This is my beloved Son, in whom I am well pleased.
Confess sin. *Perverseness.*
Hos. 8 : 12. I have written to him the great things of my law, but they were counted as a strange thing.
Job 21 : 15. What is the Almighty, that we should serve him? and what profit should we have, if we pray unto him?
Jer. 44 : 17. But we will certainly do whatsoever thing goeth forth

out of our own mouth, to burn incense unto the queen of heaven, and to pour out drink offerings unto her, as we have done, we, and our fathers, our kings, and our princes, in the cities of Judah, and in the streets of Jerusalem: for then had we plenty of victuals, and were well, and saw no evil.

Ecc. 11:9. Rejoice, O young man, in thy youth; and let thy heart cheer thee in the days of thy youth, and walk in the ways of thine heart, and in the sight of thine eyes: but know thou, that for all these things God will bring thee into judgment.

Ask for blessings. *Humility.*

Ecc. 7:9. Be not hasty in thy spirit to be angry: for anger resteth in the bosom of fools.

Eph. 4:26. Be ye angry, and sin not: let not the sun go down upon your wrath:

Tit. 3:2, 3. To speak evil of no man, to be no brawlers, but gentle, showing all meekness unto all men. For we ourselves also were sometime foolish, disobedient, deceived, serving divers lusts and pleasures, living in malice and envy, hateful and hating one another.

Thank for mercies. *Holy Spirit.*

Heb. 2:4. God also bearing them witness, both with signs and wonders, and with divers miracles, and gifts of the Holy Ghost, according to his own will?

Lk. 11:13. If ye then, being evil, know how to give good gifts unto your children; how much more shall your heavenly Father give the Holy Spirit to them that ask him?

Eph. 1:13, 14. In whom ye also trusted, after that ye heard the word of truth, the gospel of your salvation: in whom also, after that ye believed, ye were sealed with that Holy Spirit of promise, which is the earnest of our inheritance until the redemption of the purchased possession, unto the praise of his glory.

Intercede for others. *Heal divisions.*

Judg. 5:16. Why abodest thou among the sheepfolds, to hear the bleatings of the flocks? For the divisions of Reuben there were great searchings of heart.

Lk. 12:52. For from henceforth there shall be five in one house divided, three against two, and two against three.

Lam. 2:13. What thing shall I take to witness for thee? what thing shall I liken to thee, O daughter of Jerusalem? what shall I equal to thee, that I may comfort thee, O virgin daughter of Zion? for thy breach is great like the sea: who can heal thee?

Jer. 8:22. Is there no balm in Gilead? is there no physician there? why then is not the health of the daughter of my people recovered?

Ps. 60 : 2. Thou hast made the earth to tremble; thou hast broken it: heal the breaches thereof; for it shaketh.

THIRD SAB. MORN., NOVEMBER. LESSON. 1 SAM. 3.
Address to God. *To be worshiped.*

Matt. 15 : 8. This people draweth nigh unto me with their mouth, and honoreth me with their lips; but their heart is far from me.

Confess sin. *Improvidence.*

Lk. 19 : 44. And shall lay thee even with the ground, and thy children within thee; and they shall not leave in thee one stone upon another; because thou knewest not the time of thy visitation.

Prov. 6 : 6—8. Go to the ant, thou sluggard; consider her ways and be wise: which having no guide, overseer, or ruler, provideth her meat in the summer, and gathereth her food in the harvest.

Ask for blessings. *Conversion.*

Is. 56 : 4, 5. For thus saith the Lord unto the eunuchs that keep my sabbaths, and choose the things that please me, and take hold of my covenant; even unto them will I give in mine house and within my walls a place and a name better than of sons and daughters:

Jer. 50 : 5. They shall ask the way to Zion with their faces thitherward, saying, Come, and let us join ourselves to the Lord in a perpetual covenant that shall not be forgotten.

Ezek. 20 : 37. And I will cause you to pass under the rod, and I will bring you into the bond of the covenant:

Ezek. 16 : 8. Now when I passed by thee, and looked upon thee, behold, thy time was the time of love; and I spread my skirt over thee, and covered thy nakedness: yea, I sware unto thee, and entered into a covenant with thee, saith the Lord God, and thou becamest mine.

Thank for mercies. *Covenant of grace.*

Rom. 4 : 11. And he received the sign of circumcision, a seal of the righteousness of the faith which he had yet being uncircumcised: that he might be the father of all them that believe, though they be not circumcised; that righteousness might be imputed unto them also:

Acts. 2 : 38, 39. Then Peter said unto them, Repent, and be baptized every one of you in the name of Jesus Christ for the remission of sins, and ye shall receive the gift of the Holy Ghost. For the promise is unto you and to your children, and to all that are afar off, even as many as the Lord our God shall call.

Matt. 26 : 28. For this is my blood of the new testament, which is shed for many for the remission of sins.

Intercede for others. *Victory over external enemies.*

Ps. 60 : 11, 12. Give us help from trouble: for vain is the help of man. Through God we shall do valiantly: for he it is that shall tread down our enemies.

Is. 41 : 2. Who raised up the righteous man from the east, called him to his foot, gave the nations before him, and made him rule over kings? he gave them as the dust to his sword, and as driven stubble to his bow.

THIRD SAB. EVE.,   NOVEMBER.   LESSON, JOHN 15.
Address to God.   *Power.*

Deut. 33 : 31. For their rock is not as our Rock, even our enemies themselves being judges.

Is. 26 : 4. Trust ye in the Lord for ever: for in the Lord JEHOVAH is everlasting strength.

Ps. 135 : 13. Thy name, O Lord, endureth for ever; and thy memorial, O Lord, throughout all generations.

Jer. 10 : 11. Thus shall ye say unto them, The gods that have not made the heavens and the earth, even they shall perish from the earth, and from under these heavens.

Confess sin.   *Omissions.*

I Thess. 4 : 6. That no man go beyond and defraud his brother in any matter: because that the Lord is the avenger of all such, as we also have forewarned you and testified.

Job 31 : 5, 7. If I have walked with vanity, or if my foot hath hasted to deceit: * If my step hath turned out of the way, and mine heart walked after mine eyes, and if any blot hath cleaved to my hands;

Job 34 : 32. That which I see not teach thou me: if I have done iniquity, I will do no more.

Ask for blessings.   *Faith.*

Ps. 16 : 8. I have set the Lord always before me: because he is at my right hand, I shall not be moved.

Ps. 25 : 15. Mine eyes are ever toward the Lord; for he shall pluck my feet out of the net.

Heb. 11 : 26, 27. Esteeming the reproach of Christ greater riches than the treasures in Egypt: for he had respect unto the recompense of the reward. By faith he forsook Egypt, not fearing the wrath of the king: for he endured, as seeing him who is invisible.

Thank for mercies.   *Scriptures.*

Is. 29 : 11. And the vision of all is become unto you as the words of a book that is sealed, which men deliver to one that is learned, saying, Read this, I pray thee: and he saith, I cannot; for it is sealed.

Acts 2 : 11. Cretes and Arabians, we do hear them speak in our tongues the wonderful works of God.

Intercede for others. *Chief magistrate.*
Ps. 72 : 1, 4. Give the king thy judgments, O God, and thy righteousness unto the king's son. * He shall judge the poor of the people, he shall save the children of the needy, and shall break in pieces the oppressor.

FOURTH SAB. MORN., NOVEMBER. LESSON, GEN.. 32 : 9—32.
Address to God. *Omniscience.*
Ps. 139 : 1—3. O Lord thou hast searched me, and known me. Thou knowest my downsitting and mine uprising; thou understandest my thought afar off. Thou compassest my path and my lying down, and art acquainted with all my ways.

Confess sin. *Trying God's patience.*
Rom. 2 : 4. Or despisest thou the riches of his goodness and forbearance and longsuffering; not knowing that the goodness of God leadeth thee to repentance?
Ezra 10 : 2. And Shechaniah the son of Jehiel, one of the sons of Elam, answered and said unto Ezra, We have trespassed against our God, and have taken strange wives of the people of the land: yet now there is hope in Israel concerning this thing.

Ask for blessings. *Fear of the Lord.*
Jer. 32 : 40. And I will make an everlasting covenant with them, that I will not turn away from them, to do them good; but I will put my fear in their hearts, that they shall not depart from me.
Ps. 119 : 38. Stablish thy word unto thy servant, who is devoted to thy fear.
Prov. 23 : 17. Let not thine heart envy sinners; but be thou in the fear of the Lord all the day long.

Thank for mercies. *Ordinances.*
Neh. 9 : 14. And madest known unto them thy holy sabbath, and commandedst them precepts, statutes, and laws, by the hand of Moses thy servant.
Heb. 4 : 9. When your fathers tempted me, proved me, and saw my works forty years.
Eph. 4 : 8, 11—13. Wherefore he saith, When he ascended up on high, he led captivity captive, and gave gifts unto men. * And he gave some, apostles; and some, prophets; and some, evangelists; and some, pastors and teachers; for the perfecting of the saints, for the work of the ministry, for the edifying of the body of Christ: till we all come in the unity of the faith, and of the knowledge of the Son of God, unto a perfect man, unto the measure of the stature of the fulness of Christ:

Intercede for others. *Wisdom to rulers.*

Ps. 105 : 22. To bind his princes at his pleasure; and teach his senators wisdom.

Is. 11 : 3. And shall make him of quick understanding in the fear of the Lord: and he shall not judge after the sight of his eyes, neither reprove after the hearing of his ears:

FOURTH SAB., EVE. NOVEMBER. LESSON, ROM. 8 : 1—25.

Address to God. *Benefactor.*

Ps. 104 : 24, 25. O Lord, how manifold are thy works! in wisdom hast thou made them all: the earth is full of thy riches. So is this great and wide sea, wherein are things creeping innumerable, both small and great beast.

Ps. 145 : 15, 16. The eyes of all wait upon thee; and thou givest them their meat in due season. Thou openest thine hand and satisfiest the desires of every living thing.

Ps. 36 : 6. Thy righteousness is like the great mountains; thy judgments are a great deep: O Lord, thou preservest man and beast.

Confess sin. *Lack of repentance.*

I Kin. 8 : 38. What prayer and supplication soever be made by any man, or by all thy people Israel, which shall know every man the plague of his own heart, and spread forth his hands toward this house:

II Cor. 7 : 10. For godly sorrow worketh repentance to salvation not to be repented of: but the sorrow of the world worketh death.

Ezek. 16 : 63. That thou mayest remember, and be confounded, and never open thy mouth any more because of thy shame, when I am pacified toward thee for all that thou hast done, saith the Lord God.

Ask for blessings. *Love to God.*

II Cor. 2 : 15. And that he died for all, that they which live should not henceforth live unto themselves, but unto him which died for them, and rose again.

I John 2 : 15. Love not the world, neither the things that are in the world. If any man love the world, the love of the Father is not in him.

Thank for mercies. *Advance of the gospel.*

Rev. 12 : 10. And I heard a loud voice saying in heaven, Now is come salvation, and strength, and the kingdom of our God, and the power of his Christ: for the accuser of our brethren is cast down, which accused them before our God day and night.

Rev. 6 : 2. And I saw, and behold a white horse: and he that sat on him had a bow; and a crown was given unto him: and he went forth conquering and to conquer.

Is. 66 : 8. Who hath heard such a thing? who hath seen such things? Shall the earth be made to bring forth in one day? or shall a nation be born at once? for as soon as Zion travailed, she brought forth her children.

Intercede for others. *Chief magistrate.*
Ps. 132 : 18. His enemies will I clothe with shame: but upon himself shall his crown flourish.
Ps. 78 : 6, 7. That the generation to come might know them, even the children which should be born; who should arise and declare them to their children: that they might set their hope in God, and not forget the works of God, but keep his commandments:

FIFTH SAB. MORN., NOVEMBER. LESSON, II CHRON. 35 . 1—19.
Address to God. *Creator.*
Is. 64 : 8. But now, O Lord, thou art our Father; we are the clay, and thou our potter; and we are all the work of thy hand.

Confess sin. *Unbelief.*
Lk. 24 : 25. Then he said unto them, O fools, and slow of heart to believe all that the prophets have spoken:
Heb. 5 : 12. For when for the time ye ought to be teachers, ye have need that one teach you again which be the first principles of the oracles of God; and are become such as have need of milk, and not of strong meat.

Ask for blessings. *Humility.*
Col. 3 : 12. Put on therefore, as the elect of God, holy and beloved, bowels of mercies, kindness, humbleness of mind, meekness, longsuffering:
Lk. 6 : 36. Be ye therefore merciful, as your Father also is merciful.
Matt. 5 : 48. Be ye therefore perfect, even as your Father which is in heaven is perfect.

Thank for mercies. *Preservation of christianity.*
Ps. 129 : 1—4. Many a time have they afflicted me from my youth, may Israel now say: many a time have they afflicted me from my youth: yet they have not prevailed against me. The ploughers ploughed upon my back: they made long their furrows. The Lord is righteous: he hath cut asunder the cords of the wicked.
Matt. 16 : 18. And I say also unto thee, That thou art Peter, and upon this rock I will build my church; and the gates of hell shall not prevail against it.
Ps. 89 : 29. His seed also will I make to endure for ever, and his throne as the days of heaven.

Intercede for others. *Judges.*
II Sam. 23 : 3. The God of Israel said, the Rock of Israel spake to me, He that ruleth over men must be just, ruling in the fear of God.

FIFTH SAB. EVE., NOVEMBER. LESSON, MATT. 13 : 24—43.
Address to God. *God as our God.*
Ps. 119 : 94. I am thine, save me; for I have sought thy precepts.
1 Chron. 29 : 16. O Lord our God, all this store that we have prepared to build thee a house for thine holy name cometh of thine hand, and is all thine own.

Confess sin. *Justly condemned.*
Ezra 9 : 13. And after all that is come upon us for our evil deeds, and for our great trespass, seeing that thou our God hast punished us less than our iniquities deserve, and hast given us such deliverance as this;
Neh. 9 : 33. Howbeit thou art just in all that is brought upon us; for thou hast done right, but we have done wickedly:

Ask for blessings. *Hope.*
Col. 1 : 23, 27. If ye continue in the faith grounded and settled, and be not moved away from the hope of the gospel, which ye have heard, and which was preached to every creature which is under heaven; whereof I Paul am made a minister;*To whom God would make known what is the riches of the glory of this mystery among the Gentiles; which is Christ in you, the hope of glory:
Heb. 6 : 11. And we desire that every one of you do shew the same diligence to the full assurance of hope unto the end:

Thank for mercies. *Helpful examples.*
Heb. 12 : 1. Wherefore, seeing we also are compassed about with so great a cloud of witnesses, let us lay aside every weight, and the sin which doth so easily beset us, and let us run with patience the race that is set before us,
Cant. 1 : 8. If thou know not, O thou fairest among women, go thy way forth by the footsteps of the flock, and feed thy kids beside the shepherds' tents.
Heb. 11 : 2. For by it the elders obtained a good report.
Heb. 6 : 12. That ye be not slothful, but followers of them who through faith and patience inherit the promises.
I Cor. 11 : 1. Be ye followers of me, even as I also am of Christ.

Intercede for others. *Ministry.*
I Tim. 3 : 15. But if I tarry long, that thou mayest know how thou oughtest to behave thyself in the house of God, which is the church of the living God, the pillar and ground of the truth.
II Cor. 4 : 5. For we preach not ourselves, but Christ Jesus the Lord; and ourselves your servants for Jesus' sake.
II Tim. 2 : 15. Study to show thyself approved unto God, a workman that needeth not to be ashamed, rightly dividing the word of truth.

GUIDE TO PRAYER.

FIRST SAB. MORN.,   DECEMBER.   LESSON, II KIN. 20 : 1—7.
Address to God.   *I prayed to.*
Ps. 65 : 2. O thou that hearest prayer, unto thee shall all flesh come.
Job 27 : 8, 9. For what is the hope of the hypocrite, though he hath gained, when God taketh away his soul? Will God hear his cry when trouble cometh upon him?

Confess sin.   *Trying God's patience.*
Ezek. 33 : 11. Say unto them, As I live, saith the Lord God, I have no pleasure in the death of the wicked: but that the wicked turn from his way and live: turn ye, turn ye from your evil ways; for why will ye die, O house of Israel?
Joel 2 : 13, 14. And rend your heart, and not your garments, and turn unto the Lord your God: for he is gracious and merciful, slow to anger, and of great kindness, and repenteth him of the evil. Who knoweth if he will return and repent, and leave a blessing behind him; even a meat offering and a drink offering unto the Lord your God.

Ask for blessings.   *Integrity.*
Ps. 119 : 80. Let my heart be sound in thy statutes; that I be not ashamed.
Matt. 6 : 22. The light of the body is the eye: if therefore thine eye be single, thy whole body shall be full of light.

Thank for mercies.   *Communion of saints.*
John 11 : 52. And not for that nation only, but that also he should gather together in one the children of God that were scattered abroad.
Col. 1 : 18. And he is the head of the body, the church: who is the beginning, the firstborn from the dead; that in all things he might have the preeminence.
Rev. 1 : 9. I John, who also am your brother, and companion in tribulation, and in the kingdom and patience of Jesus Christ, who was in the isle that is called Patmos, for the word of God and for the testimony of Jesus Christ.

Intercede for others.   *Schools.*
Jas. 1 : 17. Every good gift and every perfect gift is from above, and cometh down from the Father of lights, with whom is no variableness, neither shadow of turning.

FIRST SAB. EVE.,   DECEMBER.   LESSON, LK. 18 : 18—43.
Address to God.   *Desired.*
Ps. 1—3, 5. O God, thou art my God; early will I seek thee: my soul thirsteth for thee, my flesh longeth for thee in a dry and thirsty land, where no water is; to see thy power and thy glory, so as I have seen thee in the sanctuary. Because thy lovingkindness is better than life,

my lips shall praise thee. * My soul shall be satisfied as with marrow and fatness; and my mouth shall praise thee with joyful lips;
Confess sin. *Lack of repentance.*
Matt. 3 : 8. Bring forth therefore fruits meet for repentance:
Ps. 85 : 8. I will hear what God the Lord will speak: for he will speak peace unto his people, and to his saints: but let them not turn again to folly.
Hos. 14 : 8. Ephraim shall say, What have I to do any more with idols? I have heard him, and observed him: I am like a green fir tree. From me is thy fruit found.
Rom. 6 : 14. For sin shall not have dominion over you: for ye are not under the law, but under grace.
Ask for blessings. *Diligence.*
Ezra 3 : 4. They kept also the feast of tabernacles, as it is written, and offered the daily burnt offerings by number, according to the custom, as the duty of every day required;
Eph. 5 : 16. Redeeming the time, because the days are evil.
Lk. 12 : 43. Blessed is that servant, whom his lord when he cometh shall find so doing.
Thank for mercies. *Hope of eternal life.*
Tit. 1 : 2. In hope of eternal life, which God, that cannot lie, promised before the world began;
I John 5 : 13. These things have I written unto you that believe on the name of the Son of God; that ye may know that ye have eternal life, and that ye may believe on the name of the Son of God.
Intercede for others. *Rulers.*
I Tim. 2 : 2. For Kings, and for all that are in authority; that we may lead a quiet and peaceable life in all godliness and honesty.

SECOND SAB. MORN., DECEMBER. LESSON, JOSH. 7 : 10—26.
Address to God. *Worshiped.*
John 4 : 23, 24. But the hour cometh, and now is, when the true worshippers shall worship the Father in spirit and in truth: for the Father seeketh such to worship him. God is a spirit: and they that worship him must worship him in spirit and in truth.
Confess sin. *Neglect.*
Job 15 : 4. Yea, thou castest off fear, and restrainest prayer before God.
Is. 64 : 7. And there is none that calleth upon thy name, that stirreth up himself to take hold of thee: for thou hast hid thy face from us, and hast consumed us, because of our iniquities.

Ask for blessings. *Submission.*

Eph. 3 : 16—19. That he would grant you, according to the riches of his glory, to be strengthened with might by his Spirit in the inner man; that Christ may dwell in your hearts by faith; that ye, being rooted and grounded in love, may be able to comprehend with all saints what is the breadth, and length, and depth, and height; and to know the love of Christ, which passeth knowledge, that ye might be filled with all the fulness of God.

Thank for mercies. *Spiritual mercies.*

Rom. 1 : 28. And even as they did not like to retain God in their knowledge, God gave them over to a reprobate mind, to do those things which are not convenient;

1 Tim. 4 : 2. Speaking lies in hypocrisy; having their conscience seared with a hot iron;

Hos. 4 : 17. Ephraim is joined to his idols: let him alone.

Gen. 6 : 3. And the Lord said, My spirit shall not always strive with man, for that he also is flesh: yet his days shall be a hundred and twenty years.

Intercede for others. *Youth.*

Ecc. 11 : 9, 10. Rejoice, O young man, in thy youth; and let thy heart cheer thee in the days of thy youth, and walk in the ways of thine heart, and in the sight of thine eyes: but know thou, that for all these things God will bring thee into judgment. Therefore remove sorrow from thy heart, and put away evil from thy flesh: for childhood and youth are vanity.

SECOND SAB. EVE., DECEMBER. LESSON, JOHN 2 : 1—11.
Address to God. *Ruler.*

Ps. 103 : 19. The Lord hath prepared his throne in the heavens; and his kingdom ruleth over all.

Neh. 9 : 6. Thou, even thou, art Lord alone; thou hast made heaven, the heaven of heavens, with all their host, the earth, and all things that are therein, the seas, and all that is therein, and thou preservest them all; and the host of heaven worshippeth thee.

Confess sin. *Condemnation.*

Ps. 51 : 4. Against thee, thee only, have I sinned, and done this evil in thy sight: that thou mightest be justified when thou speakest, and be clear when thou judgest.

Lev. 26 : 43. The land also shall be left of them, and shall enjoy her sabbaths, while she lieth desolate without them: and they shall accept of the punishment of their iniquity; because, even because they despised my judgments, and because their soul abhorred my statutes.

I Pet. 5 : 6. Humble yourselves therefore under the mighty hand of God, that he may exalt you in due time:

II Chron. 12 : 6. Whereupon the princes of Israel and the king humbled themselves; and they said, The Lord is righteous.

Ask for blessings. *Preserving grace.*

Ps. 116 : 2. Because he hath inclined his ear unto me, therefore will I call upon him as long as I live.

Job 27 : 5, 6. God forbid that I should justify you: till I die I will not remove mine integrity from me. My righteousness I hold fast, and will not let it go: my heart shall not reproach me so long as I live.

Thank for mercies. *Regeneration.*

Lk. 11 : 21, 22. When a strong man armed keepeth his palace, his goods are in peace: but when a stronger than he shall come upon him, and overcome him, he taketh from him all his armor wherein he trusted, and divideth his spoils.

Intercede for others. *Aged christian.*

Acts 21 : 16. There went with us also certain of the disciples of Cesarea, and brought with them one Mnason of Cyprus, an old disciple, with whom we should lodge.

Ps. 92 : 14, 15. They shall still bring forth fruit in old age: they shall be fat and flourishing; to shew that the Lord is upright: he is my rock, and there is no unrighteousness in him.

Ecc. 12 : 1. Remember now thy Creator in the days of thy youth, while the evil days come not, nor the years draw nigh, when thou shalt say, I have no pleasure in them;

Ps. 94 : 19. In the multitude of my thoughts within me thy comforts delight my soul.

THIRD SAB. MORN., DECEMBER. LESSON, Is. 51.
Address to God. *Preserver.*

Ps. 104 : 29. Thou hidest thy face, they are troubled: thou takest away their breath, they die, and return to their dust.

Acts 17 : 28. For in him we live, and move, and have our being; as certain also of your own poets have said, For we are also his offspring.

Confess sin. *Lack of repentance.*

Ps. 119 : 176. I have gone astray like a lost sheep: seek thy servant; for I do not forget thy commandments.

Ask for blessings. *Dying grace.*

Ps. 49 : 15. But God will redeem my soul from the power of the grave: for he shall receive me. Selah.

Ps. 73 : 24. Thou shalt guide me with thy counsel, and afterward receive me to glory.

GUIDE TO PRAYER. 105

Thank for mercies. *Remission of sins.*
Hos. 2 : 14, 15. Therefore, behold, I will allure her, and bring her into the wilderness, and speak comfortably unto her. And I will give her her vineyards from thence, and the valley of Achor for a door of hope: and she shall sing there, as in the days of her youth, and as in the day when she came up out of the land of Egypt.

Intercede for others. *Rich.*
1 Tim. 6 : 17, 19. Charge them that are rich in this world, that they be not highminded, nor trust in uncertain riches, but in the living God, who giveth us richly all things to enjoy: * Laying up in store for themselves a good foundation against the time to come, that they may lay hold on eternal life.

THIRD SAB. EVE.. DECEMBER. LESSON, MATT. 27 : 24—54.
Address to God. *Prayed to.*
Is. 8 : 19. And when they shall say unto you, Seek unto them that have familiar spirits, and unto wizards that peep and that mutter: should not a people seek unto their God? for the living to the dead?
John 6 : 68. Then Simon Peter answered him, Lord, to whom shall we go? thou hast the words of eternal life.

Confess sin. *Hypocrisy.*
Ezek. 33 : 31. And they come unto thee as the people cometh, and they sit before thee as my people, and they hear thy words, but they will not do them; for with their mouth they show much love, but their heart goeth after their covetousness.
Mal. 1 : 8, 14. And if ye offer the blind for sacrifice, is it not evil? and if ye offer the lame and sick, is it not evil? offer it now unto thy governor; will he be pleased with thee, or accept thy person? saith the Lord of hosts. * But cursed be the deceiver, which hath in his flock a male, and voweth, and sacrificeth unto the Lord a corrupt thing: for I am a great King, saith the Lord of hosts, and my name is dreadful among the heathen.

Ask for blessings. *Fit for heaven.*
Col. 3 : 2—4. Set your affection on things above, not on things on the earth. For ye are dead, and your life is hid with Christ in God. * When Christ, who is our life, shall appear, then shall ye also appear with him in glory.
1 John 3 : 2. Beloved, now are we the sons of God, and it doth not yet appear what we shall be: but we know that, when he shall appear, we shall be like him; for we shall see him as he is.
Ps. 17 : 15. As for me, I will behold thy face in righteousness: I shall be satisfied when I awake, with thy likeness.

Thank for mercies. *Preserving grace.*
Ps. 119 : 92, 93. Unless thy law had been my delights, I should then have perished in mine affliction. I will never forget thy precepts: for with them thou hast quickened me.

Intercede for others. *Poor.*
Matt. 11 : 5. The blind receive their sight, and the lame walk, the lepers are cleansed, and the deaf hear, the dead are raised up, and the poor have the gospel preached to them.

Jas. 2 : 5. Hearken, my beloved brethren. Hath not God chosen the poor of this world rich in faith, and heirs of the kingdom which he hath promised to them that love him?

FOURTH SAB. MORN., DECEMBER. LESSON, I SAM. 28 : 7—25.
Address to God. *Ruler.*
Dan. 4 : 25. That they shall drive thee from men, and thy dwelling shall be with the beasts of the field, and they shall make thee to eat grass as oxen, and they shall wet thee with the dew of heaven, and seven times shall pass over thee, till thou know that the Most High ruleth in the kingdom of men, and giveth it to whomsoever he will.

Prov. 29 : 26. Many seek the ruler's favor: but every man's judgment cometh from the Lord.

Confess sin. *Condemnation.*
Lam. 3 : 39. Wherefore doth a living man complain, a man for the punishment of his sins?

Micah 7 : 9. I will bear the indignation of the Lord, because I have sinned against him, until he plead my cause, and execute judgment for me: he will bring me forth to the light, and I shall behold his righteousness.

Ask for blessings. *Preserve from calamity.*
Job 1 : 10. Hast thou not made a hedge about him, and about his house, and about all that he hath on every side? thou hast blessed the work of his hands, and his substance is increased in the land.

Ex. 23 : 25. And ye shall serve the Lord your God, and he shall bless thy bread, and thy water; and I will take sickness away from the midst of thee.

Thank for mercies. *Ordinances.*
Cant. 2 : 3, 4. As the apple tree among the trees of the wood, so is my beloved among the sons. I sat down under his shadow with great delight, and his fruit was sweet to my taste. He brought me to the banqueting house, and his banner over me was love.

Intercede for others. *Enemies.*

Matt. 5 : 44. But I say unto you, Love your enemies, bless them that curse you, do good to them that hate you, and pray for them which despitefully use you, and persecute you;

FOURTH SAB., EVE. DECEMBER. LESSON, LK. 8 : 4—18.
Address to God. *Preserver.*
Dan. 5 : 23. But hast lifted up thyself against the Lord of heaven; and they have brought the vessels of his house before thee, and thou and thy lords, thy wives and thy concubines, have drunk wine in them; and thou hast praised the gods of silver, and gold, of brass, iron, wood, and stone, which see not, nor hear nor know: and the God in whose hand thy breath is, and whose are all thy ways, hast thou not glorified:
Jer. 10 : 23. O Lord, I know that the way of man is not in himself: it is not in man that walketh to direct his steps.
Ps. 31 : 15. My times are in thy hand: deliver me from the hand of mine enemies, and from them that persecute me.

Confess sin. *Depravity.*
Eph. 4 : 18. Having the understanding darkened, being alienated from the life of God through the ignorance that is in them, because of the blindness of their heart:

Ask for blessings. *Promised blessings.*
Ps. 119 : 132. Look thou upon me, and be merciful unto me, as thou usest to do unto those that love thy name.
Eph. 3 : 20. Now unto him that is able to do exceeding abundantly above all that we ask or think, according to the power that worketh in us.
Phil. 4 : 19. But my God shall supply all your need according to his riches in glory by Christ Jesus.

Thank for mercies. *Answer to prayer.*
Ps. 66 : 20. Blessed be God, which hath not turned away my prayer, nor his mercy from me.
I Sam. 1 : 18. And she said, Let thine handmaid find grace in thy sight. So the woman went her way, and did eat, and her countenance was no more sad.

Intercede for others. *Afflicted.*
Is. 30 : 20. And though the Lord give you the bread of adversity, and the water of affliction, yet shall not thy teachers be removed into a corner any more, but thine eyes shall see thy teachers:

FIFTH SAB. MORN., DECEMBER. LESSON, Is. 59.
Address to God. *Ruler.*
Rev. 19 : 6. And I heard as it were the voice of a great multitude,

and as the voice of many waters, and as the voice of mighty thunderings, saying, Alleluia: for the Lord God omnipotent reigneth.
Eph. 1 : 11, 12. In whom also we have obtained an inheritance, being predestinated according to the purpose of him who worketh all things after the counsel of his own will: that we should be to the praise of his glory, who first trusted in Christ.

Confess sin. *Defilement.*
Job 25 . 2—6. Dominion and fear are with him: he maketh peace in his high places. Is there any number of his armies? and upon whom doth not his light arise? How then can man be justified with God? or how can he be clean that is born of a woman? Behold even to the moon, and it shineth not; yea, the stars are not pure in his sight. How much less man, that is a worm? and the son of man, which is a worm?

Ask for blessings. *Fit for heaven.*
Lk. 16 : 9. And I say unto you, Make to yourselves friends of the mammon of unrighteousness; that, when ye fail, they may receive you into everlasting habitations.
Heb. 11 : 10. For he looked for a city which hath foundations, whose builder and maker is God.
1 Thess. 4 : 17, 18. Then we which are alive and remain shall be caught up together with them in the clouds, to meet the Lord in the air: and so shall we ever be with the Lord. Wherefore comfort one another with these words.

Thank for mercies. *Aid in affliction.*
I Pet. 1 : 6—9. Wherein ye greatly rejoice, though now for a season, if need be, ye are in heaviness through manifold temptations: that the trial of your faith, being much more precious than of gold that perisheth, though it be tried with fire, might be found unto praise and honor and glory at the appearing of Jesus Christ: whom having not seen, ye love; in whom, though now ye see him not, yet believing, ye rejoice with joy unspeakable and and full of glory: receiving the end of your faith, even the salvation of your souls.

Intercede for others. *Peace in land.*
Is. 26 : 1, 2. In that day this song shall be sung in the land of Judah; We have a strong city; salvation will God appoint for walls and bulwarks. Open ye the gates, that the righteous nation which keepeth the truth may enter in.

Fifth Sab. Eve., DECEMBER. Lesson, Matt. 15 : 21—39.
Address to God. *Omniscience.*
Ps. 139 : 4—6. For there is not a word in my tongue, but, lo, O Lord,

thou knowest it altogether. Thou hast beset me behind and before, and laid thine hand upon me. Such knowledge is too wonderful for me; it is high, I can not attain unto it.

Confess sin. *Condemned.*
Job 9 : 3, 20. If he will contend with him, he cannot answer him one of a thousand. * If I justify myself, mine own mouth shall condemn me: if I say, I am perfect, it shall also prove me perverse.

Ask for blessings. *Steadfastness.*
I Cor. 7 : 24. Brethren, let every man, wherein he is called, therein abide with God.
Prov. 3 : 6. In all thy ways acknowledge him, and he shall direct thy paths.

Thank for mercies. *Promises fulfilled.*
Ps. 34 : 1. I will bless the Lord at all times: his praise shall continually be in my mouth.
Ps. 104 : 33. I will sing unto the Lord as long as I live: I will sing praise to my God while I have my being.
Rev. 4 : 8. And the four beasts had each of them six wings about him; and they were full of eyes within: and they rest not day and night, saying, Holy, holy, holy, Lord God Almighty, which was, and is, and is to come.

Intercede for others. *Friends.*
III John 2. Beloved, I wish above all things that thou mayest prosper and be in health, even as thy soul prospereth.

——— 0 ———

GUIDE TO PRAYER.

PART II.
WEEK-DAY SERVICES.

First in   JANUARY.   Lesson, Prov. 2.
Address to God.   Eternity.

Rev. 1 : 8. I am Alpha and Omega, the beginning and the ending, saith the Lord, which is, and which was, and which is to come, the Almighty.

Confess sin.   Forsaken God's paths.

Ps. 25 : 4. Show me thy ways, O Lord; teach me thy paths.

Ask for blessings.   Hope in God.

Ps. 39 : 7, 8. And now, Lord, what wait I for? my hope is in thee. Deliver me from all my transgressions: make me not the reproach of the foolish.

Thank for mercies.   Wonderful works of mercy.

Ps. 75 : 1. Unto thee, O God, do we give thanks, unto thee do we give thanks: for that thy name is near thy wondrous works declare.

Intercede for others.   For all men.

I Pet. 2 : 17. Honor all men. Love the brotherhood. Fear God. Honor the king.

Second in JANUARY. Lesson, Acts 2 : 1—22.
Address to God. To be worshiped.
Ps. 25 : 1. Unto thee, O Lord, do I lift up my soul.
Confess sin. Perverseness
Zech. 7 : 11, 12. But they refused to hearken, and pulled away the shoulder, and stopped their ears, that they should not hear. Yea, they made their hearts as an adamant stone, lest they should hear the law, and the words which the Lord of hosts hath sent in his Spirit by the former prophets: therefore came a great wrath from the Lord of hosts.
Ask for blessings. Spirit's help in prayer.
Rom. 8 : 26, 27. Likewise the Spirit also helpeth our infirmities: for we know not what we should pray for as we ought: but the Spirit itself maketh intercession for us with groanings which cannot be uttered. And he that searcheth the hearts knoweth what is the mind of the Spirit, because he maketh intercession for the saints according to the will of God.
Thank for mercies. Benefits.
Ps. 103 : 1, 2. Bless the Lord, O my soul: and all that is within me, bless his holy name. Bless the Lord, O my soul, and forget not all his benefits:
Intercede for others. Family.
II Sam. 7 : 18—21. Then went king David in, and sat before the Lord, and he said, Who am I, O Lord God? and what is my house, that thou hast brought me hitherto? And this was yet a small thing in thy sight, O Lord God; but thou hast spoken also of thy servant's house for a great while to come. And is this the manner of man, O Lord God. And what can David say more unto thee? for thou, Lord God, knowest thy servant. For thy word's sake, and according to thine own heart, hast thou done all these great things, to make thy servant know them.

Third in JANUARY. Lesson, Ecc. 1.
Address to God. Preserver.

Ps. 22 : 9, 10. But thou art he that took me out of the womb: thou didst make me hope when I was upon my mother's breasts. I was cast upon thee from the womb: thou art my God from my mother's belly.

Confess sin. Spiritual decay.

Heb. 3 : 12. Take heed, brethren, lest there be in any of you an evil heart of unbelief, in departing from the living God.

Ask for blessings. Mercy.

Lk. 18 : 13. And the publican, standing afar off, would not lift up so much as his eyes unto heaven, but smote upon his breast, saying, God be merciful to me a sinner.

Thank for mercies. Spirit of praise.

Ps. 149 : 1, 2, 5, 6. Praise ye the Lord. Sing unto the Lord a new song, and his praise in the congregation of saints. Let Israel rejoice in him that made him: let the children of Zion be joyful in their King. * Let the saints be joyful in glory: let them sing aloud upn their beds. Let the high praises of God be in their mouth, and a two-edged sword in their hand.

Intercede for others. Conversion of unbelievers.

I Pet. 2 : 25. For ye were as sheep going astray; but are now returned unto the Shepherd and Bishop of your souls.

Fourth in JANUARY. Lesson, Matt. 2.
Address to God. Omnipresence.

Is. 66 : 1. Thus saith the Lord, The heaven is my throne, and the earth is my footstool: where is the house that ye build unto me? and where is the place of my rest?

Confess sin. Exhortation to confess unheeded.

Jer. 3 : 13. Only acknowledge thine iniquity, that thou hast transgressed against the Lord thy God, and hast scattered thy ways to the strangers under every green tree, and ye have not obeyed my voice, saith the Lord.

Ask for blessings. Cleansing.

Ps. 51 : 2, 3, 7. Wash me thoroughly from mine iniquity, and cleanse me from my sin. For I acknowledge my transgressions: and my sin is ever before me. * Purge me with hyssop, and I shall be clean: wash me, and I shall be whiter than snow.

Thank for mercies.   Christ satisfying the law.

Is. 53 : 5, 6, 10. But he was wounded for our transgressions, he was bruised for our iniquities; the chastisement of our peace was upon him; and with his stripes we are healed. All we like sheep have gone astray; we have turned every one to his own way; and the Lord hath laid on him the iniquity of us all. * Yet it pleased the Lord to bruise him: he hath put him to grief: when thou shalt make his soul an offering for sin, he shall see his seed, he shall prolong his days, and the pleasure of the Lord shall prosper in his hand.

Intercede for others.   Victory in conflict.

II Chron. 6 : 34, 35. If thy people go out to war against their enemies by the way that thou shalt send them, and they pray unto thee toward this city which thou hast chosen, and the house which I have built for thy name: then hear thou from the heavens their prayer and their supplication, and maintain their cause.

Fifth in   JANUARY.   Lesson, Acts 5 : 1—17.
Address to God.   Creator.

Job 33 : 6. Behold, I am according to thy wish in God's stead: I also am formed out of the clay.

Confess sin.   Shamefulness of sin.

Ezra 9 : 6. And said, O my God, I am ashamed and blush to lift up my face to thee, my God: for our iniquities are increased over our head, and our trespass is grown up unto the heavens.

Ask for blessings.   Sustaining grace.

Prov. 2 : 3—5. Yea, if thou criest after knowledge, and liftest up thy voice for understanding; if thou seekest her as silver, and searchest for her as for hid treasures; then shalt thou understand the fear of the Lord, and find the knowledge of God.

Thank for mercies. Regeneration.
I Cor. 1 : 9. God is faithful, by whom ye were called unto the fellowship of his Son Jesus Christ our Lord.

Intercede for others. Deliver from persecution.
Is. 51 : 9. Awake, awake, put on strength, O arm of the Lord; awake, as in the ancient days, in the generations of old. Art thou not it that hath cut Rahab, and wounded the dragon?

First in FEBRUARY. Lesson. Is. 5 : 1—19.
Address to God. Eternity.
Deut. 33 : 27. The eternal God is thy refuge, and underneath are the everlasting arms: and he shall thrust out the enemy from before thee; and shall say, Destroy them.

Confess sin. Covetousness.
I Tim. 6 : 10. For the love of money is the root of all evil: which while some coveted after, they have erred from the faith, and pierced themselves through with many sorrows.

Ask for blessings. Sense of pardon.
Is. 55 : 7. Let the wicked forsake his way, and the unrighteous man his thoughts: and let him return unto the Lord, and he will have mercy upon him; and to our God, for he will abundantly pardon.

Thank for mercies. Goodness.
Gen. 8 : 22. While the earth remaineth, seed-time and harvest, and cold and heat, and summer and winter, and day and night, shall not cease.

Intercede for others. Family.
II Sam. 7 : 26. 27. And let thy name be magnified for ever, saying, The Lord of hosts is the God over Israel: and let the house of thy servant David be established before thee. For thou, O Lord of hosts, God of Israel, hast revealed to thy servant, saying, I will build thee a house: therefore hath thy servant found in his heart to pray this prayer unto thee.

Second in FEBRUARY. Lesson, John 1 : 1--28.
Address to God. Omnipresence.
Ps. 139 : 12. Yea, the darkness hideth not from thee; but the night shineth as the day; the darkness and the light are both alike to thee.
Confess sin. Spiritual sloth.
Rom. 12 : 11. Not slothful in business; fervent in spirit; serving the Lord:
Ask for blessings. Converting grace.
II Cor. 10 : 5. Casting down imaginations, and every high thing that exalteth itself against the knowledge of God, and bringing into captivity every thought to the obedience of Christ.
Thank for mercies. Christ's resurrection.
Acts 2 : 24, 31, 36. Whom God hath raised up, having loosed the pains of death: because it was not possible that he should be holden of it. * He seeing this before, spake of the resurrection of Christ, that his soul was not left in hell, neither his flesh did see corruption. * Therefore let all the house of Israel know assuredly, that God hath made that same Jesus whom ye have crucified, both Lord and Christ.
Intercede for others. Propagation of the gospel.
Rom. 10 : 14, 15. How then shall they call on him in whom they have not believed? and how shall they believe in him of whom they have not heard? and how shall they hear without a preacher? and how shall they preach, except they be sent? as it is written, How beautiful are the feet of them that preach the gospel of peace, and bring glad tidings of good things!

Third in FEBRUARY. Lesson, Acts 13 : 16—41.
Address to God. Longsuffering.
Ps. 86 : 15. But thou, O Lord, art a God full of compassion, and gracious, longsuffering, and plenteous in mercy and truth.
Confess sin. Perverseness.
Prov. 5 : 12, 13. And say, How have I hated instruction, and my heart despised reproof; and have not obeyed the voice of my teachers, nor inclined mine ear to them that instructed me!

Ask for blessings. Instructing grace.

Eph. 1 : 17—19. That the God of our Lord Jesus Christ, the Father of glory, may give unto you the spirit of wisdom and revelation in the knowledge of him: the eyes of your understanding being enlightened; that ye may know what is the hope of his calling, and what the riches of the glory of his inheritance in the saints, and what is the exceeding greatness of his power to us-ward who believe, according to the working of his mighty power,

Thank for mercies. Temporal blessings.

Job 8 : 7. Though thy beginning was small, yet thy latter end should greatly increase.

Intercede for others. Conversion of unbelievers.

Ps. 51 : 13. Then will I teach transgressors thy ways; and sinners shall be converted unto thee.

Fourth in FEBRUARY. Lesson, John 3 : 1—21.
Address to God. Power.

Ps. 50 : 1. The mighty God, even the Lord, hath spoken, and called the earth from the rising of the sun unto the going down thereof.

Confess sin. Covetousness.

Jer. 45 : 5. And seekest thou great things for thyself? seek them not: for behold, I will bring evil upon all flesh, saith the Lord: but thy life will I give unto thee for a prey in all places whither thou goest.

Ask for blessings. Accept invitation.

Is. 53 : 3. Incline your ear, and come unto me: hear, and your soul shall live; and I will make an everlasting covenant with you, even the sure mercies of David.

Thank for mercies. Goodness.

Matt. 5 : 45. That ye may be the children of your Father which is in heaven: for he maketh his sun to rise on the evil and on the good, and sendeth rain on the just and on the unjust.

Intercede for others. Deliver from persecution.

Ps. 125 : 3. For the rod of the wicked shall not rest upon the lot of the righteous; lest the righteous put forth their hands unto iniquity.

Fifth in   FEBRUARY.   Lesson, Acts 18 : 16—34.
Address to God.   Preserver.

Lam. 3 : 22, 23. It is of the Lord's mercies that we are not consumed, because his compassions fail not. They are new every morning: great is thy faithfulness.

Confess sin.   Wilful trespass.

Ezra 9 : 7. Since the days of our father's have we been in a great trespass unto this day; and for our iniquities have we, our kings, and our priests, been delivered into the hand of the kings of the lands, to the sword, to captivity, and to a spoil, and to confusion of face, as it is this day.

Ask for blessings.   Divine favor.

Ps. 106 : 4, 5. Remember me, O Lord, with the favor that thou bearest unto thy people: O visit me with thy salvation; that I may see the good of thy chosen, that I may rejoice in the gladness of thy nation, that I may glory with thine inheritance.

Thank for mercies.   Appointment of a Redeemer.

Ps. 89 : 19—21, 27. Then thou spakest in vision to thy Holy One, and saidst, I have laid help upon one that is mighty; I have exalted one chosen out of the people. I have found David my servant; with my holy oil have I anointed him: with whom my hand shall be established: mine arm also shall strengthen him. * Also I will make him my firstborn, higher than the kings of the earth.

Intercede for others.   Family.

II Sam. 7 : 28, 29. And now, O Lord God, thou art that God, and thy words be true, and thou hast promised this goodness unto thy servant: therefore now let it please thee to bless the house of thy servant, that it may continue for ever before thee: for thou, O Lord God, hast spoken it: and with thy blessing let the house of thy servant be blessed for ever.

GUIDE TO PRAYER. 119

First in MARCH. Lesson, Is. 11.
Address to God. Unequaled absolutely.
Is. 40 : 14. With whom took he counsel, and who instructed him, and taught him in the path of judgment, and taught him knowledge, and shewed to him the way of understanding?

Confess sin. Anger.
Prov. 25 : 28. He that hath no rule over his own spirit is like a city that is broken down, and without walls.

Ask for blessings. Redeeming grace.
Zech. 9 : 11, 12. As for thee also, by the blood of thy covenant I have sent forth thy prisoners out of the pit wherein is no water. Turn you to the strong hold, ye prisoners of hope: even to-day do I declare that I will render double unto thee.

Thank for mercies. O. T. church favored.
Heb. 1 : 1. God, who at sundry times and in divers manners spake in time past unto the fathers by the prophets,

Intercede for others. Victory over external enemies.
Num. 10 : 35, 36. And it came to pass, when the ark set forward, that Moses said, Rise up, Lord, and let thine enemies be scattered; and let them that hate thee flee before thee. And when it rested, he said, Return, O Lord, unto the many thousands of Israel.

Second in MARCH. Lesson, Lk. 4 : 16—32.
Address to God. Matchless perfections.
Job 40 : 9. Hast thou an arm like God? or canst thou thunder with a voice like him?

Confess sin. Hiding faults.
Jas. 5 : 16. Confess your faults one to another, and pray one for another, that ye may be healed. The effectual fervent prayer of a righteous man availeth much.

Ask for blessings. God's sustaining power.
Job 5 : 17, 19. Behold, happy is the man whom God correcteth: therefore despise not thou the chastening of the Almighty: * He shall

deliver thee in six troubles; yea, in seven there shall no evil touch thee.

Thank for mercies.   Incarnation.

Gal. 4 : 4, 5. But when the fulness of the time was come, God sent forth his Son, made of a woman, made under the law, to redeem them that were under the law, that we might receive the adoption of sons.

Interce le for others.   All men.

Gal. 6 : 10. As we have therefore opportunity, let us do good unto all men, especially unto them who are of the household of faith.

Third in   MARCH.   Lesson, Acts 25.
Address to God.   Unequaled by men.

Jer. 10 : 7. Who would not fear thee, O King of nations? for to thee doth it appertain: forasmuch as among all the wise men of the nations, and in all their kingdoms, there is none like unto thee.

Confess sin.   Spiritual sloth.

Prov. 22 : 13. The slothful man saith, There is a lion without, I shall be slain in the streets.

Ask for blessings.   Peace of God.

Is. 32 : 17. And the work of righteousness shall be peace; and the effect of righteousness, quietness and assurance for ever.

Thank for mercies.   Goodness.

Acts 14 : 17. Nevertheless he left not himself without witness, in that he did good, and gave us rain from heaven, and fruitful seasons, filling our hearts with food and gladness.

Intercede for others.   Country.

Deut. 26 : 15. Look down from thy holy habitation, from heaven, and bless thy people Israel, and the land which thou hast given us, as thou swarest unto our fathers, a land that floweth with milk and honey.

Fourth in   MARCH.   Lesson, Is. 22 : 1—19.
Address to God.   Preserver.

GUIDE TO PRAYER.

Lam. 3 : 37, 38. Who is he that saith, and it cometh to pass, when the Lord commandeth it not? Out of the mouth of the Most High proceedeth not evil and good?

Confess sin. Original sin.

Rom. 5 : 12, 20. Wherefore as by one man sin entered into the world, and death by sin; and so death passed upon all men, for that all have sinned: * Moreover the law entered, that the offence might abound. But where sin abounded, grace did much more abound.

Ask for blessings. Deliverance from sin.

Eph. 4 : 22, 24. That ye put off concerning the former conversation the old man, which is corrupt according to the deceitful lusts; * And that ye put on the new man, which after God is created in righteousness and true holiness.

Thank for mercies. Owning Christ's work.

John 8 : 29. And he that sent me is with me: the Father hath not left me alone; for I do always those things that please him.

Intercede for others. Deliver from persecution

Ps. 74 : 21. O let not the oppressed return ashamed: let the poor and needy praise thy name.

Fifth in MARCH. Lesson, John 5 : 1—16.
Address to God. Goodness.

Ps. 86 : 5. For thou, Lord, art good, and ready to forgive; and plenteous in mercy unto all them that call upon thee.

Confess sin. Perverseness.

Is. 48 : 4. Because I knew that thou art obstinate, and thy neck is as an iron sinew, and thy brow brass;

Ask for blessings. Resist temptation.

Eph. 6 : 11—17. Put on the whole armor of God, that ye may be able to stand against the wiles of the devil. For we wrestle not against flesh and blood, but against principalities, against powers, against the rulers of the darkness of this world, against spiritual wickedness in high places. Wherefore take unto you the whole armor of God, that ye may be able to withstand in the evil day, and having done all, t stand. Stand therefore, having your loins girt about with truth, and having on the breastplate of righteousness; and your feet shod with the preparation of the gospel of peace; above all, taking the shield of faith, wherewith ye shall be able to quench all the fiery darts of the wicked. And take the helmet of salvation, and the sword of the Spirit, which is the word of God:

Thank for mercies.   Christ satisfying the law.

Heb. 9 : 12, 14, 26. Neither by the blood of goats and calves, but by his own blood he entered in once into the holy place, having obtained eternal redemption for us. * How much more shall the blood of Christ, who through the eternal Spirit offered himself without spot to God, purge your conscience from dead works to serve the living God. * For then must he often have suffered since the foundation of the world: but now once in the end of the world hath he appeared to put away sin by the sacrifice of himself.

Intercede for others.   Public pardon.

Num. 14 : 17—19. And now, I beseech thee, let the power of my Lord be great, according as thou hast spoken, saying, the Lord is longsuffering, and of great mercy, forgiving iniquity and transgression, and by no means clearing the guilty, visiting the iniquity of the fathers upon the children unto the third and fourth generation. Pardon, I beseech thee, the iniquity of this people according unto the greatness of thy mercy, and as thou hast forgiven this people, from Egypt even until now.

First in   APRIL.   Lesson, Is. 33.
Address to God.   Eternity.

Is. 63 : 16. Doubtless thou art our Father, though Abraham be ignorant of us, and Israel acknowledge us not: thou, O Lord, art our Father, our Redeemer; thy name is from everlasting.

Confess sin.   Evil passions.

Col. 3 : 5. Mortify therefore your members which are upon the earth;

GUIDE TO PRAYER. 123

fornication, uncleanness, inordinate affection, evil concupiscence, and covetousness, which is idolatry:

Ask for blessings.   Remembering grace.

Heb. 2 : 1. Therefore we ought to give the more earnest heed to the things which we have heard, lest at any time we should let them slip.

Thank for mercies.   Goodness.

Ps. 65 : 9—11. Thou visitest the earth, and waterest it: thou greatly enrichest it with the river of God, which is full of water: thou preparest them corn, when thou hast so provided for it. Thou waterest the ridges thereof abundantly: thou settlest the furrows thereof: thou makest it soft with showers: thou blessest the springing thereof. Thou crownest the year with thy goodness; and thy paths drop fatness.

Intercede for others.   Conversion of unbelievers.

Ps. 14 : 1. The fool hath said in his heart, There is no God. They are corrupt, they have done abominable works, there is none that doeth good.

Second in   APRIL.   Lesson, Matt. 6 : 1—23.
Address to God.   Holiness.

Ps. 83 : 18. That men may know that thou, whose name alone is JEHOVAH, art the Most High over all the earth.

Confess sin.   Refusal to repent.

1 Kin. 8 : 47. Yet if they shall bethink themselves in the land whither they were carried captives, and repent, and make supplication unto thee in the land of them that carried them captives, saying, We have sinned, and have done perversely, we have committed wickedness:

Ask for blessings.   Reconciliation.

Eph. 2 : 14, 16, 19. For he is our peace, who hath made both one, and hath broken down the middle wall of partition between us: * And that he might reconcile both unto God in one body by the cross, having slain the enmity thereby: * Now therefore ye are no more strangers and foreigners, but fellow-citizens with the saints, and of the household of God;

124   GUIDE TO PRAYER.

Thank for mercies.   Spiritual blessings.

Ezek. 16 : 5, 6, 8. None eye pitied thee to do any of these unto thee, to have compassion upon thee; but thou wast cast out in the open field, to the loathing of thy person, in the day that thou wast born. * And when I passed by thee, and saw thee polluted in thine own blood, I said unto thee when thou wast in thy blood, Live; yea, I said unto thee when thou wast in thy blood, Live. * Now when I passed by thee, and looked upon thee, behold, thy time was the time of love; and I spread my skirt over thee, and covered thy nakedness: yea, I sware unto thee, and entered into a covenant with thee, saith the Lord God, and thou becamest mine.

Intercede for others.   Public pardon.

Ps. 79 : 8, 9. O remember not against us former iniquities: let thy tender mercies speedily prevent us; for we are brought very low. Help us, O God of our salvation, for the glory of thy name: and deliver us, and purge away our sins, for thy name's sake.

Third in   APRIL.   Lesson, Rom. 2.
Address to God.   Power.

Rom. 4 : 21. And being fully persuaded, that what he had promised he was able also to perform.

Confess sin.   Open confession

Num. 21 : 7. Therefore the people came to Moses, and said, We have sinned, for we have spoken against the Lord and against thee; pray unto the Lord, that he take away the serpents from us. And Moses prayed for the people.

Ask for blessings.   Wisdom to do duty.

Col. 1 : 9, 10, For this cause we also, since the day we heard it, do not cease to pray for you, and to desire that ye might be filled with the knowledge of his will in all wisdom and spiritual understanding; that ye might walk worthy of the Lord unto all pleasing, being fruitful in every good work, and increasing in the knowledge of God;

Thank for mercies.   Christ's exaltation.

Phil. 2 : 8—11. And being found in fashion as a man, he humbled himself, and became obedient unto death, even the death of the cross. Wherefore God also hath highly exalted him, and given him a name which is above every name: that at the name of Jesus every knee should bow, of things in heaven, and things in earth, and things under the earth; and that every tongue should confess that Jesus Christ is Lord, to the glory of God the Father.

Intercede for others.   Welfare of God's children.

II Tim. 1 : 3, 4. I thank God, whom I serve from my forefathers with pure conscience, that without ceasing I have remembrance of thee in my prayers night and day; greatly desiring to see thee, being mindful of thy tears, that I may be filled with joy;

Fourth in   APRIL.   Lesson, Lk. 7 : 11—30.
Address to God.   Prayer hearer.

Ps. 141 : 2. Let my prayer be set forth before thee as incense; and the lifting up of my hands as the evening sacrifice.

Confess sin.   Treachery.

II Pet. 2 : 22. But it is happened unto them according to the true proverb, The dog is turned to his own vomit again; and, The sow that was washed to her wallowing in the mire.

Ask for blessings.   Show sinfulness.

Job 34 : 32. That which I see not, teach thou me: if I have done iniquity, I will do no more.

Thank for mercies.   Christ's resurrection.

I Cor. 15 : 20—23. But now is Christ risen from the dead, and become the first fruits of them that slept. For since by man came death, by man came also the resurrection of the dead. For as in Adam all die, even so in Christ shall all be made alive. But every man in his own order: Christ the first-fruits; afterward they that are Christ's at his coming.

Intercede for others.   Children.

Gen. 28 : 4. And give thee the blessing of Abraham, to thee and to thy seed with thee; that thou mayest inherit the land wherein thou art a stranger, which God gave to Abraham.

Fifth in   APRIL.   Lesson, Rom. 8 : 1—17.
Address to God.   Immutable.
Mal. 3 : 6. For I am the Lord, I change not; therefore ye sons of Jacob are not consumed.

Confess sin.   Defilement.
Is. 6 : 5. Then said I, Wo is me! for I am undone; because I am a man of unclean lips, and I dwell in the midst of a people of unclean lips: for mine eyes have seen the King, the Lord of hosts.

Ask for blessings.   Steadfastness.
Eph. 4 : 14, 15. That we henceforth be no more children, tossed to and fro, and carried about with every wind of doctrine, by the sleight of men, and cunning craftiness, whereby they lie in wait to deceive; but speaking the truth in love, may grow up into him in all things, which is the head, even Christ:

Thank for mercies.   Christ's ascension.
Ps. 68 : 18. Thou hast ascended on high, thou hast led captivity captive: thou hast received gifts for men; yea, for the rebellious also, that the Lord God might dwell among them.

Intercede for others.   Defeat church's enemies.
Is. 54 : 17. No weapon that is formed against thee shall prosper; and every tongue that shall rise against thee in judgment thou shalt condemn. This is the heritage of the servants of the Lord, and their righteousness is of me, saith the Lord.

First in   MAY.   Lesson, Is. 41.
Address to God.   Eternity.
Ps. 90 : 2. Before the mountains were brought forth, or ever thou hadst formed the earth and the world, even from everlasting to everlasting, thou art God.

Confess sin. Disobedience.

Matt. 12 : 35. A good man, out of the good treasure of the heart, bringeth forth good things: and an evil man, out of the evil treasure, bringeth forth evil things.

Ask for blessings. Direction in duty.

Ps. 119 : 133. Order my steps in thy word, and let not any iniquity have dominion over me.

Thank for mercies. Christ's exaltation.

Is. 9 : 6, 7. For unto us a child is born, unto us a son is given: and the government shall be upon his shoulder: and his name shall be called Wonderful, Counsellor, The Mighty God, The everlasting Father, The Prince of Peace. Of the increase of his government and peace there shall be no end, upon the throne of David, and upon his kingdom, to order it, and to establish it with judgment and with justice from henceforth even for ever. The zeal of the Lord of hosts will perform this.

Intercede for others. Propagation of gospel.

Is. 11 : 9. They shall not hurt nor destroy in all my holy mountain: for the earth shall be full of the knowledge of the Lord, as the waters cover the sea.

Second in MAY. Lesson, John 6 : 1—41.
Address to God. Justice.

Job 34 : 10, 11. Therefore hearken unto me, ye men of understanding: far be it from God, that he should do wickedness; and from the Almighty, that he should commit iniquity. For the work of a man shall he render unto him, and cause every man to find according to his ways.

Confess sin. Afflictive sin.

Neh. 1 : 6. Let thine ear now be attentive, and thine eyes open, that thou mayest hear the prayer of thy servant, which I pray before thee now, day and night, for the children of Israel thy servants, and confess the sins of the children of Israel, which we have sinned against thee: both I and my father's house have sinned.

Ask for blessings. Sanctification.

I Thess. 5 : 23, 24. And the very God of peace sanctify you wholly; and I pray God your whole spirit and soul and body be preserved blameless unto the coming of our Lord Jesus Christ. Faithful is he that calleth you, who also will do it.

Thank for mercies. Second advent.

Acts 17 : 31. Because he hath appointed a day, in the which he will judge the world in righteousness, by that man whom he hath ordained: whereof he hath given assurance unto all men, in that he hath raised him from the dead.

Intercede for others. Captive sinners.

II Chron. 6 : 36—39. If they sin against thee, (for there is no man which sinneth not,) and thou be angry with them, and deliver them over before their enemies, and they carry them away captives unto a land far off or near; yet if they bethink themselves in the land whither they are carried captive, and turn and pray unto thee in the land of their captivity, saying, We have sinned, we have done amiss, and have dealt wickedly; if they return to thee with all their heart and with all their soul in the land of their captivity, whither they have carried them captives, and pray toward their land, which thou gavest unto their fathers, and toward the city which thou hast chosen, and toward the house which I have built for thy name: then hear thou from the heavens, even from thy dwellingplace, their prayer and their supplications, and maintain their cause, and forgive thy people which have sinned against thee.

Third in MAY. Lesson, I Cor. 2.
Address to God. Greatness.

Ps. 93 : 1. The Lord reigneth, he is clothed with majesty; the Lord is clothed with strength, wherewith he hath girded himself: the world also is stablished, that it cannot be moved.

Confess sin. Condemnation

Hos. 2 : 3, 9. Lest I strip her naked, and set her as in the day that she was born, and make her as a wilderness, and set her like a dry land, and slay her with thirst. * Therefore will I return, and take away my corn in the time thereof, and my wine in the season thereof, and I will recover my wool and my flax given to cover her nakedness.

Ask for blessings. Divine presence.

Ps. 51 : 11. Cast me not away from thy presence; and take not thine Holy Spirit from me.

Thank for mercies. Covenant of grace.

Ps. 89 : 32—34. Then will I visit their transgression with the rod, and their iniquity with stripes. Nevertheless my loving-kindness will I not utterly take from him, nor suffer my faithfulness to fail. My covenant will I not break, nor alter the thing that is gone out of my lips.

Intercede for others. All men.

1 Tim. 2 : 1. I exhort therefore, that, first of all, supplications, prayers, intercessions, and giving of thanks, be made for all men.

Fourth in MAY. Lesson, Mark. 7 : 1—23.
Address to God. Preserver.

Ps. 71 : 6. By thee have I been holden up from the womb: thou art he that took me out of my mother's bowels: my praise shall be continually of thee.

Confess sin. Condemnation

Is. 51 : 17. Awake, awake, stand up, O Jerusalem, which hast drunk at the hand of the Lord the cup of his fury; thou hast drunken the dregs of the cup of trembling, and wrung them out.

Ask for blessings. God's mercy.

Ps. 86 : 5, 15. For thou, Lord, art good, and ready to forgive; and plenteous in mercy unto all them that call upon thee. * But thou, O Lord, art a God full of compassion, and gracious, long-suffering, and plenteous in mercy and truth.

Thank for mercies. Aid in affliction.

Ps. 31 : 7, 21. I will be glad and rejoice in thy mercy for thou hast considered my trouble, thou hast known my soul in adversities; * * *

Blessed be the Lord: for he hath showed me his marvelous kindness in a strong city.
Intercede for others. Favor under punishment.
I Kin. 8 : 30, 50. And hearken thou to the supplication of thy servant, and of thy people Israel, when they shall pray toward this place: and hear thou in heaven thy dwelling place: and when thou hearest, forgive. * And forgive thy people that have sinned against thee, and all their transgressions wherein they have transgressed against thee, and give them compassion before them who carried them captive, that they may have compassion on them.

Fifth in　　　　　　　　　MAY.　　　　　　Lesson, II Cor. 1.
Address to God. Wrath.
Job 21 : 9. Their houses are safe from fear, neither is the rod of God upon them.
Confess sin. Sins of tongue.
Ps. 64 : 8. So they shall make their own tongue to fall upon themselves all that see them shall flee away.
Ask for blessings. Encouragement.
Is. 44 : 22. I have blotted out, as a thick cloud, thy transgressions, and, as a cloud, thy sins; return unto me; for I have redeemed thee.
Thank for mercies. Answer to prayer.
Ps. 10 : 17. Lord, thou hast heard the desire of the humble: thou wilt prepare their heart, thou wilt cause thine ear to hear.
Intercede for others. Stay of divine punishment.
I Kin. 8 : 33, 34. When thy people Israel be smitten down before the enemy, because they have sinned against thee, and shall turn again to thee, and confess thy name, and pray, and make supplication unto thee in this house: then hear thou in heaven, and forgive the sin of thy people Israel, and bring them again unto the land which thou gavest unto their fathers.

First in　　　　　　　　　JUNE.　　　　　　Lesson, Is. 52.
Address to God. Goodness.

Ps. 34 : 3. O magnify the Lord with me, and let us exalt his name together.

Confess sin. Treachery.
Jer. 2 : 20. For of old time I have broken thy yoke, and burst thy bands: and thou saidst, I will not transgress; when upon every high hill and under every green tree thou wanderest, playing the harlot.

Ask for blessings. Enlightening grace.
Acts 26 : 18. To open their eyes, and to turn them from darkness to light, and from the power of Satan unto God, that they may receive forgiveness of sins, and inheritance among them which are sanctified by faith that is in me.

Thank for mercies. God's preserving care.
Ps. 66 : 9. Which holdeth our soul in life, and suffereth not our feet to be moved.

Intercede for others. Prisoners.
Ps. 79 : 11. Let the sighing of the prisoner come before thee; according to the greatness of thy power preserve thou those that are appointed to die;

Second in JUNE. Lesson, Matt. 17.
Address to God. Omnipotence.
Rev. 11 : 17. Saying, we give thee thanks, O Lord God Almighty, which art, and wast, and art to come; because thou hast taken to thee thy great power, and hast reigned.

Confess sin. Uncharitableness.
Rom. 14 : 10. But why dost thou judge thy brother? or why dost thou set at naught thy brother? for we shall all stand before the judgment seat of Christ.

Ask for blessings. Divine goodness.
Num. 14 : 17—19. And now, I beseech thee, let the power of my Lord be great according as thou hast spoken, saying, the Lord is longsuffering, and of great mercy, forgiving iniquity and transgression, and by no means clearing the guilty, visiting the iniquity of the fathers

upon the children unto the third and fourth generation. Pardon, I beseech thee, the iniquity of this people according unto the greatness of thy mercy, and as thou hast forgiven this people, from Egypt even until now.

Thank for mercies. Christ's ascension.

John 20 : 17. Jesus saith unto her, Touch me not: for I am not yet ascended to my Father: but go to my brethren, and say unto them, I ascend unto my Father and your Father, and to my God and your God.

Intercede for others. Nations.

Is. 49 : 23. And kings shall be thy nursing fathers, and their queens thy nursing mothers: they shall bow down to thee with their face toward the earth, and lick up the dust of thy feet; and thou shalt know that I am the Lord: for they shall not be ashamed that wait for me.

Third in JUNE. Lesson, II Cor. 4.
Address to God. To be worshiped.

Ps. 115 : 4. Their idols are silver and gold, the work of men's hands.

Confess sin. Humiliated by sin.

Job 40 : 4, 5. Behold, I am vile; what shall I answer thee? I will lay mine hand upon my mouth. Once have I spoken; but I will not answer: yea, twice; but I will proceed no further.

Ask for blessings. Preserving grace.

Jude 1 : 20, 21. But ye, beloved, building up yourselves on your most holy faith, praying in the Holy Ghost, keep yourselves in the love of God, looking for the mercy of our Lord Jesus Christ unto eternal life.

Thank for mercies. Covenant of grace.

Heb. 6 : 17, 18. Wherein God, willing more abundantly to shew unto the heirs of promise the immutability of his counsel, confirmed it by an oath: that by two immutable things, in which it was impossible for God to lie, we might have a strong consolation, who have fled for refuge to lay hold upon the hope set before us.

Intercede for others. Universal church.

II Thess. 3 : 1. Finally, brethren, pray for us, that the word of the Lord may have free course, and be glorified, even as it is with you;

GUIDE TO PRAYER.

Fourth in   JUNE.   Lesson, John 8 : 1—30.
Address to God.   Preserver.
Matt. 10 : 29. Are not two sparrows sold for a farthing? and one of them shall not fall on the ground without your Father.

Confess sin.   Secret faults.
Ps. 19 : 12. Who can understand his errors? cleanse thou me from secret faults.

Ask for blessings.   Faith.
Col. 2 : 6, 7. As ye have therefore received Christ Jesus the Lord, so walk ye in him: rooted and built up in him, and stablished in the faith, as ye have been taught, abounding therein with thanksgiving.

Thank for mercies.   Scriptures.
Lk. 10 : 21, 24. In that hour Jesus rejoiced in spirit, and said, I thank thee, O Father, Lord of heaven and earth, that thou hast hid these things from the wise and prudent, and hast revealed them unto babes: even so, Father; for so it seemed good in thy sight. * For I tell you, That many prophets and kings have desired to see those things which ye see, and have not seen them; and to hear those things which ye hear, and have not heard them.

Intercede for others.   Children.
Gen. 32 : 9, 10. And Jacob said, O God of my father Abraham, and God of my father Isaac, the Lord which saidst unto me, Return unto thy country, and to thy kindred, and I will deal well with thee: I am not worthy of the least of all the mercies, and of all the truth, which thou hast shewed unto thy servant; for with my staff I passed over this Jordan; and now I am become two bands.

Fifth in   JUNE.   Lesson, II Cor. 9.
Address to God.   To be worshiped.
Jer. 30 : 21. And their nobles shall be of themselves, and their governor shall proceed from the midst of them; and I will cause him to draw near, and he shall approach unto me: for who is this that engaged his heart to approach unto me? saith the Lord.

Confess sin. Sin's degradation.
Gen. 18 : 27. And Abraham answered and said, Behold now, I have taken upon me to speak unto the Lord, which am but dust and ashes:

Ask for blessings. Plead Christ's righteousness.
1 John 2 : 1, 2. And if any man sin, we have an advocate with the Father, Jesus Christ the righteous: and he is the propitiation for our sins: and not for ours only, but also for the sins of the whole world.

Thank for mercies. God's bounties.
Ps. 23 : 2, 5. He maketh me to lie down in green pastures: he leadeth me beside the still waters. * Thou preparest a table before me in the presence of mine enemies: thou anointest my head with oil; my cup runneth over.

Intercede for others. Universal church.
Ps. 80 : 14, 15. Return, we beseech thee, O God of hosts: look down from heaven, and behold, and visit this vine; and the vineyard which thy right hand hath planted, and the branch that thou madest strong for thyself.

First in JULY. Lesson, Is. 59.
Address to God. Creator.
Gen. 2 : 7. And the Lord God formed man of the dust of the ground, and breathed into his nostrils the breath of life; and man became a living soul.

Confess sin. Folly of sin.
Ps. 73 : 22. So foolish was I and ignorant; I was as a beast before thee.

Ask for blessings. Love to God.
Deut. 30 : 6. And the Lord thy God will circumcise thine heart, and the heart of thy seed, to love the Lord thy God with all thine heart, and with all thy soul, that thou mayest live.

Thank for mercies. God's goodness.
Ps. 147 : 9, 10. He giveth to the beast his food, and to the young ra-

GUIDE TO PRAYER. 135

vens which cry. He delighteth not in the strength of the horse: he taketh not pleasure in the legs of a man.

Intercede for others.   Deliver from persecution.

Ps. 12 : 5. For the oppression of the poor, for the sighing of the needy, now will I arise, saith the Lord; I will set him in safety from him that puffeth at him.

Second in   JULY.   Lesson, Lk. 10 : 17—42.
Address to God.   Preserver.

Acts 17 : 26. And hath made of one blood all nations of men for to dwell on all the face of the earth, and hath determined the times before appointed, and the bounds of their habitation;

Confess sin.   Unfaithfulness.

Ecc. 10 : 2. A wise man's heart is at his right hand; but a fool's heart at his left.

Ask for blessings.   Tender conscience.

Ezek. 11 : 19. And I will give them one heart, and I will put a new spirit within you: and I will take the stony heart out of their flesh, and will give them an heart of flesh:

Thank for mercies.   Helpful examples.

Rev. 12 : 11. And they overcame him by the blood of the Lamb, and by the word of their testimony; and they loved not their lives unto the death.

Intercede for others.   All men.

Rev. 11 : 15. And the seventh angel sounded; and there were great voices in heaven, saying, The kingdoms of this world are become the kingdoms of our Lord and of his Christ; and he shall reign for ever and ever.

Third in   JULY.   Lesson, Eph. 1.
Address to God.   Trinity.

I John 5 : 7. For there are three that bear record in heaven, the

Father, the Word, and the Holy Ghost: and these three are one.

Confess sin.   Public sins.

Jer. 14 : 7. O Lord, though our iniquities testify against us, do thou it for thy name's sake; for our backslidings are many; we have sinned against thee.

Ask for blessings.   Brotherly love.

I Pet. 1 : 22. Seeing ye have purified your souls in obeying the truth through the Spirit unto unfeigned love of the brethren, see that ye love one another with a pure heart fervently:

Thank for mercies.   Regeneration.

Col. 3 : 13. Who hath delivered us from the power of darkness, and hath translated us into the kingdom of his dear Son:

Intercede for others.   Saints.

Ps. 40 : 16. Let all that seek thee rejoice and be glad in thee: let such as love thy salvation say continually, The Lord be magnified.

Fourth in   JULY.   Lesson, John 10.

Address to God.   Eternity.

Ps. 102 : 26. They shall perish, but thou shalt endure: yea, all of them shall wax old like a garment; as a vesture shalt thou change them, and they shall be changed:

Confess sin.   Corrupt nature.

Is. 1 : 5. Why should ye be stricken any more? ye will revolt more and more: the whole head is sick, and the whole heart faint.

Ask for blessings.   Self-denial.

Rom. 14 : 7, 8. For none of us liveth to himself, and no man dieth to himself. For whether we live, we live unto the Lord; and whether we die, we die unto the Lord: whether we live therefore, or die, we are the Lord's.

Thank for mercies.   Preserving grace.

Ps. 138 : 3. In the day when I cried thou answeredst me, and strengthenedst me with strength in my soul.

GUIDE TO PRAYER.

Intercede for others. Heal divisions.
II Cor. 13 : 11. Finally, brethren, farewell. Be perfect, be of good comfort, be of one mind, live in peace; and the God of love and peace shall be with you.

Fifth in JULY. Lesson, Eph. 6.
Address to God. Omniscient.
Amos 4 : 13. For, lo, he that formeth the mountains, and createth the wind, and declareth unto man what is his thought, that maketh the morning darkness, and treadeth upon the high places of the earth, The Lord, the God of hosts, is his name.

Confess sin. Public sins.
Jer. 3 : 25. We lie down in our shame, and our confusion covereth us: for we have sinned against the Lord our God, we and our fathers, from our youth even unto this day, and have not obeyed the voice of the Lord our God.

Ask for blessings. Govern tongue.
Jas. 3 : 2. For in many things we offend all. If any man offend not in word, the same is a perfect man, and able also to bridle the whole body.

Thank for mercies. Ordinances.
Matt. 28 : 20. Teaching them to observe all things whatsoever I have commanded you: and lo I am with you alway, even unto the end of the world. Amen.

Intercede for others. Defeat of church's enemies.
Ps. 83 : 13, 16, 18. O my God, make them like a wheel; as the stubble before the wind. * Fill their faces with shame; that they may seek thy name, O Lord. * That men may know that thou, whose name alone is JEHOVAH, art the Most High over all the earth.

First in AUGUST. Lesson, Is. 65.
Address to God. Faithfulness.

GUIDE TO PRAYER.

Deut. 7 : 9. Know therefore that the Lord thy God, he is God, the faithful God, which keepeth covenant and mercy with them that love him and keep his commandments to a thousand generations:

Confess sin.   Stubbornness.

Is. 26 : 11. Lord, when thy hand is lifted up, they will not see: but they shall see, and be ashamed for their envy at the people; yea, the fire of thine enemies shall devour them.

Ask for blessings.   Preserve from sin.

Ps. 19 : 13. Keep back thy servant also from presumptuous sins; let them not have dominion over me: then shall I be upright, and I shall be innocent from the great transgression.

Thank for mercies.   Christ satisfying the law.

Eph. 2 : 14—16. For he is our peace, who hath made both one, and hath broken down the middle wall of partition between us: having abolished in his flesh the enmity, even the law of commandments contained in ordinances: for to make in himself of twain one new man, so making peace; and that he might reconcile both unto God in one body by the cross, having slain the enmity thereby:

Intercede for others.   Hear others' prayers.

II Chron. 6 : 28, 29. If there be dearth in the land, if there be pestilence, if there be blasting or mildew, locusts or caterpillars; if their enemies besiege them in the cities of their land; whatsoever sore, or whatsoever sickness there be: then what prayer or what supplication soever shall be made of any man, or of all thy people Israel, when every one shall know his own sore and his own grief, and shall spread forth his hands in this house: then hear thou from heaven thy dwellingplace, and forgive,

Second in   AUGUST.   Lesson, Lk. 18.
Address to God.   Creator.

Job 10 : 11, 12. Thou hast clothed me with skin and flesh, and hast fenced me with bones and sinews. Thou hast granted me life and favor, and thy visitation hath preserved my spirit.

GUIDE TO PRAYER.

Confess sin.   Refusal to hear.
Ps. 58 : 4, 5. Their poison is like the poison of a serpent: they are like the deaf adder that stoppeth her ear; which will not hearken to the voice of charmers, charming never so wisely.

Ask for blessings.   Humility.
Matt. 11 : 29. Take my yoke upon you, and learn of me; for I am meek and lowly in heart: and ye shall find rest unto your souls.

Thank for mercies.   Goodness.
Ps. 19 : 4, 5. Their line is gone out through all the earth, and their words to the end of the world. In them hath he set a tabernacle for the sun, which is as a bridegroom coming out of his chamber, and rejoiceth as a strong man to run a race.

Intercede for others.   Not be cast off.
Jer. 11 : 14. Therefore pray not thou for this people, neither lift up a cry or prayer for them: for I will not hear them in the time that they cry unto me for their troubles.

Third in   AUGUST.   Lesson, II Thess. 1.
Address to God.   Knowledge.
1 Sam. 2 : 3. Talk no more so exceeding proudly; let not arrogancy come out of your mouth: for the Lord is a God of knowledge, and by him actions are weighed.

Confess sin.   Offensiveness of sin.
Is. 65 : 3. A people that provoketh me to anger continually to my face; that sacrificeth in gardens, and burneth incense upon altars of brick;

Ask for blessings.   Dying grace.
Ps. 23 : 4. Yea, though I walk through the valley of the shadow of death, I will fear no evil; for thou art with me; thy rod and thy staff they comfort me.

Thank for mercies.   Answer to prayer.
Ps. 116 : 1, 2. I love the Lord, because he hath heard my voice and my supplications. Because he hath inclined his ear unto me, therefore will I call upon him as long as I live.

Intercede for others.   Church universal.

Is. 57 : 19. I create the fruit of the lips; Peace, peace to him that is far off, and to him that is near, saith the Lord; and I will heal him.

Fourth in   AUGUST.   Lesson, I Tim. 4.
Address to God.   Preserver.

Gen. 48 : 15. And he blessed Joseph, and said, God, before whom my fathers Abraham and Isaac did walk, the God which fed me all my life long unto this day,

Confess sin.   Self-condemned.

Dan. 9 : 7. O Lord, righteousness belongeth unto thee, but unto us confusion of faces, as at this day: to the men of Judah, and to the inhabitants of Jerusalem, and unto all Israel, that are near, and that are far off, through all the countries whither thou hast driven them, because of their trespass that they have trespassed against thee.

Ask for blessings.   Contentment.

I Cor. 7 : 29—31. But this I say, brethren, The time is short. It remaineth, that both they that have wives, be as though they had none; and they that weep, as though they wept not; and they that rejoice, as though they rejoiced not; and they that buy, as though they possessed not: and they that use this world, as not abusing it. For the fashion of this world passeth away.

Thank for mercies.   Preserving grace.

Ps. 94 : 17—19. Unless the Lord had been my help, my soul had almost dwelt in silence. When I said, My foot slippeth; thy mercy, O Lord, held me up. In the multitude of my thoughts within me thy comforts delight my soul.

Intercede for others.   Reviving church.

Mal. 3 : 3, 4. And he shall sit as a refiner and purifier of silver; and he shall purify the sons of Levi, and purge them as gold and silver, that they may offer unto the Lord an offering in righteousness. Then shall the offering of Judah and Jerusalem be pleasant unto the Lord, as in the days of old, and as in former years.

Fifth in AUGUST. Lesson, II Tim. 3.
Address to God. Mercy.
Dan. 9 : 9. To the Lord our God belong mercies and forgivnesses, though we have rebelled against him.

Confess sin. Perverseness.
Gen. 6 : 5. And God saw that the wickedness of man was great in the earth, and that every imagination of the thoughts of his heart was only evil continually.

Ask for blessings. Hope.
Ps. 146 : 5. Happy is he that hath the God of Jacob for his help, whose hope is in the Lord his God:

Thank for mercies. Communion.
Ps. 36 : 8, 9. They shall be abundantly satisfied with the fatness of thy house; and thou shalt make them drink of the river of thy pleasures. For with thee is the fountain of life; in thy light shall we see light.

Intercede for others. Wicked asking God's mercy
Gen. 10 : 17. Now therefore forgive, I pray thee, my sin only this once, and entreat the Lord your God, that he may take away from me this death only.

First in SEPTEMBER. Lesson, Jer. 5.
Address to God. Omniscience.
Amos 9 : 3. And though they hide themselves in the top of Carmel, I will search and take them out thence; and though they be hid from my sight in the bottom of the sea, thence will I command the serpent, and he shall bite them:

Confess sin. Treachery.
II Sam. 19 : 19. And said unto the king, Let not my lord impute iniquity unto me, neither do thou remember that which thy servant did perversely the day that my lord the king went out of Jerusalem, that the king should take it to his heart.

Ask for blessings. Supply needs

Deut. 28 : 3, 5, 6. Blessed shalt thou be in the city, and blessed shalt thou be in the field. * Blessed shall be thy basket and thy store. Blessed shalt thou be when thou comest in, and blessed shalt thou be when thou goest out.

Thank for mercies.   Incarnation.

John 1 : 14. And the Word was made flesh, and dwelt among us, (and we beheld his glory, the glory as of the only begotten of the Father,) full of grace and truth.

Intercede for others.   All men.

Ps. 98 : 2, 3. The Lord hath made known his salvation: his righteousness hath he openly shewed in the sight of the heathen. He hath remembered his mercy and his truth toward the house of Israel: all the ends of the earth have seen the salvation of our God.

Second in   SEPTEMBER.   Lesson, John 12 : 1—36.
Address to God.   Knowledge.

Is. 46 : 10. Declaring the end from the beginning, and from ancient times the things that are not yet done, saying, My counsel shall stand, and I will do all my pleasure:

Confess sin.   Damage of sin.

Prov. 14 : 9. Fools make a mock at sin: but among the righteous there is favor.

Ask for blessings.   Fit for heaven.

II Thess. 2 : 16, 17. Now our Lord Jesus Christ himself, and God, even our Father, which hath loved us, and hath given us everlasting consolation and good hope through grace, comfort your hearts, and stablish you in every good word and work.

Thank for mercies.   Temporal prosperity.

Job 1 : 10. Hast thou not made a hedge about him, and about his house, and about all that he hath on every side? thou hast blessed the work of his hands, and his substance is increased in the land.

Intercede for others.   Defeat church's enemies.

Ps. 129 : 5, 6. Let them all be confounded and turned back that hate

Zion. Let them be as the grass upon the housetops, which withereth afore it groweth up:

Third in   SEPTEMBER.   Lesson, Heb. 4.
Address to God.   Irresistible.
Job 34 : 29. When he giveth quietness, who then can make trouble? and when he hideth his face, who then can behold him? whether it be done against a nation, or against a man only:

Confess sin.   Treachery.
Prov. 26 : 11. As a dog returneth to his vomit, so a fool returneth to his folly.

Ask for blessings.   Wisdom.
Jas. 3 : 15, 17. This wisdom descendeth not from above, but is earthly, sensual, devilish. * But the wisdom that is from above is first pure, then peaceable, gentle, easy to be entreated, full of mercy and good fruits, without partiality, and without hypocrisy.

Thank for mercies.   God's goodness.
Ps. 8 : 3, 4. When I consider thy heavens, the work of thy fingers, the moon and the stars, which thou hast ordained; what is man that thou art mindful of him? and the son of man, that thou visitest him?

Intercede for others.   Children.
I Chron. 22 : 12. Only the Lord give thee wisdom and understanding, and give thee charge concerning Israel, that thou mayest keep the law of the Lord thy God.

Fourth in   SEPTEMBER.   Lesson, Matt. 23.
Address to God.   Eternity.
Dan. 4 : 3. How great are his signs! and how mighty are his wonders! his kingdom is an everlasting kingdom, and his dominion is from generation to generation.

Confess sin.   Condemnation.
Ps. 95 : 11. Unto whom I sware in my wrath, that they should not enter into my rest.

Ask for blessings. Sincerity.

II Cor. 1 : 12. For our rejoicing is this, the testimony of our conscience, that in simplicity and godly sincerity, not with fleshly wisdom, but by the grace of God, we have had our conversation in the world, and more abundantly to you-ward.

Thank for mercies. Spirit of praise.

Ps. 145 : 1, 2, 7. I will extol thee, my God, O King; and I will bless thy name for ever and ever. Every day will I bless thee; and I will praise thy name for ever and ever. * They shall abundantly utter the memory of thy great goodness, and shall sing of thy righteousness.

Intercede for others. Propagation of gospel.

Matt. 4 : 16. The people which sat in darkness, saw a great light; and to them which sat in the region and shadow of death, light is sprung up.

Fifth in SEPTEMBER. Lesson, Heb. 11.
Address to God. Unchangeable.

Num. 23 : 19. God is not a man, that he should lie; neither the son of man, that he should repent: hath he said, and shall he not do it? or hath he spoken, and shall he not make it good?

Confess sin. Misplaced affection.

Prov. 23 : 5. Wilt thou set thine eyes upon that which is not? for riches certainly make themselves wings: they fly away as an eagle toward heaven.

Ask for blessings. Conscientiousness.

Ps. 119 : 5, 6. O that my ways were directed to keep thy statutes! Then shall I not be ashamed, when I have respect unto all thy commandments.

Thank for mercies. God's goodness.

Ps. 104 : 14, 15. He causeth the grass to grow for the cattle, and herb for the service of man: that he may bring forth food out of the earth: and wine that maketh glad the heart of man, and oil to make his face to shine, and bread, which strengtheneth man's heart.

GUIDE TO PRAYER.

Intercede for others. All men.
1 Tim. 2 : 3, 4. For this is good and acceptable in the sight of God our Saviour; who will have all men to be saved, and to come unto the knowledge of the truth.

First in OCTOBER. Lesson, Jer. 19.
Address to God. Unworthy suppliants.
Gen. 18 : 27, 30. And Abraham answered and said, Behold now, I have taken upon me to speak unto the Lord, which am but dust and ashes: * And he said unto him, Oh, let not the Lord be angry, and I will speak: Peradventure there shall thirty be found there. And he said, I will not do it if I find thirty there.

Confess sin. Stubbornness.
Amos 4 : 11. I have overthrown some of you, as God overthrew Sodom and Gomorrah, and ye were as a firebrand plucked out of the burning: yet have ye not returned unto me, saith the Lord.

Ask for blessings. Perfecting grace.
Ps. 138 : 8. The Lord will perfect that which concerneth me: thy mercy, O Lord, endureth for ever: forsake not the works of thine own hands:

Thank for mercies. Hope of eternal life.
1 Pet. 1 : 4. To an inheritance incorruptible, and undefiled, and that fadeth not away, reserved in heaven for you,

Intercede for others. Afflicted heard.
1 Kin. 8 : 37—39. If there be in the land famine, if there be pestilence, blasting, mildew, locust, or if there be caterpillar; if their enemy besiege them in the land of their cities; whatsoever plague, whatsoever sickness there be: what prayer and supplication soever be made by any man, or by all thy people Israel, which shall know every man the plague of his own heart, and spread forth his hands toward this house: then hear thou in heaven thy dwellingplace, and forgive, and do, and give to every man according to his ways, whose heart thou knowest; (for thou, even thou only, knowest the hearts of all the children of men:)

GUIDE TO PRAYER.

Second in   OCTOBER.   Lesson, Matt. 25 : 1—30.
Address to God.   Wisdom.

Ps. 94 : 9. He that planted the ear, shall he not hear? he that formed the eye, shall he not see?

Confess sin.   Offense of sin.

Eph. 4 : 30. And grieve not the Holy Spirit of God, whereby ye are sealed unto the day of redemption.

Ask for blessings.   Grace.

Phil. 3 : 12—14. Not as though I had already attained, either were already perfect: but I follow after, if that I may apprehend that for which also I am apprehended of Christ Jesus. Brethren, I count not myself to have apprehended; but this one thing I do, forgetting those things which are behind, and reaching forth unto those things which are before, I press toward the mark for the prize of the high calling of God in Christ Jesus.

Thank for mercies.   Favors to O. T. church.

Ps. 44 : 3. For they got not the land in possession by their own sword, neither did their own arm save them: but thy right hand, and thine arm, and the light of thy countenance, because thou hadst a favor unto them.

Intercede for others.   Deliver from persecution.

Ps. 14 : 7. Oh that the salvation of Israel were come out of Zion! when the Lord bringeth back the captivity of his people, Jacob shall rejoice, and Israel shall be glad.

Third in   OCTOBER.   Lesson, I Pet. 5
Address to God.   Knows heart.

II Chron. 6 : 30. Then hear thou from heaven thy dwellingplace, and forgive, and render unto every man according unto all his ways, whose heart thou knowest; (for thou only knowest the hearts of the children of men;)

Confess sin.   Sin realized.

II Chron. 6 : 12. For our transgressions are multiplied before thee,

GUIDE TO PRAYER. 117

and our sins testify against us: for our transgressions are with us; and as for our iniquities, we know them:

Ask for blessings. Diligence.

I Cor. 15 : 58. Therefore, my beloved brethren, be ye steadfast, unmoveable, always abounding in the work of the Lord, forasmuch as ye know that your labor is not in vain in the Lord.

Thank for mercies. Appointment of a Redeemer.

John 3 : 16. For God so loved the world, that he gave his only-begotten Son, that whosoever believeth in him, should not perish but have everlasting life.

Intercede for others. Ministers of the gospel.

Phil. 4 : 3. And I entreat thee also, true yokefellow, help those women which labored with me in the gospel, with Clement also, and with other my fellow laborers, whose names are in the book of life.

Fourth in OCTOBER. Lesson, John 15.

Address to God. Unequalled by idols.

Ex. 15 : 11. Who is like unto thee, O Lord, among the gods? who is like thee, glorious in holiness, fearful in praises, doing wonders?

Confess sin. Treachery.

Ps. 85 : 8. I will hear what God the Lord will speak: for he will speak peace unto his people, and to his saints: but let them not turn again to folly.

Ask for blessings. Courage.

Acts 20 : 23, 24. Save that the Holy Ghost witnesseth in every city, saying, that bonds and afflictions abide me. But none of these things move me, neither count I my life dear unto myself, so that I might finish my course with joy, and the ministry which I have received of the Lord Jesus, to testify the gospel of the grace of God.

Thank for mercies. Christ's work owned.

John 3 : 2. The same came to Jesus by night, and said unto him, Rabbi, we know that thou art a teacher come from God: for no man can do these miracles that thou doest, except God be with him.

Intercede for others. Saints.
Ps. 36 : 10. O continue thy lovingkindness unto them that know thee; and thy righteousness to the upright in heart.

Fifth in OCTOBER. Lesson, II Pet. 3.
Address to God. Invisible.
John 1 : 18. No man hath seen God at any time; the only begotten Son, which is in the bosom of the Father, he hath declared him.
Confess sin. Remorse.
I Chron. 21 : 8. And David said unto God, I have sinned greatly, because I have done this thing: but now, I beseech thee, do away the iniquity of thy servant; for I have done very foolishly.
Ask for blessings. Submission.
Ecc. 7 : 14. In the day of prosperity be joyful, but in the day of adversity consider: God also hath set the one over against the other, to the end that man should find nothing after him.
Thank for mercies. God's goodness.
Job 29 : 3, 4. When his candle shined upon my head, and when by his light I walked through darkness; as I was in the days of my youth, when the secret of God was upon my tabernacle;
Intercede for others. Universal church.
Rom. 10 : 1. Brethren, my heart's desire and prayer to God for Israel is, that they might be saved.

First in NOVEMBER. Lesson, Jer. 26.
Address to God. Eternity.
Is. 57 : 15. For thus saith the high and lofty One that inhabiteth eternity, whose name is Holy; I dwell in the high and holy place, with him also that is of a contrite and humble spirit, to revive the spirit of the humble, and to revive the heart of the contrite ones.
Confess sin. Burden of guilt.
Ps. 31 : 10. For my life is spent with grief, and my years with sigh-

ing: my strength faileth because of mine iniquity, and my bones are consumed.

Ask for blessings. Cheerfulness.

Deut. 28 : 47. Because thou servedst not the Lord thy God with joyfulness, and with gladness of heart, for the abundance of all things;

Thank for mercies. Aid in affliction.

II Cor. 1 : 4. Who comforteth us in all our tribulation, that we may be able to comfort them which are in any trouble by the comfort wherewith we ourselves are comforted of God.

Intercede for others. Asking prayers of God's people.

Acts 8 : 24. Then answered Simon, and said, Pray ye to the Lord for me, that none of these things which ye have spoken come upon me.

Second in NOVEMBER. Lesson, Matt. 26 : 26—46.
Address to God. Eternity.

Hab. 3 : 6. He stood and measured the earth: he beheld, and drove asunder the nations; and the everlasting mountains were scattered, the perpetual hills did bow: his ways are everlasting.

Confess sin. Confession neglected.

Lev. 5 : 5. And it shall be, when he shall be guilty in one of these things, that he shall confess that he hath sinned in that thing:

Ask for blessings. Dying grace.

Lk. 12 : 35, 40. Let your loins be girded about, and your lights burning; * Be ye therefore ready also: for the Son of man cometh at an hour when ye think not.

Thank for mercies. Incarnation.

I Tim. 1 : 15. This is a faithful saying, and worthy of all acceptation, that Christ Jesus came into the world to save sinners; of whom I am chief.

Intercede for others. Seek divine favor.

Mal. 1 : 9. And now, I pray you, beseech God that he will be gracious unto us: this hath been by your means: will he regard your persons? saith the Lord of hosts.

Third in NOVEMBER. Lesson, II John.
Address to God. Mitigation of wrath.
Ezek. 16 : 42. So will I make my fury toward thee to rest, and my jealousy shall depart from thee, and I will be quiet, and will be no more angry.
Confess sin. Sensuality.
Rom. 8 : 5. For they that are after the flesh do mind the things of the flesh: but they that are after the Spirit, the things of the Spirit.
Ask for blessings. Sanctifying grace.
II Thess. 1 : 11. Wherefore also we pray always for you, that our God would count you worthy of this calling, and fulfil all the good pleasure of his goodness, and the work of faith with power:
Thank for mercies. Spiritual blessings.
II Sam. 14 : 14. For we must needs die, and are as water spilt on the ground, which cannot be gathered up again; neither doth God respect any person: yet doth he devise means, that his banished be not expelled from him.
Intercede for others. Children.
I Chron. 29 : 19. And give unto Solomon my son a perfect heart, to keep thy commandments, thy testimonies, and thy statutes, and to do all these things, and to build the palace, for the which I have made provision.

Fourth in NOVEMBER. Lesson, Matt. 27 : 1—37.
Address to God. Omniscience.
Job 34 : 22. There is no darkness, nor shadow of death, where the workers of iniquity may hide themselves.
Confess sin. Recognizing sinfulness.
Ps. 38 : 18. For I will declare mine iniquity; I will be sorry for my sin.
Ask for blessings. Supply needs.
Job 5 : 21, 23, 24. Thou shalt be hid from the scourge of the tongue; neither shalt thou be afraid of destruction when it cometh. * For thou

shalt be in league with the stones of the field: and the beasts of the field shall be at peace with thee. And thou shalt know that thy tabernacle shalt be in peace; and thou shalt visit thy habitation, and shalt not sin.

Thank for mercies. God's goodness.

Job 38 : 26. To cause it to rain on the earth, where no man is; on the wilderness, wherein there is no man;

Intercede for others. Asking prayers of God's people.

Ex. 9 : 28. Entreat the Lord (for it is enough) that there be no more mighty thunderings and hail; and I will let you go, and ye shall stay no longer.

Fifth in NOVEMBER. Lesson, Jude.
Address to God. Power.

II Chron. 20 : 6. And said, O Lord God of our Fathers, art thou not God in heaven? and rulest not thou over all the kingdoms of the heathen? and in thine hand is there not power and might, so that none is able to withstand thee?

Confess sin. Humble confession.

Lev. 26 : 40—42. If they shall confess their iniquity, and the iniquity of their fathers, with their trespass which they trespassed against me, and that also they have walked contrary unto me; and that I also have walked contrary unto them, and have brought them into the land of their enemies; if then their uncircumcised hearts be humbled, and they then accept of the punishment of their iniquity: then will I remember my covenant with Jacob, and also my covenant with Isaac, and also my covenant with Abraham will I remember; and I will remember the land.

Ask for blessings. Supply needs.

Ps. 37 : 3, 6. Trust in the Lord, and do good; so shalt thou dwell in the land, and verily thou shalt be fed. * And he shall bring forth thy righteousness as the light, and thy judgment as the noon-day.

Thank for mercies. God's goodness.

Ps. 104 : 10—12. He sendeth the springs into the valleys, which run among the hills. They give drink to every beast of the field: the wild asses quench their thirst. By them shall the fowls of the heaven have their habitation, which sing among the branches.

Intercede for others.   Restrain from unpardonable sin.

Jer. 7 : 16. Therefore pray not thou for this people, neither lift up cry nor prayer for them, neither make intercession to me: for I will not hear thee.

First in   DECEMBER.   Lesson, Jer. 36.
Address to God.   Omniscience.

Dan. 2 : 22. He revealeth the deep and secret things: he knoweth what is in the darkness, and the light dwelleth with him.

Confess sin.   Mercy sought through confession.

Ps. 41 : 4. I said, Lord, be merciful unto me: heal my soul; for I have sinned against thee.

Ask for blessings.   Supply needs.

Ps. 144 : 12, 13, 15. That our sons may be as plants grown up in their youth; that our daughters may be as corner-stones, polished after the similitude of a palace: that our garners may be full, affording all manner of store; that our sheep may bring forth thousands and ten thousands in our streets: * Happy is that people, that is in such a case: yea, happy is that people, whose God is the Lord.

Thank for mercies.   Incarnation.

John 3 : 8. He that committeth sin is of the devil; for the devil sinneth from the beginning. For this purpose the Son of God was manifested, that he might destroy the works of the devil.

Intercede for others.   Prayers of God's servants sought.

I Sam. 7 : 8. And the children of Israel said to Samuel, Cease not to cry unto the Lord our God for us, that he will save us out of the hand of the Philistines.

Second in   DECEMBER.   Lesson, Lk. 23 : 1—33.
Address to God.   Holiness.

GUIDE TO PRAYER. 153

Is. 5 : 16. But the Lord of hosts shall be exalted in judgment, and God that is holy shall be sanctified in righteousness.
Confess sin. Undone by sin.
Lam. 5 : 16. The crown is fallen from our head: woe unto us, that we have sinned!
Ask for blessings. Preserve from sin.
Ps. 141 : 4. Incline not my heart to any evil thing, to practise wicked works with men that work iniquity: and let me not eat of their dainties.
Thank for mercies. Christ satisfying the law.
Gal. 3 : 13. Christ hath redeemed us from the curse of the law, being made a curse for us; for it is written, Cursed is every one that hangeth on a tree:
Intercede for others. Preservation of ministry.
Rom. 15 : 30, 31. Now I beseech you, brethren, for the Lord Jesus Christ's sake, and for the love of the Spirit, that ye strive together with me in your prayers to God for me;

Third in DECEMBER. Lesson, Rev. 3.
Address to God. Mercy.
Deut. 4 : 31. (For the Lord thy God is a merciful God;) he will not forsake thee, neither destroy thee, nor forget the covenant of thy fathers, which he sware unto them.
Confess sin. Burden of guilt.
Ps. 32 : 3, 4. When I kept silence, my bones waxed old through my roaring all the day long. For day and night thy hand was heavy upon me: my moisture is turned into the drought of summer. Selah.
Ask for blessings. Faith.
Gal. 2 : 20. I am crucified with Christ: nevertheless, I live; yet not I, but Christ liveth in me: and the life which I now live in the flesh, I live by the faith of the son of God, who loved me, and gave himself for me.
Thank for mercies. Christ satisfying the law.

Rev. 5 : 9, 12. And they sung a new song, saying, Thou art worthy to take the book, and to open the seals thereof: for thou wast slain, and hast redeemed us to God by thy blood out of every kindred, and tongue, and people and nation; * Saying with a loud voice, Worthy is Lamb that was slain to receive power, and riches, and wisdom, and strength, and honor, and glory and blessing.

Intercede for others. All saints.

Ps. 67 : 1, 2. God be merciful unto us, and bless us; and cause his face to shine upon us; Selah. That thy way may be known upon earth, thy saving health among all nations.

Fourth in DECEMBER. Lesson, John 21.
Address to God. Faithful to oath.

Is. 45 : 23. I have sworn by myself, the word is gone out of my mouth in righteousness, and shall not return, That unto me every knee shall bow, every tongue shall swear.

Confess sin. Burden of guilt.

Ps. 38 : 6. I am troubled; I am bowed down greatly: I go mourning all the day long.

Ask for blessings. Cleansing.

Is. 1 : 18. Come now and let us reason together, saith the Lord: though your sins be as scarlet, they shall be as white as snow; though they be red like crimson, they shall be as wool.

Thank for mercies. Christ satisfying the law.

Col. 2 : 14, 15. Blotting out the hand-writing of ordinances that was against us, which was contrary to us, and took it out of the way, nailing it to his cross; and having spoiled principalities and powers, he made a shew of them openly, triumphing over them in it.

Intercede for others. Saints everywhere.

II Chron. 6 : 41. Now therefore arise, O Lord God, into thy resting place, thou, and the ark of thy strength: let thy priests, O Lord God, be clothed with salvation, and let thy saints rejoice in goodness.

GUIDE TO PRAYER. 155

Fifth in   DECEMBER.   Lesson, Rev. 22.
Address to God.   Longsuffering.

Ps. 78 : 38. But he, being full of compassion, forgave their iniquity, and destroyed them not: yea, many a time turned he his anger away, and did not stir up all his wrath.

Confess sin.   Burden of guilt.

Ps. 38 : 3, 4. There is no soundness in my flesh because of thine anger; neither is there any rest in my bones because of my sin. For mine iniquities are gone over mine head: as a heavy burden they are too heavy for me.

Ask for blessings.   Pardon.

Hos. 14 : 2—4. Take with you words, and turn to the Lord: say unto him, Take away all iniquity, and receive us graciously: so will we render the calves of our lips. Asshur shall not save us; we will not ride upon horses: neither will we say any more to the work of our hands, Ye are our gods: for in thee the fatherless findeth mercy. I will heal their backsliding, I will love them freely: for mine anger is turned away from him.

Thank for mercies.   Christ satisfying the law.

Rev. 1 : 5, 6. And from Jesus Christ, who is the faithful Witness, and the First begotten of the dead, and the Prince of the kings of the earth. Unto him that loved us, and washed us from our sins in his own blood, and hath made us kings and priests unto God and his Father;

Intercede for others.   Saints everywhere.

Ps. 70 : 4. Let all those that seek thee rejoice and be glad in thee: and let such as love thy salvation say continually, Let God be magnified.

——— 0 ———

INDEX TO SCRIPTURE TEXTS.

In this Index the figure before the page number refers to the general division of the prayer under which the text is used, i. e., 1. Address to God; 2. Confess sin; 3. Ask for blessings; 4. Thank for mercies; 5. Intercede for others.

GENESIS.		33 : 19,	1 83	28 : 47,	3 149	7 : 26, 27,	5 115
1 : 3, 6, 7,	1 45	34 : 6, 7,	1 42	29 : 20,	4 74	7 : 28, 29,	5 118
2 : 7,	1 134	34 : 7,	3 4	29 : 20,	2 89	11 : 27,	2 20
3 : 15.	4 11			30 : 6,	3 134	12 : 14,	2 24
3 : 19,	2 7	LEVITICUS.		32 : 4,	1 66	14 : 14,	4 150
6 : 3,	4 103	5 : 5,	2 149	32 : 5, 6,	2 55	15 : 20,	3 81
6 : 5,	2 141	10 : 3,	1 26	32 : 18,	2 35	19 : 19,	2 141
6 : 12,	2 93	13 : 45,	2 31	32 : 32,	2 62	23 : 3,	5 99
8 : 22,	4 115	16 : 21,	2 22	32 : 39,	1 66	23 : 5,	3 78
10 : 17,	5 141	16 : 22,	3 55	33 : 18,	5 66	24 : 10,	2 73
12 : 3,	4 83	25 : 4, 5,	5 44	33 : 19,	5 2		
18 : 27,	2 134	26 : 40-42,	2 151	33 : 27,	3 43	I KINGS.	
18 : 27, 30,	1 145	26 : 43,	2 103	33 : 27,	1 115	3 : 9,	3 22
27 : 38,	3 60			33 : 29,	5 63	4 : 25,	5 29
28 : 4,	5 125	NUMBERS.		33 : 31,	1 96	8 : 30, 50,	5 130
32 : 9, 10.	5 133	6 : 24—26,	3 59			8 : 33, 34,	5 130
32 : 10,	4 43	10 : 35, 36,	5 119	JOSHUA.		8 : 37—39,	1 145
32 : 10,	1 89	14 : 4,	5 17	7 : 19,	2 1	8 : 38,	2 98
32 : 26,	3 60	14 : 17—19,	5 122			8 : 47,	2 123
42 : 21,	2 14	14 : 17-19,	3 131	JUDGES.		8 : 56,	4 49
48 : 15,	1 140	15 : 30,	2 148	5 : 11,	4 43	10 : 9,	5 43
49 : 10,	4 83	21 : 7,	2 124	5 : 16,	5 94		
49 : 24,	5 47	23 : 19,	1 144	5 : 18,	5 15	II KINGS.	
49 : 25,	5 75			5 : 31,	5 6	2 : 21,	5 58
		DEUTERONOMY.		13 : 23,	2 90		
EXODUS.		4 : 7,	1 53			I CHRONICLES.	
5 : 2,	2 48	4 : 7,	4 69	I SAMUEL.		4 : 10,	3 10
9 : 28,	5 151	4 : 31,	1 153	1 : 18,	4 107	17 : 27,	3 10
14 : 25,	5 63	6 : 4,	1 57	2 : 3,	1 139	21 : 8,	2 148
15 : 2,	1 29	7 : 9,	1 138	7 : 8,	5 152	22 : 12,	5 143
15 : 11,	1 6	8 : 2,	4 77	7 : 12,	4 77	29 : 15,	3 46
15 : 11,	1 147	8 : 10,	4 8	12 : 19,	3 2	29 : 16,	1 100
18 : 11,	5 72	11 : 12,	4 9	20 : 3,	4 41	29 : 19,	5 150
18 : 21,	5 19	15 : 19,	2 86				
23 : 25,	3 106	26 : 15,	5 120	II SAMUEL.		II CHRONICLES.	
28 : 36,	5 51	26 : 17-19,	1 71	2 : 24, 25,	1 50	6 : 12,	2 146
29 : 43,	4 61	26 : 19,	5 49	7 : 14,	2 56	6 : 18,	1 22
33 : 15,	3 11	28 : 3, 5, 6,	3 142	7 : 18—21,	5 112	6 : 28, 29,	5 138
33 : 19,	4 2	28 : 23,	5 44	7 : 25,	3 78	6 : 30,	1 146

GUIDE TO PRAYER.

6 : 34, 35,	5 114	12 : 6,	4 42	7 : 9,	5 93	31 : 1,	1 24
6 : 36—39,	5 128	12 : 10,	1 38	8 : 3, 4,	4 143	31 : 7, 21,	4 129
6 : 41,	5 154	12 : 20,	5 60	8 : 4,	1 72	31 : 10,	2 148
12 : 6,	2 104	14 : 4,	2 82	8 : 5,	4 39	31 : 15,	1 107
15 : 5,	5 29	15 : 4,	2 102	9 : 20,	5 72	31 : 22,	2 69
16 : 9,	1 37	15 : 15, 16,	2 60	10 : 4,	2 35	32 : 3, 4,	2 153
19 : 6, 7,	5 59	17 : 9,	3 42	10 : 17,	4 130	32 : 5, 6,	2 61
20 : 6,	1 151	21 : 9,	4 8	10 : 18,	5 35	33 : 9,	1 45
20 : 12,	3 71	21 : 9,	1 30	11 : 7,	3 4	33 : 11,	5 8
24 : 22,	2 13	21 : 15,	2 93	12 : 5,	5 135	34 : 1,	4 109
30 : 8,	1 87	22 : 21,	3 7	14 : 1,	1 4	34 : 3,	1 131
32 : 25,	2 76	25 : 2—6,	2 108	14 : 1,	5 123	34 : 8,	1 83
32 : 26,	2 10	25 : 6,	1 22	14 : 3,	2 93	34 : 19,	5 23
		26 : 9,	1 16	14 : 7,	5 146	34 : 20,	4 6
EZRA.		26 : 14,	1 15	16 : 2,	1 20	35 : 10,	4 6
3 : 4,	3 102	27 : 5, 6,	3 104	16 : 5, 6,	1 23	35 : 27,	5 57
9 : 6,	2 114	27 : 8, 9,	1 101	16 : 8,	3 96	36 : 6,	1 41
9 : 7,	2 118	29 : 3, 4,	4 148	17 : 15,	3 105	36 : 6,	1 98
9 : 10,	2 29	31 : 5, 7,	2 96	18 : 11,	1 3	36 : 8, 9,	4 141
9 : 13,	2 100	31 : 24,	2 68	18 : 16, 17, 19,	5 87	36 : 10,	5 148
9 : 14,	2 79	32 : 8,	4 39	18 : 34, 35,	5 15	37 : 3, 6,	3 151
9 : 15,	1 27	33 : 4,	1 70	19 : 1,	1 4	37 : 4,	3 26
10 : 2,	2 97	33 : 6,	1 114	19 : 4, 5,	4 139	37 : 30,	3 35
		33 : 14,	2 63	19 : 12,	2 133	37 : 31,	3 23
NEHEMIAH.		33 : 17,	3 30	19 : 13,	3 138	38 : 3, 4.	2 155
1 : 6,	2 127	33 : 24,	4 45	20 : 7,	1 74	38 : 4,	2 91
9 : 5,	1 43	33 : 27,	2 18	21 : 4—7	5 62	38 : 6,	2 154
9 : 6,	1 103	34 : 10, 11,	1 127	22 : 3,	1 13	38 : 18,	2 150
9 : 14,	4 97	34 : 22,	1 150	22 : 7,	5 65	39 : 3,	1 34
9 : 17,	3 3	34 : 29,	1 143	22 : 9, 10,	1 113	39 : 4, 5,	3 46
9 : 26,	2 48	34 : 32,	2 96	22 : 28,	5 88	39 : 7, 8,	3 111
9 : 33,	2 100	34 : 32,	3 125	23 : 2, 5,	4 134	40 : 7, 8,	4 10
		35 : 7,	1 20	23 : 4,	3 139	40 : 8,	3 23
ESTHER.		35 : 10, 11,	1 86	23 : 6,	3 81	40 : 12,	2 66
10 : 3,	4 79	37 : 19,	1 3	24 : 1,	1 11	40 : 12, 13,	3 6
		37 : 23,	1 43	24 : 4,	2 63	40 : 16,	5 136
		38 : 6,	1 70	25 : 1,	1 112	41 : 4,	2 152
JOB.		38 : 8, 11,	4 3	25 : 3,	1 24	41 : 12,	3 90
1 : 10,	3 106	38 : 26,	4 151	25 : 4,	2 111	42 : 1, 2, 8,	1 73
1 : 10,	4 142	39 : 6,	5 89	25 : 15,	3 96	43 : 3,	1 76
5 : 17, 19,	3 119	40 : 4, 5,	2 132	25 : 21,	3 6	44 : 1,	5 68
5 : 21, 23, 24,	3 150	40 : 9,	1 119	25 : 24,	3 90	44 : 3,	4 146
6 : 24,	3 20	42 : 2,	1 12	26 : 3,	1 83	44 : 4,	1 49
7 : 20,	2 29	42 : 5, 6,	2 59	27 : 8,	1 56	45 : 6,	5 92
8 : 7,	4 117			28 : 1,	1 75	46 : 4,	5 58
9 : 3, 20,	2 109	PSALMS.		28 : 9,	5 3	46 : 9,	5 69
9 : 4,	1 38	2 : 1—5,	5 86	29 : 2,	1 56	47 : 9,	5 18
10 : 4, 5,	1 34	2 : 6,	4 92	29 : 11,	5 3	48 : 8, 9,	5 69
10 : 11, 12,	1 138	2 : 8,	5 24	30 : 4,	1 13	49 : 7,	4 45
11 : 2,	2 14	3 : 5,	4 40	30 : 5,	3 9	49 : 11, 13,	2 35
11 : 7,	1 5	4 : 6, 7,	1 25	30 : 5,	3 57	49 : 12, 20,	2 4
11 : 12,	2 49	5 : 4,	1 40	30 : 5,	2 12	49 : 13,	2 73
11 : 44,	2 31	5 : 12,	5 3	30 : 6,			

GUIDE TO PRAYER.

49 : 15,	3 104	73 : 2, 3,	4 68	93 : 1,	1 125	116 : 1. 2.	4 131.
50 : 1,	1 117	73 : 22,	2 134	93 : 5.	1 83	116 : 2.	3 104
50 : 10,	1 11	73 : 24,	3 104	94 : 9.	1 146	116 : 3—9,	4 76
50 : 15,	1 25	73 : 25, 26,	1 28	94 : 15.	5 85	116 : 7, 12, 13,	4 71
50 : 23,	4 36	73 : 28,	4 32	94 : 16.	5 93	116 : 16.	1 87
50 : 23,	1 88	74 : 16, 17,	1 68	94 : 17—19.	4 140	117 : 2,	1 14
51 : 2, 3, 7,	3 113	74 : 21,	5 121	94 : 19.	5 104	118 : 15,	4 8
51 : 4,	1 13	75 : 1,	4 111	95 : 3, 4, 5,	1 11	118 : 25,	3 50
51 : 4,	2 39	76 : 7,	2 81	95 : 6.	1 19	118 : 27,	1 1
51 : 4,	2 103	77 : 7, 8, 10,	2 69	95 : 9, 10.	2 74	119 : 5, 6,	3 144
51 : 5,	2 82	78 : 6, 7,	5 99	95 : 11.	2 143	119 : 11,	3 33
51 : 10—12,	3 61	78 : 38,	1 155	97 : 1. 2.	1 41	119 : 33—36,	3 85
51 : 11,	3 129	79 : 8, 9.	3 56	98 : 2, 3,	5 142	119 : 38,	3 97
51 : 13,	3 17	79 : 8, 9,	5 124	99 : 17,	3 50	119 : 43, 74,	1 91
51 : 13,	5 117	79 : 11,	5 131	100 : 3.	1 19	119 : 58,	3 9
51 : 15,	1 93	80 : 2, 3,	5 67	100 : 5.	1 14	119 : 58,	1 25
51 : 17,	2 32	80 : 8, 9,	4 12	100 : 5.	4 71	119 : 64,	4 4
51 : 18,	5 83	80 : 14, 15,	5 134	102 : 13, 16, 17,	5 28	119 : 65,	4 35
52 : 8. 9,	1 74	81 : 12,	3 33	102 : 18.	5 30	119 : 67, 71,	4 70
58 : 4, 5,	2 139	82 : 1,	5 18	102 : 25—27.	1 61	119 : 68,	1 67
58 : 11,	1 4	82 : 5,	2 34	102 : 26,	1 136	119 : 80,	3 101
60 : 2,	5 95	83 : 13, 16, 18,	5 137	103 : 1, 2.	4 112	119 : 91,	1 45
60 : 11, 12,	5 95	83 : 18,	1 123	103 : 3. 4.	4 67	119 : 92, 93,	4 106
61 : 5,	4 33	84 : 9,	1 93	103 : 9.	3 3	119 : 94,	1 100
61 : 7, 8,	5 61	84 : 10—12,	4 68	103 : 10,	2 58	119 : 124,	
62 : 1. 2,	1 24	85 : 1.	5 68	103 : 12,	3 55	125, 169,	3 68
62 : 11,	1 12	85 : 5. 6.	3 58	103 : 19.	1 16	119 : 132,	3 107
63 : 1,	1 29	85 : 7—13,	5 11	103 : 19.	1 103	119 : 133,	3 127
63 : 1—3, 5,	1 101	85 : 8.	2 102	103 : 20, 21,	1 44	119 : 176,	2 104
63 : 3,	3 9	85 : 8.	2 147	104 : 1. 2.	1 3	121 : 4—8,	3 80
63 : 3,	3 58	85 : 12.	5 89	104 : 4.	1 44	122 : 7,	5 66
64 : 8,	2 139	86 : 5.	1 121	104 : 5. 9.	4 3	122 : 7, 8,	5 83
65 : 2,	1 101	86 : 5. 15.	3 129	104 : 10—12,	4 152	125 : 3,	5 117
65 : 5,	5 75	86 : 8. 10.	1 60	104 : 14, 15,	4 144	126 : 4,	5 75
65 : 9—11,	4 123	86 : 9.	1 26	104 : 24,	1 64	126 : 5, 6,	2 80
65 : 9,	4 131	86 : 11,	3 73	104 : 24, 25.	1 98	128 : 5, 6,	5 74
66 : 20,	4 107	86 : 15.	1 116	104 : 29,	1 104	129 : 1—4,	4 99
67 : 1, 2,	5 154	89 : 6 8.	1 33	104 : 27—31,	4 38	129 : 5, 6,	5 142
67 : 2,	5 78	89 : 17. 18,	1 24	104 : 33,	4 109	130 : 1, 2,	4 33
67 : 3, 4,	5 78	89 / 19—21, 27,	4 118	105 : 8.	4 35	130 : 3,	1 28
68 : 6,	4 43	89 : 29,	4 99	105 : 22,	5 98	130 : 3, 4, 7, 8	2 3
68 : 18,	4 126	89 : 32, 34,	4 129	106 : 2,	1 59	132 : 15,	5 48
69 : 5,	2 17	90 : 2,	1 35	106 : 4, 5,	3 118	132 : 18,	5 16
69 : 31,	4 36	90 : 2.	1 126	106 : 30,	5 13	132 : 18,	5 99
69 : 31.	1 88	90 : 9.	2 84	106 : 33,	2 11	133 : 1, 3,	3 40
69 : 35, 36,	5 61	90 : 11,	2 81	107 : 42,	5 13	133 : 3,	3 10
70 : 4,	5 155	91 : 2, 4, 9, 10, 3	49	110 : 3,	3 8	135 : 13,	1 96
71 : 6,	1 129	91 : 12, 13,	4 75	110 : 3.	5 21	136 : 1,	1 14
71 : 17, 18,	5 22	91 : 14,	3 26	111 : 9,	1 13	138 : 2,	5 73
72 : 1, 4,	5 97	92 : 1. 2,	4 1	111 : 10,	3 68	138 : 3,	4 136
72 : 5, 7,	5 30	92 : 14, 15,	5 104	115 : 4.	1 132	138 : 8,	3 145
73 : 1,	1 67	92 : 15,	1 67	115 : 16,	1 11	139 : 1—3,	1 97

Ref	Pg	Ref	Pg	Ref	Pg	Ref	Pg	Ref	Pg
139 : 4—6,	1 108	14 : 34.		5 31	11 : 9,	2 94	30 : 18.	2 58	
139 : 7—10,	1 62	15 : 3,		1 37	11 : 9, 10.	5 103	30 : 20.	5 107	
139 : 12,	1 116	15 : 3,		1 62	11 : 10,	2 84	30 : 21.	3 71	
139 : 14,	4 5	15 : 8,		1 88	12 : 1,	5 104	32 : 15,	5 85	
139 : 14—16,	1 47	15 : 16, 17,		3 31	12 : 13.	3 73	32 : 17,	3 120	
140 : 7,	5 15	15 : 33,		3 25			33 : 6,	5 30	
140 : 13,	3 61	16 : 7,		5 24	SOLOMONS SONG.		33 : 20-22,	5 34	
141 : 2,	1 92	16 : 31,		5 38	1 : 8.	4 100	33 : 24,	3 57	
141 : 2,	1 125	17 : 5.		2 44	2 : 3, 4,	4 106	34 : 8,	5 7	
141 : 4,	3 153	17 : 16,		2 65	5 : 10, 16,	3 74	38 : 10, 17,	4 41	
142 : 4, 5,	1 52	17 : 22.		3 87			38 : 17.	4 67	
143 : 1,	1 53	17 : 24,		2 6	ISAIAH.		40 : 14,	1 119	
143 : 8,	3 13	18 : 10,		1 42	1 : 2.	2 25	40 : 15, 17,	1 80	
144 : 12, 13, 15,	3 152	19 : 3,		2 13	1 : 3, 4,	2 20	40 : 28,	1 81	
145 : 1, 2, 7,	4 144	19 : 21,		5 8	1 : 4,	2 33	41 : 2,	5 96	
145 : 3,	1 32	20 : 27,		4 39	1 : 4,	5 90	42 : 1.	4 82	
145 : 8,	4 37	20 : 28,		5 62	1 : 5,	2 136	42 : 21,	5 73	
145 : 9,	1 67	22 : 13,		2 120	1 : 18,	3 154	43 : 21,	4 74	
145 : 10,	4 2	22 : 15,		2 27	1 : 25, 26,	5 75	44 : 22,	3 130	
145 : 15, 16,	1 98	22 : 15,		2 49	2 : 4,	5 70	45 : 19,	1 53	
145 : 17,	1 83	23 : 5,		2 63	4 : 4,	5 65	45 : 23,	1 154	
146 : 5,	3 141	23 : 5.		2 144	4 : 5,	5 93	46 : 4,	5 55	
147 : 1,	4 1	23 : 17,		3 97	5 : 1,	5 89	46 : 10.	1 142	
147 : 4, 5,	1 10	24 : 9,		2 6	5 : 4.	2 8	48 : 1, 2,	2 24	
147 : 9,	1 75	24 : 10,		2 48	5 : 16,	1 153	48 : 4,	2 121	
147 : 9, 10,	4 134	25 : 5.		5 62	6 : 1, 2,	1 16	48 : 8,	2 33	
147 : 11,	4 73	25 : 28.		2 119	6 : 5,	2 71	48 : 18,	5 31	
147 : 14.	4 43	26 : 11.		2 143	6 : 5,	2 126	49 : 4.	5 52	
147 : 19, 20,	4 25	26 : 14,		2 47	8 : 8,	5 9	49 : 6,	5 24	
149 : 1, 2, 5, 6,	4 113	28 : 13,		2 60	8 : 19,	1 105	49 : 8,	4 82	
		28 : 26,		2 40	8 : 20,	5 73	49 : 14.	2 69	
PROVERBS.		29 : 1,		2 26	9 : 4 8,	5 88	49 : 23.	5 16	
1 : 7,	3 25	29 : 5,		2 51	9 : 6, 7,	4 127	49 : 23,	5 132	
2 : 3—5,	3 114	29 : 26,		1 105	9 : 13,	2 57	50 : 1.	2 21	
3 : 5,	2 40	31 : 26,		3 90	11 : 3,	5 98	51 : 7.	3 39	
3 : 5, 7,	3 77				11 : 6, 9, 13,	5 39	51 : 9.	5 115	
3 : 6,	3 109	ECCLESIASTES.			11 : 9,	5 127	51 : 17,	2 129	
3 : 11,	2 43	1 : 4,		4 74	12 : 5,	5 2	52 : 11.	5 51	
5 : 12, 13,	2 116	5 : 2,		3 34	12 : 3.	3 78	53 : 3,	3 117	
5 : 19,	4 78	7 : 9,		2 11	14 : 32.	5 74	53 : 5, 6, 10,	4 114	
6 : 6—8,	2 95	7 : 9,		3 94	22 : 1,	5 9	53 : 12	4 19	
6 : 10,	2 47	7 : 14,		3 148	24 : 16,	2 28	54 : 2,	5 77	
8 : 36,	2 21	7 : 29,		2 4	26 : 1, 2,	5 108	54 : 9,	4 3	
10 : 19,	2 14	8 : 1, 18,		3 37	26 : 4,	1 96	54 : 10,	4 23	
10 : 20, 21,	3 90	8 : 11,		2 79	26 : 8, 9,	1 51	54 : 17.	5 126	
10 : 21, 32,	2 45	9 : 7,		3 40	26 : 11,	2 138	55 : 3,	4 23	
10 : 32,	3 90	9 : 9,		4 78	26 : 13,	1 49	55 : 7,	3 115	
12 : 25,	3 87	9 : 10,		3 38	27 : 4, 5,	3 7	55 : 9.	1 60	
14 : 8,	3 22	9 : 18,		2 65	28 : 13,	2 77	56 : 4, 5.	3 95	
14 : 9,	2 142	10 : 2.		2 135	28 : 17.	2 89	56 : 7,	4 32	
14 : 17,	2 11	10 : 10.		3 22	28 : 20,	1 37	56 : 12,	2 12	
14 : 27,	3 25	11 : 4.		2 47	29 : 11,	4 96	57 : 15.	2 32	

GUIDE TO PRAYER. 161

57 : 15,	1 148	10 : 7,	5 88	16 : 8,	3 67	AMOS.	
57 : 16,	3 43	10 : 7,	1 120	16 : 8,	3 95	2 : 13,	2 74
57 : 17,	2 26	10 : 10,	1 57	16 : 42,	1 150	4 : 11,	2 145
57 : 19,	5 140	10 : 11,	1 96	16 : 63,	2 98	4 : 13,	1 137
58 : 1,	5 47	10 : 15, 16,	1 78	18 30,	3 2	5 : 24,	5 19
58 : 7,	2 86	10 : 23,	1 107	20 : 37,	3 95	6 : 3,	2 12
58 : 9,	4 69	11 : 14,	5 136	33 : 11,	2 101	7 : 5,	5 42
58 : 12,	5 34	12 : 1,	1 13	33 : 31,	2 105	8 : 11, 12,	5 12
59 : 2,	2 52	13 : 11,	1 71	36 : 37,	3 1	9 : 3,	1 141
59 : 21,	3 35	14 : 7,	2 139	37 : 26,	4 61		
60 : 7, 8,	5 2	14 : 7—9,	5 91	37 : 26, 27,	5 9	OBADIAH.	
60 : 17, 18,	5 12	17 : 9,	2 64			1 : 3,	2 73
62 : 4,	5 12	17 : 10,	1 63	DANIEL.			
62 : 9,	5 48	17 : 12,	5 92	2 : 22,	1 152	JONAH.	
63 : 4,	5 7	17 : 14,	3 58	2 : 44,	5 8	2 : 8,	2 36
63 : 7,	4 72	22 : 21,	2 85	4 : 3,	1 143		
63 : 10,	2 74	23 : 6,	1 28	4 : 25,	1 106	MICAH.	
63 : 16,	1 122	23 : 23, 24,	1 8	4 : 34, 35,	1 65	2 : 1,	2 6
64 : 6,	3 4	30 : 21,	1 133	5 : 23,	2 9	3 : 8,	5 47
64 : 7,	1 56	31 : 3,	4 66	5 : 23,	1 107	6 : 8,	2 10
64 : 7,	2 102	31 : 33,	3 23	7 : 10,	1 44	7 : 9,	2 106
64 : 8,	1 99	32 : 39,	5 40	7 : 14,	4 57	7 : 18, 19,	3 54
65 : 3,	2 139	32 : 40,	3 97	9 : 7,	2 140		
65 : 8,	4 81	34 : 18,	2 28	9 : 8,	2 2	HABAKKUK.	
65 : 24,	4 69	38 : 16,	1 70	9 : 9,	1 141	1 : 13,	1 40
66 : 1,	1 113	44 : 4, 5,	2 56	9 : 10,	2 39	1 : 16,	2 40
66 : 1, 2,	2 32	44 : 17,	2 93	9 : 17,	5 42	3 : 2,	5 5
66 : 8,	4 98	45 : 5,	2 117	9 : 18,	1 27	3 : 6,	1 149
66 : 11,	3 78	50 : 5,	1 87	9 : 24,	4 54		
		50 : 5,	3 95			ZEPHANIAH.	
JEREMIAH.		50 : 20,	3 5	HOSEA.		3 : 9,	5 45
2 : 13,	2 36	51 : 5,	5 10	2 : 3, 9,	2 128	7 : 11, 12,	2 112
2 : 19,	2 75			2 : 9,	5 44		
2 : 20,	2 131	LAMENTATIONS.		2 : 14, 15,	4 105	HAGGAI.	
2 : 21,	2 62	2 : 13,	5 94	4 : 17,	4 103	1 : 9,	5 48
2 : 32,	2 35	3 : 22, 23,	1 118	6 : 3,	3 19		
3 : 4,	3 58	3 : 26,	5 71	6 : 4,	2 88	ZECHARIAH.	
3 : 13,	2 113	3 : 29,	2 31	7 : 16,	2 64	2 : 5,	5 92
3 : 19,	5 9	3 : 32, 33,	4 37	8 : 12,	2 93	4 : 10,	4 31
3 : 19,	3 58	3 : 37, 38,	1 121	11 : 4,	4 66	6 : 13,	4 47
3 : 22,	2 79	3 : 39,	2 106	11 : 7,	2 64	9 : 11, 12,	3 119
3 : 25,	2 137	3 : 41,	1 29	11 : 9,	1 34	11 : 11,	5 54
4 : 14,	2 6	4 : 1,	2 62	12 : 14,	2 20	12 : 1,	1 70
4 : 22,	2 34	5 : 16,	2 153	13 : 9,	4 10	12 : 3,	5 6
5 : 3,	2 27			14 : 2—4,	3 155	12 : 10,	1 54
5 : 4, 5,	2 53	EZEKIEL.		14 : 5, 6,	3 84	12 : 10,	5 76
5 : 24,	5 44	6 : 9,	2 51	14 : 8,	2 102	13 : 2,	5 45
6 : 7,	2 85	7 : 16,	2 52				
7 : 12,	5 66	9 : 4,	5 90			MALACHI.	
7 : 16,	5 152	11 : 19,	3 135	JOEL.		1 : 8, 14,	2 105
8 : 22,	5 94	16 : 2, 3,	2 33	2 : 23,	5 44	1 : 9,	5 149
9 : 1,	2 80	16 : 5, 6, 8,	4 124	2 : 13, 14,	2 101	1 : 11,	5 25

3:3, 4,	5 140	22:37,	3 26	1:1—3, 14,	1 18	20:17,	4 132
3:6,	1 126	24:12,	5 68	1:14,	4 142	ACTS.	
3:10, 12,	5 48	25:18, 25,	2 38	1:16,	3 64	2:11,	4 96
4:2,	3 84	26:28,	4 95	1:18,	1 148	2:24, 31, 36,	4 116
		26:41,	3 15	1:29,	4 16	2:33,	4 59
MATTHEW.		28:18,	4 20	3:2,	4 147	2:38, 39,	4 95
1:21,	4 16	28:18,	1 39	3:6,	2 7	2:47,	5 77
3:2,	2 30	28:20,	4 137	3:8,	4 152	5:31,	2 30
3:8,	2 102			3:16,	4 147	6:4,	5 20
3:10,	2 8	MARK.		3:33,	3 73	7:60,	5 53
3:17,	1 93	8:24,	2 63	3:35,	4 47	8:24,	5 149
4:16,	5 144	8:38,	3 39	4:23, 24,	1 102	8:39,	3 40
5:6,	1 90	11:24,	3 1	4:34,	4 52	10:35,	5 57
5:44,	3 76	11:25,	5 53	5:22, 26, 27,	4 47	11:21,	5 52
5:44,	5 107	16:16,	5 81	5:23,	1 46	13:39,	3 53
5:45,	4 117	16:20,	4 26	5:36,	4 87	14:17,	4 120
5:48,	3 99			5:39,	4 24	17:25,	4 4
6:7, 8,	3 51	LUKE.		6:6,	3 1	17:26,	1 135
6:21,	2 7	1:17,	3 17	6:37,	4 53	17:27,	1 36
6:22,	3 101	1:33,	4 92	6:39,	4 81	17:28,	1 104
6:31, 32,	2 37	1:37,	1 12	6:68,	1 105	17:31,	4 128
6:32, 33,	3 48	1:38,	3 51	6:69,	4 13	18:24,	5 59
7:7,	1 49	1:53,	1 90	7:16,	4 15	18:24,	3 70
7:29,	4 15	6:33,	3 99	7:17,	3 69	19:20,	4 62
8:27,	4 87	7:47, 50,	3 57	7:18,	2 67	20:23, 24,	3 147
9:6, 13,	4 15	10:18,	4 26	7:37,	4 88	21:4,	3 31
9:38,	5 81	10:21, 24,	4 133	7:38,	4 59	21:16,	5 104
10:16,	3 37	11:13,	4 94	8:29,	4 121	26:18,	3 131
10:29,	1 133	11:21, 22,	4 104	8:32, 36,	3 69	26:22,	4 32
11:5,	4 87	12:19, 20,	2 42	8:56,	4 83	ROMANS.	
11:5,	5 106	12:35, 40,	3 149	9:4,	3 38	1:4,	4 18
11:19,	4 16	12:43,	3 102	10:10,	4 50	1:20,	1 4
11:25,	1 18	12:47,	2 23	11:52,	4 101	1:28,	4 103
11:28,	4 53	12:52,	5 94	12:31,	5 80	1:32,	2 76
11:28,	2 91	13:6, 7,	2 8	13:36,	4 91	2:4,	2 29
11:29,	4 15	15:18,	2 9	14:2, 3,	4 91	2:4,	2 97
11:29,	3 139	15:19,	3 58	14:16, 17,	4 22	2:15,	4 65
12:20,	4 31	15:21,	2 92	14:26,	3 21	2:21,	2 88
12:35,	3 35	16:1,	2 65	14:26,	1 85	2:23,	2 20
12:35,	2 127	16:9,	3 108	15:26,	1 85	3:2,	4 49
12:36, 37,	2 71	18:13,	3 113	16:13,	3 20	3:19,	2 78
13:14,	2 63	19:10,	4 50	16:14,	4 22	3:23,	2 9
13:41, 43,	4 58	19:14,	2 48	16:23,	1 55	3:24,	3 53
15:3,	5 72	19:42,	5 60	16:23, 24,	3 52	4:11,	4 95
15:8,	1 95	19:44,	2 95	17:1	1 29	4:21,	1 124
15:19,	2 6	21:12—15,	4 27	17:2,	4 86	4:25,	4 18
15:26, 27,	1 89	22:35,	4 7	17:3,	3 19	5:4, 5,	3 32
16:18,	4 99	23:34,	5 53	17:6,	4 80	5:8,	4 18
16:24,	3 29	24:25,	2 99	17:15, 17,	3 82	5:12, 20,	2 121
16:26,	2 50	29:19,	3 93	17:20, 21,	4 19	6:4,	3 66
18:26,	3 4			17:20, 21,	5 40	6:6, 12, 13,	3 14
19:23, 26,	5 55	JOHN.		18:37,	4 13	6:9,	4 55

GUIDE TO PRAYER.

6:14,	4 82	15:5,6,	5 14	5:14,15,	3 42	4:4—6,	5 40
6:14,	2 102	15:16,	5 25	5:19,	4 14	4:8,11—13,	4 97
6:17,	3 72	15:30,31,	5 153	5:21,	3 4	4:14,15,	3 126
6:21,	2 50	16:20,	3 65	6:4,	4 27	4:18,	2 107
6:23,	2 57	16:25,26,	4 26	6:4,7,8,	3 88	4:21,	5 84
7:11,	2 19			6:10,	3 83	4:22,24,	3 121
7:12,	2 39	**I CORINTHIANS.**		7:10,	3 87	4:26,	3 94
7:13,	2 16	1:2,	4 28	7:10,	2 98	4:29,	2 45
7:18,19,	2 7	1:9,	4 115	10:4,	4 26	4:30,	2 146
7:21—23,	2 38	1:10,	5 64	10:5,	3 116	4:31,	2 11
7:22,	3 23	1:30,	3 4	11:12,	3 91	5:4,	2 46
8:1,	3 7	1:30,	3 16	12:9,	3 33	5:6,	2 57
8:5,	2 67	2:11,	4 5	12:9,10,	3 18	5:15,	3 91
8:5,	2 150	2:14,	2 5	13:11,	5 33	5:16,	3 102
8:7,	2 83	4:3,4,	3 88	13:11,	5 137	6:10,	3 18
8:15,	1 54	4:4,	2 92			6:11—17,	3 121
8:16,17,	3 62	5:2,	2 67	**GALATIANS.**		6:13,	5 79
8:24,	3 32	6:19,	4 39	2:20,	3 153	6:18,	1 21
8:26,	1 25	6:19,	1 87	3:10,	2 57	6:19,20,	5 36
8:26,27,	3 112	7:24,	3 109	3:13,	4 153	6:24,	5 26
8:28,	3 79	7:25,	5 36	3:14,	3 60		
8:36,37,	4 63	7:29—31,	3 140	3:22,	2 79	**PHILIPPIANS.**	
9:4,	4 49	7:35,	1 77	4:4,5,	4 120	1:6,	3 68
9:5,	1 78	9:27,	3 29	4:15,	2 72	1:29,	3 24
10:1,	5 148	10:12,	3 75	4:18,	3 89	2:3,	5 46
10:12,	1 89	10:13,	3 15	4:19,	5 21	2:8—11,	4 125
10:14,15,	5 116	10:17,	4 64	5:26,	2 70	2:11,	1 69
11:5,	4 46	11:1,	4 100	6:10,	3 28	3:12—14,	3 146
11:23—26,	5 81	12:4—6,	4 64	6:10,	5 120	3:20,21,	3 80
11:26,	5 65	13:4,5,	2 44	6:14,	3 64	4:3,	5 147
11:27,	3 5	14:24,25,	5 5			4:4,	3 39
11:33,	1 82	15:20—23,	4 125	**EPHESIANS.**		4:5,	5 46
11:36,	1 55	15:24,25,28,	4 92	1:3,	4 80	4:6,	1 21
12:1,	1 1	15:38,	3 147	1:4—6,	4 46	4:7,	3 63
12:2,	3 72	15:49,	2 7	1:6,	1 56	4:11,	2 41
12:3,	2 10			1:7,	4 31	4:12,	3 30
12:11,	2 116	**II CORINTHIANS.**		1:7,8,	3 7	4:19,	3 107
12:18,	3 28	1:4,	4 149	1:11,	1 64		
13:1,5,	3 86	1:9,	4 41	1:11,12,	1 108	**COLOSSIANS.**	
13:3,	5 43	1:12,	3 144	1:13,14,	4 94	1:9,10,	3 124
13:4,	5 35	1:20,	3 51	1:17—19,	3 117	1:12,	3 47
13:4,	4 79	2:11,	3 27	2:1,	3 67	1:17,	1 85
13:14,	2 86	2:15,	3 98	2:2,3,	2 82	1:18,	4 101
14:3,19,	5 33	3:3,	3 23	2:4,	4 89	1:19,	3 64
14:7,8,	3 136	3:6,	5 36	2:8,	3 24	1:23,27,	3 100
14:9,	4 90	3:16,	5 76	2:12,	5 78	2:6,7,	3 133
14:10,	2 131	4:4,	5 80	2:14—16,	4 138	2:14,15,	4 154
14:17,	5 5	4:5,	5 100	2:14,16,19,	3 123	2:19,	3 42
14:19,	2 14	4:8,	3 83	2:18,	1 50	3:1,	2 7
14:19,	3 28	4:18,	2 63	3:16—19,	3 103	3:2—4,	3 105
15:4,	3 32	5:5,	3 47	3:18,19,	4 89	3:5,	2 122
15:4,	4 60	5:9,	1 25	3:20,	3 107	3:12,	3 99

GUIDE TO PRAYER.

3 : 13,	5	53	2 : 3,	3	38	4 : 14,	1	76	1 : 23, 24,	2	77
3 : 13,	3	76	2 : 15,	5	100	4 : 16,	3	14	1 : 27,	5	5
3 : 13,	4	136	2 : 19,	5	26	4 : 16,	1	72	2 : 5,	5	106
3 : 15,	3	63	2 : 19,	2	54	5 : 1, 2, 9,	4	91	2 : 6,	2	24
3 : 16,	3	21	2 : 24, 25,	5	50	5 : 12,	2	99	2 : 7,	2	87
3 : 23,	3	89	2 : 25, 26,	5	84	6 : 11,	3	100	3 : 2,	2	66
4 : 2,	1	21	3 : 2,	3	77	6 : 12,	4	100	3 : 2,	3	137
4 : 6,	3	35	3 : 4,	2	86	6 : 17, 18,	4	132	3 : 15, 17,	3	143
			3 : 14,	5	38	6 : 19, 20,	3	92	4 : 7,	3	65
I THESSALON'S.			3 : 16,	4	24	6 : 20,	4	18	4 : 17,	2	38
1 : 2, 5,	4	30	3 : 17,	5	59	7 : 25,	4	56	5 : 5,	2	67
1 : 9,	4	62	3 : 17,	3	70	7 : 25,	1	76	5 : 16,	2	119
2 : 2,	4	62	4 : 18,	3	45	7 : 26,	4	52			
4 : 6,	2	96				8 : 1,	4	55	**I PETER.**		
4 : 9, 10,	3	28	**TITUS**			8 : 6,	4	59	1 : 3,	3	92
4 : 14,	4	22	1 : 1,	5	84	8 : 10,	3	8	1 : 4,	4	145
4 : 17 18,	3	108	1 : 2,	4	102	8 : 11,	3	19	1 : 6—9,	4	108
5 : 10,	4	90	1 : 5,	5	72	9 : 10,	5	5	1 : 8,	3	74
5 : 16,	3	39	1 : 13,	5	50	9 : 12, 14, 26,	4	122	1 : 10—12,	4	84
5 : 22,	3	27	1 : 15,	2	52	9 : 14,	3	12	1 : 14,	3	72
5 : 23, 24,	3	128	1 : 16,	2	88	9 : 24,	4	18	1 : 21,	1	85
			2 : 1,	5	50	10 : 5, 6, 7	4	10	1 : 22,	3	136
II THESSALON'S.			2 : 6,	5	56	10 : 19,	1	77	2 : 3,	3	13
1 : 7, 8, 10,	4	21	2 : 7,	5	59	10 : 24,	2	70	2 : 5,	1	55
1 : 11,	3	150	2 : 10,	3	91	11 : 2,	4	100	2 : 7,	3	74
2 : 2 3 8 10 11	5	27	2 : 11—14,	3	36	11 : 2, 4, 39,	4	48	2 : 11,	2	86
2 : 13,	4	46	3 : 2, 3,	3	94	11 : 6,	1	31	2 : 14,	5	36
2 : 16, 17,	3	142	3 : 3,	2	17	11 : 10,	3	108	2 : 15,	3	91
3 : 1,	5	132	3 : 4, 5,	4	9	11 : 10, 16,	4	64	2 : 17,	3	86
						11 : 26, 27,	3	96	2 : 17,	5	111
I TIMOTHY.			**PHILEMON.**			12 : 1,	4	100	2 : 21—23	4	52
1 : 15,	4	149	1 : 25,	5	52	12 : 3, 4,	5	32	2 : 25,	5	113
1 : 17,	1	7				12 : 9,	1	70	3 : 4,	5	5
2 : 1,	5	129	**HEBREWS.**			12 : 10, 11,	4	34	3 : 5,	3	30
2 : 2,	5	102	1 : 1,	4	119	12 : 11,	5	28	3 : 7,	3	41
2 : 3, 4,	5	145	1 : 2,	4	15	12 : 18, 19, 24,	3	54	3 : 22,	4	55
3 : 15,	5	100	1 : 3,	1	84	12 : 22, 23,	1	44	4 : 1,	4	52
4 : 2,	4	103	1 : 3, 6,	1	46	12 : 29,	2	81	5 : 5,	3	30
4 : 8,	3	48	1 : 12,	1	81	13 : 3,	5	87	5 : 6,	2	104
4 : 12,	5	51	1 : 14,	4	75	13 : 5,	3	11	5 : 7,	3	48
4 : 13, 15, 16,	5	20	2 : 1,	3	123	13 : 5,	3	31	5 : 9,	3	65
6 : 6,	3	31	2 : 4,	4	94	13 : 5,	2	41			
6 : 9,	2	17	2 : 7, 8, 9,	4	20	13 : 8,	1	35	**II PETER.**		
6 : 10,	2	115	2 : 9, 14,	4	17	13 : 14,	4	64	1 : 4,	5	37
6 : 15, 16,	1	79	2 : 11, 14,			13 : 15,	4	36	1 : 4,	3	51
6 : 17,	4	42	16, 17,	4	85	**JAMES.**			1 : 4,	4	59
6 : 17,	2	68	3 : 12,	2	113	1 : 4,	3	93	1 : 19,	4	60
6 : 17, 19,	5	105	3 : 13,	2	19	1 : 5,	3	37	1 : 21,	4	84
			4 : 2,	3	73	1 : 12,	4	29	2 : 4,	4	81
II TIMOTHY.			4 : 9,	4	97	1 : 14,	2	19	2 : 10,	2	50
1 : 3, 4,	5	125	4 : 12,	1	9	1 : 17,	1	58	2 : 22,	2	125
1 : 12,	5	37	4 : 13,	1	6	1 : 17,	5	101	3 : 9,	2	30

GUIDE TO PRAYER. 165

3 : 13, 14,	4	93	3 : 20,	2	92	1 : 5, 6,	4 155	8 : 4,	1	56
3 : 15,	2	90	4 : 9,	4	51	1 : 8,	1 111	11 : 15,	5	135
3 : 18,	3	42	4 : 10,	4	17	1 : 9,	4 101	11 : 17,	1	131
			4 : 16,	1	30	1 : 11, 12,	5 82	12 : 10,	4	98
I JOHN.			4 : 17,	4	52	1 : 18,	4 54	12 : 11,	4	135
1 : 5,	1	30	5 : 7,	1	135	2 : 1,	5 82	13 : 8,	4	12
1 : 7,	4	28	5 : 13,	4	102	2 : 4,	2 72	13 : 10,	5	70
1 : 8, 9,	2	61	5 : 19,	5	80	2 : 4, 5,	5 66	13 : 11, 12, 13.	5	17
2 : 1,	4	56				2 : 11,	3 2	14 : 7,	1	45
2 : 1, 2,	3	134	III JOHN.			2 : 21,	2 79	17 : 13,	5	41
2 : 2,	4	17	1 : 2,	5	109	3 : 2,	2 15	18 : 2, 21,	5	41
2 : 14,	5	56	JUDE.			4 : 8,	1 2	19 : 1, 5,	1	69
2 : 15,	3	98	1 : 3,	5	14	4 : 8,	4 109	19 : 6,	1	107
3 : 2,	3	105	1 : 20, 21,	3	132	4 : 11,	1 17	19 : 16,	4	57
3 : 4,	2	16	1 : 24,	3	45	5 : 6,	4 19	21 : 3,	4	61
3 : 8,	4	50				5 : 9, 12,	4 154	21 : 24,	5	41
3 : 17,	2	86	REVELATION.			6 : 2,	4 98	22 : 20,	4	93

INDEX TO SCRIPTURE LESSONS.

GENESIS.		JUDGES.		2		8	JEREMIAH.	
1	58	2		82	37		3 5	141
3	80				PROVERBS.		9 : 1—16,	10
8	68	I SAMUEL.		2		111	19	145
12	53	3		95	8		1 23 : 5—22,	34
22 : 1—19,		26	13 : 5—23,	85			26	148
32 : 9—32,		97	28 : 7—25,	106	ECCLESIASTES.		28	51
42 : 1—24,		17			1		112 35	73
		II SAMUEL.					36	152
EXODUS.		6 : 1—19,		78	ISAIAH.			
3 : 1—18,		41	17 : 1—24,	56	5 : 1—19,		115	LAMENTATIONS.
16 : 1—21,		61			8		5	2 : 1—19, 13
20	75	I KINGS.			11		119	
32 : 15—35,	87	6 : 1—22,		45	14 : 1—20,		76	EZEKIEL.
		8 : 1—21,		37	22 : 1—19,		120	2 12
LEVITICUS.		19		21	25		89	10 49
25 : 1—24,	65				33		122	17 : 1—21, 19
		II KINGS.			35		93	33 : 1—16, 25
NUMBERS.		5 : 1—19,		91	41		126	37 : 1—19, 39
16 : 12—35,	72	20 : 1—19,		101	51		104	43 : 1—12, 36
24	47				52		130	
		II CHRONICLES.			53		6	DANIEL.
DEUTERONOMY.		35 : 1—19,		99	59		107	3 : 1—18, 23
6	83				59		134	5 : 1—16, 28
		EZRA.			63		30	12 32
JOSHUA.		3		15	65		137	
7 : 10—26,	102	JOB.						HOSEA.

10		43	7 : 11---30,	125	5 : 1----17,	114	139
			8 : 4---18,	107	6	49	
AMOS.			10 : 17---42,	135	9 : 1----22,	37	I TIMOTHY.
5		55	11 : 1---26,	86	13 : 16 ----41,	116	1 7
			14 : 1---24,	72	18 : 16 ---- 34,	118	4 140
MICAH.			15 : 11---32,	46	21 : 17 ----39,	25	
7		79	16 : 19---31,	93	25	120	II TIMOTHY.
ZEPHANIAH.			17 : 1---19,	62	26 : 1 ----29,	2 3	141
2		68	18	138			
			18 : 18---43,	101	ROMANS.		HEBREWS.
ZECHARIAH.			23 : 1---33.	152	2	124	4 143
12		63			8 : 1 ----17,	126	9 : 11 ----28, 14
			JOHN.		8 : 1 ----25,	98	11 144
MALACHI.			1 : 1---28,	116	12	59	
3		60	2 : 1---11,	103	13	40	JAMES.
			3 : 1---21,	117			1 29
MATTHEW.			3 : 14---36,	27	I CORINTHIANS.		
2		113	5 : 1---16,	121	2	128	I PETER.
3		24	5 : 1---24,	50	9 : 11 ----27,	52	2 60
4		54	6 : 1---21,	57	13	11	4 33
6 : 1--23,		123	6 : 1-- 41,	127			5 13
8 : 1--13,		83	8 : 1--30,	133	II CORINTHIANS.		5 146
10 : 1--24,		90	8 : 33--59,	74	1	130	
13 : 24--43,		100	9 : 1---38,	66	4	136	II PETER.
15 : 21--39,		108	10	136	6	57	3 148
17		131	10 : 1---30,	88	9	133	
20 : 1---16,		38	12 : 1---36,	142	11 : 12 ----33,	4	I JOHN.
23		143	13 : 1---26,	42		3	9
24 : 23---42,		69	14	35	EPHESIANS.	4	77
25 : 1---30,		146	15	96	1	135	5 22
26 : 26---46,		149	15	147	5 : 6 ----33,	20	II JOHN.
27 : 1---37,		150	16 : 1---20,	92	6	137	1 150
27 : 24---54,		105	20 : 1---18,	84			JUDE.
			20 : 19---31,	79	PHILIPPIANS.	1	151
MARK.			21	154	2	16	
7 : 1---23,		129					REVELATION.
16		75	ACTS.		COLOSSIANS.	3	153
			1	11	2	18	4 6
LUKE.			2 : 1--22	112	3	44	8 55
2 : 39---52,		31	2 : 14---36,	81			22 155
4 : 16---32,		119	4 : 32 ---- 5 : 11, 64		II THESSALON'S.		

INDEX TO SUBJECTS.

In this Index the figure before the page number refers to the general division of the prayer under which the text is used, i. e., 1. Address to God; 2. Confess sin; 3. Ask for blessings; 4. Thank for mercies; 5. Intercede for others. The figure in brackets after the page number shows how often the subject appears on the page.

Above other beings, God, see.
Absolutely unequaled, God, see.
Accept invitation, 3 117.
Accept services, 1 25, 1 53, 1 92.
Accusing, sin self, see
Adoption, 3 62.
Advance of the gospel, 4 26, 4 62, 4 98.
Advent, second, see.
Affections misplaced, 2 7, 2 36. See misplaced.
Afflicted, 5 23, 5 42, 5 107. Heard, 5 145.
Affliction, aid in, see.
Afflictive sin, 2 127.
Aged christian, 5 22. 5 55, 5 104.
Aid in affliction, 4 34, 4 70, 4 108, 4 129, 4 149.
  Divine, see.
  In prayer, see.
All men, 5 78. 5 80, 5 111, 5 120, 5 129, 5 135, 5 142, 5 145.
  Saints, 5, 154.
Anger, 2 11, 2 119.
Answer to prayer, 4 33, 4 69, 4 107, 4 130, 4 139.
Apostasy, heal, see,
Appointment of a Redeemer, 4 118, 4 147.
Ascension, Christ's, see.
  Our Lord's, see.
Asking prayers of God's people, 5 149, 5 151.
Assurance of faith, 5 37.

Being, man a rational, see.
  Recognized, God, see.
Beings, God above other, see.
Benefactor, God, see.
Benefits, 4 112.
Blessing, divine, see,
  Fatherly, see.
Blessings, grant promised, see.
  Promised, grant, see.
  Promised, see.
  Spiritual, see.
  Temporal, see.
  To land, 4 43, 4 79.
Blest, land, see.
Bodies, present, see.
Bounties, God's, see.
Brotherly love, 3 28, 3 76, 3 136.
Burden of guilt, 2 148, 2 153, 2 154, 2 155.
Calamity, preserve from, see.
Captive sinners, 5 128.
Care, preserving, see,
  God's preserving, see.
Carnal security, 2 12, 2 42, 2 68.
Cast off, not to be, see.
Cheerfulness, 3 87, 3 149.
Chief magistrate, 5 62, 5 97, 5 99.
Children, 5 125, 5 133, 5 143, 5 150.
Christ's ascension, 4 18 4 91, 4 126, 4 132.
  Doctrine, 4 15.
  Encouraged to seek (Saviour), see.
  Exaltation, 4 20, 4 57, 4

92, 4 124. 4 127.
Holy life, 4 52.
Incarnation, 4 13.
Intercession, 4 19, 4 56, 4 91.
Love to, see.
Reliance upon, see.
Resurrection, 4 18, 4 90, 4 116, 4 125.
Righteousness, 3 16, 3 54.
  " plead, see.
  " reliance on, see.
Satisfying the law, 4 16, 4 54, 4 89, 4 114, 4 122, 4 138, 4 153 [2], 4 154, 4 155.
Work, owned, 4 86, 4 147.
  " owning, see.
Christian, aged, see.
Christian fellowship, 3 40.
Christianity, preservation of, see.
Church favored, O. T., see.
  In distant parts, 5 2.
  In ends of world, 5 75.
  O. T. favored, see.
  Revival of, see.
  Reviving, see.
  Universal, 5 3, 5 26, 5 40. 5 140.
  Universal, see.
Church's, defeat enemies, see.
Enemies, defeat, see.
Civil rulers, godly, see.
Cleansing, 3 113, 3 154.
Common people, 5 57.
Communion, 4 141.
Communion of saints, 4 28,

4 64, 4 101.
Condemnation, 2 89, 2 105.
 2 106, 2 128, 2 140, 2 143.
Seal, see.
Under, see.
Condemned, 2 109.
 Justly, see.
 Self, see.
Confess, exhortation to unheeded, see.
 Slow to, see.
Confession, humble, see.
 Mercy sought through, see.
 Neglected, 2 149.
 Open, see.
Confidence, God, see.
 In God, see.
Conflict, victory in, see.
Conscience, peace of, see.
 Tender, see.
Conscientiousness, 3 144.
Contentment, 3 30, 3 140.
Continuance of godly rule, 5 17, 5 61.
 Of gospel, 5 92.
  " in the land, 5 12, 5 30, 5 66.
 Of peace, 5 92.
  " in the land, 5 12, 5 65.
Continued, godly rule, see.
Contrition, lack of, see.
Conversion, 3 95.
 Of unbelievers, 5 5, 5 73, 5 81, 5 113, 5 117, 5 128.
Converting grace, 3 8, 3 17, 3 58, 3 116.
Corrupt nature, 2 7, 2 38, 2 64, 2 136.
Corruption of nature, 2 33.
Country, 5 120.
Country's peace, plenty and righteousness, 5 44.
 Plenty, 5 48.
Courage, 3 38, 3 88, 3 147.
Covenant of grace, 4 23, 4 59, 4 95, 4 129, 4 132.
Covetousness, 2 41, 2 115, 2 117.
Creation, man's wonderful, see.

Creator, God, see.
Creature, man made rational, see.
Damage of sin, 2 21, 2 142.
Danger, ignored, see.
 Of sin, 2 52, 2 75.
Decay, spiritual, see.
Deceitfulness of sin, 2 19, 2 50, 2 73.
Deed, word and, see.
Defeat church's enemies, 5 6, 5 27, 5 41, 5 71, 5 86, 5 126, 5 137, 5 142.
Defiled, 2 60.
Defilement, 2 108, 2 126.
Degeneracy through original sin, 2 62.
Degradation, sin's, see.
Deliver from persecution, 5 7, 5 28, 5 70, 5 115, 5 117, 5 121, 5 135, 5 146.
Deliverance from sin, 3 14, 3 15, 3 64, 3 121.
 From sickness, 4 76.
 In peril, 4 41.
Denial, self, see.
Deplorableness of sin, 2 76.
Depravity, 2 5, 2 34, 2 63, 2 82, 2 93, 2 107.
Desired, God, see.
 " to be, see.
Despising God's longsuffering, 2 90.
Diligence, 3 38, 3 89, 3 102, 3 147.
Direction in duty, 3 71, 3 127.
Disobedience, 2 85, 2 127.
Disobedient, 2 39.
Distant parts, church in, see.
Divine aid, 3 6, 3 14, 3 63.
 Blessing, 3 10.
 Enlightenment, 3 69.
 Favor, 3 9, 3 59, 3 118.
 " seek, see.
 Goodness, 3 131.
 Guidance, 4 77.
 Panoply, 5 79.
 Patience, tried, see.
 Presence, 3 11, 3 129.
 Punishment, stay of, see.
 Divisions, heal, see.

Doctrine, Christ's, see.
Duty, direction in, see.
 Wisdom to do, see.
Dying grace, 3 46, 3 81, 3 104, 3 139, 3 149.
Earliest days, salvation in, see.
Early indications of grace, 4 11.
 " of mercy, 4 83.
Encouraged to pray, 3 51.
 To seek Christ, 4 88.
 " Saviour, 4 15.
Encouragement, 3 130.
 To seek Christ, 4 53.
Ends of the world, church in, see.
Enemies, 5 23, 5 39, 5 53, 5 106.
 Defeat church's, see.
 Victory over, see.
 " " external, see.
Enlightening grace, 3 131.
Enlightenment, divine, see.
Eternal, immutable, invisible, God, see.
Eternal life, hope of see.
Eternity, God, see.
Everywhere, saints, see.
Evil passions, 2 122.
Exaltation, Christ's, see.
Examples, helpful, see.
Exhortation to confess unheeded, 2 113.
External enemies, victory over, see.
Faith, 3 24, 3 73, 3 96, 3 133, 3 153.
 Assurance of see.
Faithful, God, see.
 To oath, God, see.
Faithfulness, God, see.
False security, warned of, see.
Family, 5 112, 5 115, 5 118.
Fatherly blessing, 3 60.
Faults, hiding, see.
 Secret, see.
Favor, 3 57.
 Divine see.
 Seek divine, see.
 Under punishment, 5 130.

Favored, O. T. church, see.
Favors to O. T. church, 4 146.
Fear God, 3 25, 3 73.
  Of the Lord, 3 97.
Fellowship, christian, see.
Fit for heaven, 3 47, 3 80, 3 105, 3 108, 3 142.
Folly of sin, 2 17, 2 49, 2 72, 2 134.
Forbearance, God's, see.
Forgetfulness of God, 2 35.
Forgiveness, pardon and, see.
For own and other nations, 5 69.
Forsaken God's paths, 2 111.
Friends, 5 109.
Fulfill promises, 3 51.
Fulfilled, promises, see.
Fulfillment of God's promises. 4 71.
Glorified, God, see.
Glory, God, see.
God, above other beings, 1 60, 1 80.
  Aid in prayer, 1 25, 1 54, 1 75, 1 93.
  As our God, 1 20, 1 49, 1 71, 1 87, 1 100.
  Being recognized, 1 31.
  Benefactor, 1 98.
  Bounties, 4 7, 4 134.
  Confidence. 1 24, 1 52, 1 74, 1 91.
  Creator, 1 19, 1 45, 1 47, 1 68, 1 70, 1 86, 1 99, 1 114, 1 134, 1 138.
  Desired, 1 23, 1 51, 1 73, 1 90, 1 101.
  Eternal, immortal, invisible, 1 7.
  Eternity, 1 35, 1 111, 1 115, 1 122, 1 126, 1 136, 1 143, 1 148, 1 149.
  Faithful, 1 75.
  Faithfulness, 1 137.
  Faithful to oath, 1 154.
  Fear, 3 25, 3 73.
  Forbearance, 3 3.
  Forgetfulness of, see.
  Glorified, 1 26.
  Glory, 1 3, 1 16, 1 17, 1 44, 1 55.
  Goodness, 4 2, 4 3, 4 4, 1 14, 4 37, 4 38, 1 42, 1 67, 4 73, 4 74, 1 83, 1 121, 4 123, 1 130, 4 134, 4 139, 4 143, 4 144, 4 148, 4 151 [2].
  Greatness, 1 128.
  Holiness, 1 2, 1 13, 1 40, 1 83, 1 123, 1 152.
  Hope in, see.
  Immortal, 1 7.
  Immutability, 1 61.
  Immutable, 1 58, 1 81, 1 126.
  Incomprehensible, 1 5, 1 15, 1 32, 1 43, 1 59.
  Invisible, 1 7, 1 148.
  Irresistible, 1 143.
  Justice, 1 13, 1 41, 1 127.
  Knowledge, 1 139, 1 142.
  Knows heart, 1 146.
  Longsuffering, 1 116, 1 155.
  " despising, see.
  Love to, see.
  Lovingkindness, 4 72.
  Matchless perfections, 1 6, 1 60, 1 119.
  Mercy, 3 129, 1 141, 1 153.
  Mitigation of wrath, 1 150.
  Omnipotence, 1 131.
  Omnipresence, 1 8, 1 36, 1 37, 1 62, 1 113, 1 116.
  Omniscience, 1 6, 1 9, 1 63, 1 97, 1 108, 1 137, 1 141, 1 150, 1 152.
  Only potentate, 1 79.
  Owning Christ's work, 1 14.
  Paths, forsaken, see.
  Patience, tried, see.
   " trying, see.
  Peace of, see.
  Perfection, 1 30.
  Perfections matchless, 1 33.
  Power, 1 12, 1 39, 1 66, 1 93, 1 117, 1 124 1 151.
  Prayed to, 1 21, 1 49, 1 72, 1 88, 1 101, 1 105.
  Prayer hearer, 1 125.
  Preserver, 1 84, 1 104, 1 107, 1 112, 1 118, 1 120, 1 129, 1 133, 1 135, 1 140.
  Preserving care, 4 6, 4 75, 4 131.
  Promises, fulfillment of, see.
   " performance of, see.
  Revealed in works, 1 4.
  Righteous, 1 66.
  Ruler, 1 103, 1 106, 1 107.
  Sovereignty, 1 11, 1 38, 1 65.
  Supreme, 1 34.
  Sustaining power, 3 83, 3 119.
  To be desired, 1 29.
  To be worshiped, 1 28, 1 95, 1 112, 1 132, 1 133.
  Trinity, 1 18, 1 46, 1 69, 1 135.
  True God, 1 57, 1 78.
  Unchangeable, 1 144.
  Unequaled absolutely, 1 119.
  Unequaled by idols, 1 147.
  Unequaled by men, 1 120.
  Wisdom, 1 10, 1 3 37 [2], 1 64, 1 146.
  Wisdom unsearchable, 1 82.
  Worshiped, 1 56, 1 77, 1 102.
  Wrath, 1 130.
Godly civil rulers, 5 16.
Godly rule, continuance of, see.
Godly rule continued, 5 34.
God's children, welfare of, see.
God's people, asking prayers of, see.
  Goodness, 4 115, 4 117, 4 120.
  Divine, see.
  God's, see.
Gospel, advance of, see.
  Continuance of, see.
  " in land, see.
  Propagation of, see.
Govern tongue, 3 34, 3 35, 3 96, 3 137.

Grace, 3 42, 3 84, 3 146.
  Converting, see.
  Covenant of, see.
  Dying, see.
  Early indications of, see.
  Enlightening, see.
  Instructing, see.
  Perfecting, see.
  Preserving, see.
  Redeeming, see.
  Remembering, see.
  Renewing, see.
  Sanctifying, see.
  Sustaining, see.
  To help, 3 36, 3 66.
Grant promised blessings, 3 77.
Greatness, God, see.
Guidance, divine, see.
Guide of life, 5 38.
Guilt, burden of, see.
Heal apostasy, 5 75.
  Divisions, 5 14, 5 33, 5 46, 5 64, 5 94, 5 137.
  Hear others' prayers, 5 138.
  Refusal to, see.
Heard, afflicted, see.
Hearer, prayer God, see.
Heart, God knows, see.
  Sinful, see.
Heathen, 5 24.
Heaven, fit for, see.
Help, grace to, see.
  In prayer, Spirit's, see.
Helpful examples, 4 27, 4 63, 4 100, 4 135.
Hiding faults, 2 119.
Holiness, God, see.
Holy life, Christ's, see.
Holy Spirit, 4 22, 4 59, 1 85, 4 94.
Hope, 3 32, 3 92, 3 100, 3 141.
  In God, 3 111.
  Of eternal life, 4 29, 4 64, 4 102, 4 145.
Humble confession, 2 151.
  For nat onal sins, 5 10.
Humiliated by sin, 2 132.
Humiliation for national sins, 5 68, 5 90.
  Of sin, 2 2.

Humility, 3 30, 3 94, 3 99, 3 139.
Hypocrisy, 2 88, 2 105.
Idols, unequal to God, see.
Ignorance, sinful, see.
Ignored, danger, 2 81.
Immortal, eternal, invisible, God, see.
Immutable, God, see.
Impatience, 2 43, 2 69.
Improvidence, 2 95.
Incarnation, 4 50, 4 85, 4 120, 4 142, 4 149, 4 152.
  Christ's, see.
Incomprehensible, God, see.
Inconsistency, 2 24.
In profession, 2 54.
Indications of mercy, early, see.
Ingratitude, 2 13, 2 25, 2 55, 2 76.
Instructing grace, 3 19, 3 20, 3 68, 3 117.
Integrity, 3 90, 3 101.
Intercession of Christ, 4 56.
  Christ's see.
Invisible, eternal immortal, God, see.
Invitation, accept, see.
Irresistible, God, see.
Jews, 5 76, 5 81.
Joyousness, 3 39.
Judges, 5 19, 5 35, 5 59, 5 99.
Justice, God, see.
Justification, 3 53.
Justly condemned, 2 100.
Knowledge, God, see.
Knows heart, God, see.
Lack of contrition, 2 32.
  Of repentance, 2 98, 2 102, 2 104.
Land, blessings to, see.
  Blest, 4 8.
Continuance of gospel in, see.
  Of peace in, see.
  Our, see.
  Our own, see.
  Peace in, see.
Law, Christ satisfying see.
Life, Christ's holy, see.

Guide of, see.
Hope of eternal, see.
Longsuffering, despising God's, see.
God's, see.
Lord, fear of the, see.
Lord's, our, resurrection, (Christ's), see.
Love, brotherly, see.
Lovingkindness, God's, see.
Love to Christ, 3 74.
  To God, 3 26, 3 98, 3 134.
Magistrate, chief, see.
Man a rational being, 4 73.
Made a rational creature, 4 39.
Wonderful creation, 4 5.
Matchless perfections, God, see.
Men, all, see.
  God unequaled by, see.
  Mercies, national, see.
  Spiritual, see.
Mercy, 3 53, 3 56, 3 113.
  Early indications of, see.
  God's, see.
  " wicked asking, see.
  Sought through confession, 2 152.
  Wonderful works of, see.
Ministry, 5 20, 5 36, 5 47, 5 50, 5 51, 5 52, 5 59, 5 100, 5 147.
  Preservation of, see.
Miracles, 4 87.
Misplaced affections, 2 37, 2 63, 2 144.
  Affections, see.
Mitigation of wrath, God, see.
Mohammedans, 5 82.
National mercies, 5 11, 5 67, 5 91.
Peace and righteousness, 5 31.
Sins, humble for, see.
  " humility for, see.
  " humiliation for, see.
Nations, 5 8, 5 132.
  For own and other, see.
  Other, see.
Nature, corrupt, see.

GUIDE TO PRAYER. 171

Need of repentance, 2 91.
Needs, supply, see.
Neglect, 2 102.
Neglected confession, see.
Not be cast off, 5 139.
Oath, faithful to, God, see.
Offense of sin, 2 20, 2 51, 2 74, 2 146.
Offensiveness of sin, 2 139.
Omissions, 2 96.
Omnipotence, God, see.
Omnipresence, God, see.
Omniscience, God, see.
Only potentate, God, see.
Open confession, 2 124.
Ordinances, 4 25, 4 82, 4 61, 4 68, 4 97, 4 106, 4 137.
Original sin, 2 4, 2 121.
 Degeneracy through, see.
O. T. church favored, 4 12, 4 49, 4 84, 4 119.
 Favors to, see.
Other beings, God above, see.
Other nations, 5 88.
Our land, 5 9.
Our Lord's ascension, 4 55.
 Resurrection, 4 54.
Our own land, 5 29.
Our unworthiness, 1 22.
Own land, 5 43, 5 68, 5 89.
Owned, Christ's work, see.
Owning Christ's work, 4 51. 4 121.
 God's, see.
Panoply, divine, see.
Pardon, 3 5, 3 7, 3 55, 3 57, 3 153.
 And forgiveness, 3 2.
 Public, see.
 Sense of, see.
Passions, evil, see.
Paths, God's forsaken, see.
Patience, 3 93.
 Divine, tried, see.
 Trying God's, see.
Peace and righteousness, national, see.
 Country's, see.
 In land, 5 108.
  " continuance of, see.

Of conscience, 3 13, 3 63.
Of God, 3 120.
Plenty and righteousness, country's, see.
People, common, see.
Asking prayers of God's, see.
Perfecting grace, 3 145.
Perfection, God, see.
 Matchless, see.
Performance of God's promises, 4 35.
Peril, deliverance in, see.
Persecuted, 5 87.
Persecution, deliver from, see.
Perverseness, 2 26, 2 56, 2 77, 2 83, 2 93, 2 112, 2 116, 2 121, 2 141.
Plead Christ's righteousness, 3 134.
Promises, 2 3.
Plenty, country's, see.
 Peace and righteousness, country's, see.
Polluted, 2 31.
Poor, 5 54, 5 106.
Potentate, God only, see.
Power, God, see.
 Sustaining, see.
Praise, spirit of, see.
Pray, encouraged to, see.
Prayed to, God, see.
Prayer, aid in, God, see.
 Answer to, see.
 Hearer, God, see.
 Spirit of, see.
 Spirit's help in, see.
Prayers, hear others', see.
 Of God's people, asking, see.
 Servants sought, 5 152.
Predestination, 4 46, 4 80.
Presence, divine, see.
Present bodies, 1 1.
Preservation of Christianity, 4 99.
 Of ministry, 5 153.
Preserve from calamity, 3 49, 3 79, 3 106.
 From sin, 3 33, 3 91, 3 138, 3 153.

Preserver, God, see.
Preserving care, 4 40.
 God's, see.
Grace, 4 31, 3 45, 3 67, 3 82, 3 104, 4 106, 3 132, 4 136, 4 140.
Presumptuous sin, 2 48.
Pride, 2 10, 2 67.
Prisoners, 5 131.
Profession, inconsistency in, see.
Promised blessings, 3 107.
 Grant, see.
Promises, fulfill, see.
 Fulfillment of God's, see.
 Fulfilled, 4 109.
 Performance of God's, see.
 Also, fulfilled, see.
Plead, see.
Propagation of gospel, 5 2, 5 25, 5 77, 5 81, 5 116, 5 124, 5 144.
Prosperity, temporal, see.
Provided, Redeemer, see.
Public pardon, 5 122, 5 124.
 Sins, 2 136, 2 137.
Punishment, divine, stay of, see.
 Favor under, see.
Quarrelsome, 2 70.
Rational creature, man made, see.
 Being, man a, see.
Realized, sin, see.
Recognizing sinfulness, 2 150.
Reconciliation, 3 7, 3 123.
 Sense of, see.
Redeemer, appointment of, see.
 Provided, 4 47, 4 82.
Redeeming grace, 3 119.
Redemption, 4 10.
Refusal to hear, 2 139.
 To repent, 2 123.
Regeneration, 4 30, 4 66, 4 104, 4 115, 4 136.
Reliance on Christ, 1 27, 1 55, 1 76.
 Christ's righteousness, 3 4.
 On the Saviour, 1 93.
Remembering grace, 3 21,

3 70, 3 123.
Remission of sins, 4 31, 4 67, 4 105.
Remorse, 2 148.
Renewing grace, 3 67.
Repent, refusal to, see.
Repentance, lack of, see.
Need of, see.
Resignation, 3 31.
Resist temptation, 3 65, 3 121.
Restrain from unpardonable sin, 5 152.
Resurrection, Christ's, see. Our Lord's, see.
Revealed in works, God, see.
Reviving church, 5 5, 5 72, 5 85, 5 140.
Rich, 5 55, 5 105.
Righteousness and peace, national, see.
Christ's, see.
Country's, see.
Plead Christ's, see.
Reliance on Christ's, see.
Rule, continuance of godly, see.
Ruler, God, see.
Rulers, 5 102.
Godly civil, see.
Wisdom to, see.
Saints, 5 136, 5 148.
All, see.
Communion of, see.
Everywhere, 5 154, 5 155.
Salvation in earliest days, 4 48.
Sanctification, 3 23, 3 61, 3 72, 3 128.
Sanctifying grace, 3 150.
Satisfying the law, Christ's, see.
Saviour, encouraged to seek, see.
Reliance on, see.
Schools, 5 58, 5 101.
Scriptures, 4 24, 4 60, 4 96, 4 133.
Second advent, 4 21, 4 58, 4 93, 4 128.
Secret faults, 2 133.
Sins, 2 22.

Security, carnal, see.
Warned of false, see.
Seek Christ, encouraged to, see. Also Saviour.
Divine favor, 5 149.
Self-condemnation, 2 29, 2 78, 2 140.
Denial, 3 29, 3 77, 3 136.
Trusting in, see.
Sense of pardon, 3 115.
Of reconciliation, 3 12.
Sensuality, 2 67, 2 86, 2 150.
Servants, of God, prayers sought, see.
Services, accept, see.
Shamefulness of sin, 2 114.
Show sinfulness, 3 125.
Sickness, deliverance from, see.
Sin, afflictive, see.
Damage of, see.
Danger of, see.
Deceitfulness of, see.
Degradation of, 2 134.
Deliverance from, see.
Deplorableness of, see.
Folly of, see.
Humiliation of, see.
Offense of, see.
Original, see.
" degeneracy from, see.
Preserve from, see.
Presumptuous, see.
Realized, 2 146.
Self-accusing, 2 1.
Shamefulness of, see.
Sinfulness of, 2 16.
Undone by, see.
Unprofitableness of, see.
Willfulness of, see.
Sins, humility for national, see.
Of tongue, 2 14, 2 71, 2 130.
Public, see.
Remission of, see.
Secret, see.
Sinful heart, 2 6.
Ignorance, 2 92.
Sinfulness, recognizing, see.
Show, see.

Sinners, captive, see.
Sincerity, 3 144.
Sloth, spiritual, see.
Slothfulness, 2 46.
Slow to confess, 2 60.
Sought, prayers of God's servants, see.
Sovereignty, God, see.
Spirit, Holy, see.
Of praise, 4 1, 4 36, 4 113, 4 144.
Of prayer, 3 1.
Spirit's help in prayer, 3 112.
Spiritual blessings, 4 45, 4 80, 4 81, 4 124, 4 150.
Decay, 2 15, 2 88, 2 113.
Mercies, 4 9, 4 65, 4 103.
Sloth, 2 72, 2 116, 2 120.
Stay of divine punishment, 5 130.
Steadfastness, 3 109, 3 126.
Stubbornness, 2 27, 2 56, 2 138, 2 145.
Submission, 3 42, 3 85, 3 86, 3 103, 3 148.
Suppliants, unworthy, see.
Supply needs, 3 50, 3 79. 3 141. 3 150, 3 151, 3 152.
Supppressed, wickedness, see.
Supreme, God, see.
Sustaining grace, 3 18. 4 68, 3 114.
Power. 3 43. God's, see.
Temporal blessings. 4 8. 4 43, 3 48. 4 78, 4 117.
Prosperity, 4 142.
Temptation, resist, see.
Tender conscience, 3 27. 3 75. 3 135.
Tongue, 2 45. Govern, see.
Sins of, see.
Treachery, 2 28. 2 125. 2 131, 2 141. 2 143, 2 147.
Trespass, willful.
Tried divine patience. 2 58.
God's, 2 29.
Trinity. God. see.
True God. God, see.
Trusting in self. 2 40.
Trying God's patience, 2 79.

2 97, 2 101.
Unbelief, 2 99.
Unbelievers, conversion of, see.
Uncharitableness. 2 14, 2 44, 2 86, 2 131.
Under condemnation, 2 57.
Undone by sin, 2 153.
Unequaled absolutely, God. Also by men. Idols, see.
Unfaithfulness. 2 8, 2 38, 2 65, 2 84, 2 135.
Unheeded, exhortation to confess, see.
Universal church. 5 74, 5 83, 5 132, 5 134, 5 148. Church, see.
Unprofitableness of sin. 2 18, 2 49.
Unpardonable sin, restrain from, see.
Unrepentant. 2 30, 2 59, 2

80.
Unsearchable, wisdom. God. see.
Unworthiness. 2 9, 1 50.
Our, see.
Unworthy suppliants, 1 72, 1 89, 1 145.
Victory in conflict, 5 114.
Over enemies, 5 15.
External. 5 63, 5 95, 5 119.
Warned of false security, 4 42.
Welfare of God's children, 5 125.
Wickedness suppressed, 5 13, 5 32, 5 45, 5 49 5, 65, 5 93.
Wicked asking God's mercy, 5 141.
Willfulness, 3 23.
Of sin, 2 53.

Willful trespass, 2 118.
Wisdom 1 3 37 [2], 3 143.
God's, see.
To do duty, 3 22, 3 124.
To rulers, 5 18, 5 34, 5 60, 5 97.
Unsearchable, God, see.
Wonderful creation, man's, see.
Works of mercy, 4 111.
Word and deed, 2 66.
Work, Christ's owned, see.
World, church in ends of, see.
Works, God revealed in, see.
Of mercy, wonderful, see.
Worshiped, God, see.
Wrath, God, see.
Mitigation of, God, see.
Youth, 5 21, 5 56, 5 103.

www.ingramcontent.com/pod-product-compliance
Lightning Source LLC
Chambersburg PA
CBHW020253170426
43202CB00008B/356